BEYOND
DANCING

BEYOND DANCING

A Veteran's Struggle—A Woman's Triumph

ANITA BLOOM ORNOFF

Silver Spring, Maryland

Printed in the United States of America

Published by:

Bartleby Press
JACKSON WESTGATE, INC.
11141 Georgia Avenue
Silver Spring, Maryland 20902
(800) 953-9929
www.BartlebythePublisher.com

Library of Congress Cataloging-in-Publication Data

Ornoff, Anita Bloom.
    Beyond dancing : a veteran's struggle, a woman's
    triumph / Anita Bloom Ornoff.
        p.   cm.
    ISBN 0-910155-50-X
    1. Ornoff, Anita Bloom—Health. 2. World War, 1939-1945—
Personal narratives, American. 3. United States. Army. Women's
Army Auxiliary Corps—Biography. 4. World War, 1939-1945—
Veterans—United States—Biography. 5. Spinal cord—Infections—
Patients—United States—Biography. I. Title.

D811.5.O76 2003
940.54'8173—dc21

                                                        2003002543

To Hal,
with all my love

Acknowledgments

First, let me tell you about my editor Joan Pollack. Joan led me into one of the most fascinating adventures of my life, guiding me gently into those waters of pain and anguish as I recalled the details of what happened from my entrance into the WAAC up through the passage of the bill that granted me veteran's status. Her patience and guidance was both humane, non-critical, non-judgmental and sprinkled with her delightful sense of humor. I am proud to tout Joan Pollack as one of the finest editors I could have chosen.

In the mid-seventies I was fortunate to have Sister Maura Eichner at the College of Notre Dame as my teacher and mentor and it was under her tutoring that I began seriously writing. She and Sister Ruth Miriam, my taskmaster, taught me the basics of creative writing, and they have been a beacon for me ever since.

Today I am thankful for the medical skills of my urologist Dr. Henry J. Weiss, as well as my internist for twenty-two years, Dr. Ira Tublin. My dearest friend and physical therapist Carolyn Dockins, in Silver Spring, has been a great source of encouragement for many years, as has Sean Borman in Boca Raton.

My most ardent champion for *Beyond Dancing* was my husband Harold (Hal). Our grandchildren, Toby Treem and Meredeth Dash, and Meredeth's husband Randy Dash, were all responsible for finding some sense of order in the work I had already completed but was too ill to organize.

Beverly Bowersox was my typist, my angel when I was unable to use the computer due to illness. My cousin Mildred Hird has been a constant stalwart of encouragement and has provided me with wise counsel. Another cousin, Dr. Samuel J. Mann, gave me great encouragement and it was ultimately through him that I contacted Joan Pollack. My two daughters, Ellen Treem and Naomi

Willey, and Aunt Florence (Flo) Freidenreich have been constant in their encouragement as have the rest of my family and friends. I am grateful to all of them for all their kindness and patience throughout this undertaking.

Words cannot describe the exultation I felt when Jeremy Kay at Bartleby Press agreed to publish my memoir. In the process of finalizing the text, Jeremy taught me new techniques that enhanced my writing immensely and I found working with him challenging and exciting. This highly intelligent gentleman became my guiding light when it counted the most.

Getting in touch with memories, sad and happy, has been a momentous experience. That I have lived to write my memoir, of course, has been in the hands of The One above who walked with me all the way. Hallelujah! You said we'd make it and we did!

Chapter 1

I did. I enlisted. Dad almost fainted. Aunt Flo was shocked beyond words. But I was overjoyed. The chief physician, after his examination of me, said I was the healthiest specimen he had seen and the admitting Lieutenant said she was certain I was OCS (Officer's Candidate School) material. On January 8, 1943, the official letter arrived. I was to report to Fort Oglethorpe, Georgia for a six and a half week basic training course starting on January 28. My heart pounded as I contemplated my new adventure.

On a cold dismal Sunday morning with menacing dark clouds hovering, Mom, Dad, my younger sister Marilyn, and our Rabbi piled into my father's automobile. The weather matched the demeanor of the long faces of my parents and the Rabbi. Only 16-year-old Marilyn, who was sure I would be killing Nazis soon, shared a sense of my zeal.

"Drive faster, faster," I wanted to scream at my father. God, what if I missed my train? I was getting a headache listening to Dad and Rabbi Rosenthal making trite conversation about the local activities in our synagogue. I shut my eyes to blot out their talk. The grand adventure that loomed ahead was uppermost in my mind. One day they would all be proud of this Jewish gal who served when her country needed her. I took a deep breath, determined not to let their attitude dampen my exuberance.

"Neet, you'll carry a gun, won't you?" Marilyn asked excitedly. I smiled inwardly. Dad's shoulders tensed. I was sure he was going to have conniptions, but, thank God, not a sound.

"No, Mar, I doubt it. I'm going to release a man for active duty. I won't be fighting."

Mom sitting between both of us on the back seat patted my hand. "Nita, darling, you won't go overseas either? You promised?"

1

"Oh, sure, Mom. Now don't you worry about me. I'll be fine. I promise to write all about the service." Finally, after what seemed an eternity, we arrived at the station, all of us standing awkwardly, struggling with the moment. The roar of the locomotive in the distance imposed a heavier silence. Suddenly it was all very real.

"Nita, dear, you will write often?" Rabbi pleaded. "Call once in a while. You won't forget us?"

"Oh, Rabbi, I promise to give you a blow by blow description of everything." The train huffed and puffed past us. I straightened my shoulders, then gave everyone a quick kiss.

"Darling, please take care of yourself." Mom was struggling to control tears.

My stomach felt stiff as a rock "I promise, Mom. Don't worry, I'll be fine." The train stopped. "So long, folks. Got to go now." My heart pounded as I leaped up the steps. I took the nearest seat waving frantically.

They stood like pall bearers as the train began to move. Mom and Dad were wiping their eyes.

"It's hard to say goodbye, isn't it?"

The young woman facing me was incredibly beautiful without a trace of makeup. Her skin was as smooth as a fine piece of satin. She wore her light brown hair in a tightly pulled back page boy that surely would have made the average woman look drab, but on her, the style was stunning.

"Name's Helen Worth."

"Anita Bloom. Everyone calls me Nita." I extended my hand which she shook warmly.

"Yes, it's hard, especially when they don't understand why I had to enlist." I sighed, feeling totally exhausted. "Will you forgive me? I need to take a catnap. I've been partying for days. I think everything's caught up with me."

Helen smiled. "Same here. Thanks. See you in a while."

Chapter 2

Never in my wildest imagination could I have dreamed what my future would become.

Three weeks after my seventeenth birthday in June 1938, I graduated from Suffern High School in the small town of Suffern, New York, about twenty-six miles northwest of New York City. Then I went, or I should say, was sent to live with Uncle Irv, my mom's brother and his wife, Aunt Flo, in Paterson, New Jersey, the city where I was born on May 30,1921.

This change of address occurred because I was head over heels in love with a young man whom my Jewish father had forbidden me to see. He was a Christian. We were going to elope on my 18th birthday the following year. Aunt Flo and Uncle Irv had a baby girl and were totally absorbed with Ruth. They were unaware of my tryst and I continued my relationship surreptitiously. They didn't have a clue about it. I had met several Jewish boys whom I dated while I lived with them but none of them interested me. My bedroom was a converted porch that was separated from the rest of the large apartment. I had no plans for my future except to marry Herm.

My uncle insisted I enroll in the local night college to prepare myself for an accounting degree, which he felt would guarantee a good future. I took several accounting courses that were totally boring. My uncle ran a small advertising business and I begged him to teach me that profession but he told me he would never employ a family member. When I finally brought myself to tell him how much I hated the night courses, he said I would have to find a job or return home. It was the height of the depression; no jobs, especially for one of the Jewish faith. For two weeks I went in and out of every store on Main Street as well as the side streets. No jobs. The twenty-five dollars I had received for graduation was practically gone. Herm offered to give me money but I didn't want to depend on him. We would meet two or three times a week. We had codes on the telephone: he was Morris, Paul or Harry. No one paid any attention to those calls.

At last I found an ad saying that Woolworth's Five and Ten-Cent Store was hiring. A prim squeamish manager approached me when I went in for the interview... "What did you say your name was? Blum or Bloom?"

"Bloom."

The woman's nose twitched. I knew I was out. She looked down at her papers. "There's been some mistake. This job has already been filled."

I was humiliated. For a minute I felt like choking her. I turned around and left. Maybe my father was right. America was a great place but not always for the Jews.

My boyfriend Herm tried to divert my mind from the difficulty of job-seeking. He was learning to become a piano tuner until he became a famous pianist. He taught me to appreciate classical music and took me to the Lewisohn Stadium in New York for their summer concerts. Herm was a poor dancer and because I was an excellent dancer, I was overjoyed that he agreed to let me teach him the latest dance, the Lindy. His parents liked me a lot and his mom often fixed wonderful lunches for us to take when we went picnicking.

Herm was a peach of a guy. He was three and a half years older than me. Not handsome–not a standout—just pleasant to look at. He was honest, caring and, plainly put, adored me. Herm was studying to become a concert pianist and taking lessons from a well known piano teacher in Paterson. He was realistic and knew he would have to earn a living in order to pay for his expensive lessons. I was very excited because his teacher had arranged for him to play at a piano concert at the Aolian Hall in New York. Herm treated me like a princess: always loving and giving. His demeanor was that of a man well-bred, intelligent, and very patient. I was flattered by all his attention and love but I hated the fact that my relationship had to be conducted surreptitiously. I knew my parents would have loved him too, if only they overlooked the fact that he wasn't Jewish. He assured me that he would convert before we were married.

Herm's family owned property in upper New York State, I had been there before and on those occasions, I always told my aunt I was visiting a girlfriend overnight. On a beautiful August morning, we left Paterson heading toward the Catskill Mountains. I fingered my magnificent Marquise cut diamond ring, delighted by the sparkles that glistened into a myriad of colors. Herm had saved and scrimped to give the ring to me for my seventeenth birthday. Usually I wore it underneath my bra. No one had ever seen it. One day I would proudly show it to the world. Herm purchased deli sandwiches for lunch. Usually he did all the cooking and never asked me to help.

"You'll have plenty of time after we're married," he teased. I didn't object. Housework and cooking were not my cup of tea.

It was mid morning when we reached the cabin. "How I wish you could come when the family's here." Herm lamented. His family liked me but I couldn't sneak away that much."Let's take a walk up to the rock."

I agreed willingly. It was heaven just to be there with him. We walked leisurely up the steep path where wild flowers danced in the sunlight. I had changed into a light-blue halter that tied around my waist and a pair of white shorts. Herm took my hand, leading me up to the top of the hill where a huge flat rock overlooked the deep green mountains.

"What a spectacular view," I gasped. Herm pulled me to him gently lifting my chin up for a long kiss. We stayed together enjoying the view, embracing and kissing all afternoon.

Herm had stretched out, resting his head on my abdomen. We remained silent for a long time until he spoke."America will be at war soon," Herm said somberly. "I'll have to enlist rather than be drafted." He had spent a summer at a Civilian Conservation Camp, (CCC) where the first soldiers were to be choosen if war were declared.

"How do you know?" I murmured lazily. The penetrating rays of the sun had lulled me into a luxurious stupor.

"When I went to the reserves, a couple of weeks ago, it wasn't like any other time. I didn't feel I was practicing. It was different. The orders were different. All of us noticed."

"Well," I announced, "you can be sure if there's going to be a war, I'll go too."

Herm laughed heartily. "My little Pupshen, what are you going to do? Shoot daisies in a beer can?" He had tried to teach me to shoot but somehow we always ended up necking.

Using a gun was offensive to me. I would never kill an animal for sport. It was against my philosophy. "I'm serious. I'm not talking about dumb daisies in a beer can. If my country goes to war I'm going to enlist, even if I have to pretend I am a boy."

He laughed again. "Oh, you are cute. That's why I love you so much." I struggled to get away from him. "Hon, what's wrong?"

"I am dead serious. Women would have a lot to offer."

"You bet they would," Herm smiled sheepishly. "Show me, show me."

I was on my feet. "Men," ugh. "Is that your total conception of a woman?" I jumped off the rock, running down the steep hill. I was not going to tolerate his patronizing attitude. I was as good as any man. If he didn't appreciate me as a woman, I'd stop seeing him—which I should have done a long time ago! The day was shot. He could not appease me. I hated to hear a man ridicule a woman. That's what my father did to me and my sister, and to my mother in particular. I insisted that we return to Paterson.

Two weeks later I found a job in a local department store selling infant's wear but I had to settle a score first. I rubbed off my lipstick, pinned my hair on top of my head, donned a pair of clear eye glasses that I stole from Aunt Flo and went back to Woolworth's. Articulating the same tone I used when I played a society matron in the senior play, I asked for the manager, certain she would be the same woman who had made the snide remark previously. Only this time my name was Amy Brown. I was hired on the spot.

"Madam," I said haughtily, as I unpinned my hair and removed my glasses, while Miss Prissy gasped,"I wouldn't take your darned job if I was starving!" And I pranced out proudly.

Selling in the department store was no problem for me. I'd had lots of practice when I worked after school in my father's baby shop. I earned four dollars a day, three days a week. One day the manager and an assistant stood observing me and shaking their heads approvingly. I was chosen to be Snow White and greet children over the Christmas holidays. I had an entire Snow White entourage with seven dwarfs and a lovely little house. The children were awed each time they came. Following that job, I was chosen to be Miss Valentine for that special weekend. I wore gorgeous outfits for both of these roles. Then the job was finished.

In mid-January of 1939, one Sunday morning after breakfast, Uncle Irv approached me. "When are you going to think about a serious job? A steady full time job?"

For a moment I didn't say anything. "Uncle Irv, I would like to work for you."

He scowled, "You know I would never hire anyone in the family. However, I have a friend who is second in command in his brother's shoe concern. I'll inquire to see if he can find a job for you."

His friend Joe, who was also a client of my uncle's, hired me as a unit control worker, paying ten dollars a week. Boring, boring, boring. Thankfully, within the month, I was transferred to the main floor to work the cash register. As much as I appreciated the promotion, it exposed me to an uncomfortable situation. My uncle's friend always managed to get close to me when I turned my back to work the register. I glared at Joe, fearful that the money wouldn't balance and annoyed that he would take advantage of me.

I had been eyeing the hosiery and pocketbook department directly across from where I was stationed and at the first opportunity, I requested a job as a salesgirl there. Occasionally I would fill in and it didn't take long for my talents to be recognized. I was transferred. Behind this showcase, I was virtually unapproachable by that wretched man. I worked in hosiery and handbags for a long time without being harassed. I had limited contact with my uncle's friend Joe. Whenever he and his wife visited my aunt and uncle, I managed to avoid any contact with him.

The night before my 18th birthday, I cried all night. I had reached the decision to sever my relationship with my sweetheart. The war in Europe, my father's hysterics and the fear that my parents would disown me was unbearable; I knew the next day would be the last one I would ever see Herm. I was overcome with grief when I told him we would have to part. As much as he regretted my decision, he carefully told me that we could not see each other again. We cried and cried, clutching each other as if holding on to life-preservers. I don't know how I managed the stairs to Aunt Flo's that day, struggling to keep calm for fear my aunt and uncle would detect something and force me to explain. For weeks and weeks, it was an effort to put on a happy face. I vowed never to date a gentile boy again.

In time, I brought myself to date several Jewish men and the following summer I actually went steady for a few months with an older man. TJ Friedman lived right next door to my parents' home, but he stood me up on New Year's Eve, which finished that relationship. I dated a lot, but no one could replace Herm.

About once a month, I would take the train home to visit my parents. On a late November afternoon, in 1939, I had just placed my foot on the train going to Suffern, when quite suddenly I was jerked off the train's steps. I was petrified and shocked when I saw the big grin on the face of my uncle's friend Joe, who had harassed me at work.

"What are you doing? I've missed my train."

"I'll take you home," holding my elbow tightly while he engineered me toward his car. "Get in and stop screaming." Lowering his voice, "I won't hurt you. I like you a lot. You're exciting. You're alive." He paused, "You know I'm responsible for your job." He opened the door, but I quickly ran to open the back one. He was quicker than me and pushed me toward the front seat. "Come in. Come, sit close." Joe tried putting his arm around me. I huddled over to the right side, practically leaning on the door. I was very frightened and sick to my stomach with fear that he could do something so dastardly with no shame whatsoever. He made light conversation; I answered minimally. I was nervous and lit a cigarette, dreading the forty five-minute drive. At one exit, he started to pull off the highway but I pleaded to continue driving. Some time later, when he stopped for the red light on the Suffern line, I jumped out of the car. Joe tried to follow but I dashed in back of someone's home and lost him. Although no one knew about the incident, it haunted me day and night.

Three days later I took a daring risk. I was granted an appointment to see the big boss who was the owner of all the three stores to alert him about what his brother had done. Nervous and shaky, I went up to his office and told him briefly about the train incident and Joe's conduct. The man glared at me unbelievingly. I was certain I had lost my job.

Two days later, my employer sent for me. "Nita, you are very young, how old?"

"About 19," I said with tongue in cheek.

"You have shown respect and concern for me and my business even though you knew it would bring a great deal of pain to me. There were so many other routes you could have taken, but you chose wisely. Now I have a grand surprise for you. I looked over your sales during the months of September, October, and November. They were very impressive. The manager of my Passaic, N.J. store is leaving at the first of the year. How would you like to take over her job?" My legs started to shake. I could hardly contain myself. "A nice raise, a commission, a great opportunity for advancement. I want you to take her job. The women you will supervise are older and you will need to have a meeting with them. How does it sound? You will need to commute but it's a short ride and I know you will get along with my younger brother just fine. He has agreed to teach you the rudiments of managing that department." His deep dark eyes searched mine.

My face flushed. In a million years I never dreamed this could happen. I was so thankful I had not vacillated. This man had observed me at the counter many times and I would often see him smiling approvingly. All my experience in Dad's baby shop finally paid off. I managed to whisper, "Thank you. I'll try to make you proud of me." We shook hands.

His brother Joe from the Paterson store threatened me again. "You know I come over to Passaic quite often." I did not respond.

My new position worked out very well. I had called a meeting with the women and everything was falling into place. In a relatively short time I brought in more sales than the previous manager and my boss began teaching me the rudiments of buying. I had a good relationship with the women that I supervised and a good relationship with the other employees, earned a good salary and, in general, was content.

My father was very concerned about his brother and his two young nieces in Germany. Dad was exerting pressure on any influential person that he or anyone else knew, to assist in bringing his family to the States. Whenever I was home and read the newspapers or heard about the horrors taking place, I was deeply affected. I began to have nightmares about Hitler that frightened and disturbed me no end. One night I would find myself crawling on the ground with a gun in my hand trying to kill Hitler; another night I'd be a member of the Nazi Gestapo carrying guns for Hitler. I awoke totally exhausted. It was an effort to go to work. On Sunday, December 7th, we learned of the hell at Pearl Harbor and the declaration of war. Many men I knew were drafted. I was still living with my aunt and uncle, earning a good salary, dating occasionally.

In the spring of 1942, the Women's Auxiliary Army Corps (WAAC) was formed. My cousin's Aunt Rose had enlisted. I was determined to do something for the war effort. Although I detested hospitals, I attempted to volunteer at the local Red Cross but unfortunately, the classes were held in the morning, which interfered with my work. I joined the USO at the YWHA and enjoyed teaching young soldiers how to dance. Although women volunteers were not allowed to date servicemen, Aunt Flo would give me the keys to her car and I would drive over to the barracks where a young soldier from Chicago would be waiting for me. I had a lot of fun taking him and other out-of-town soldiers who had never been to New York before on their first visit.

Then I thought about going to New York to interview for a job in a resident buyer agency that would eventually put me in a managerial position in that city at a tremendous increase in salary. The manager said, "Your experience in New Jersey doesn't count for one iota. If you come into the city for six months, I'll teach you all you need to know, but I cannot pay you a penny." How could I afford to live in New York and commute back and forth from Paterson? Downhearted, I went back to my aunt and uncle's.

A few days later I happened to be behind the counter at work when a stunning-looking WAAC in uniform entered the store. I was mesmerized, following her every move. Now, I rationalized, there was a woman of sterling qualities. As though in a trance, I left the counter unattended, dashed up the stairs, threw my coat over my shoulders and when I saw her walking out of the store, I raced down the stairs, despite my boss's glare and followed her for several blocks.

At last I knew my calling. This is what I had to do. Enlist in the Women's Auxiliary Army Corps!

Chapter 3

When we awoke, Helen Worth and I talked all the way to Georgia. "I don't plan on dating until basic is over and I am assigned a job," I said emphatically. "I'm not even going to take a drink. I want to concentrate on my army career."

"I feel exactly the same way," her pale green eyes looked sincerely into mine.

We had a lot in common. Each of us had a sibling: Helen had a younger brother Connie, who had enlisted in the army. We had each parted with a sweetheart; we both had foreign-born parents (although, I proudly told her, my mom didn't have a trace of any accent), each of us had held responsible jobs. Helen had a regal quality. It wouldn't have surprised me to learn she was a princess.

"Helen, would you like a piece of candy? My friends gave me a surprise party the other night and one of the gifts was my favorite: a box of Fanny Farmer chocolates. I'm afraid I ate too many but I brought a few with me." She nodded enthusiastically and I held out my little treat bag. "Tell me about Connie." I loved the name and I understood he spoke several languages, was very intelligent and quite handsome. He had just enlisted and had not been assigned yet.

"And your sister?"

"Marilyn is four and a half years younger than me. She's graduating high school this year. She took the state award in the debating teams. Sis is big boned compared to me. We aren't very close." I didn't tell her I always considered her a big pest. Soon it was time for dinner, and we continued to talk until we fell asleep.

Arrival at Fort Oglethorpe on January 28, the following morning, was indescribable.

Dark wooden barracks surrounded the area. Obviously it had been male quarters. There was absolute and complete pandemonium at first. Helen and I got separated. Herds of women kept bumping into one another, like chickens without heads. Women, all shapes, sizes and ages, running around trying to interpret vague instructions about whether and when to go here or there or some other place. I spied Helen. "Am I glad to see you."

She walked over, "We're in one of these drab wooden barracks. I don't think we're in the same building."

"Oh, shucks."

An attractive short woman whose eyes sparkled brilliantly, joked, "You're in those gorgeous quarters," pointing to a large dark brown wooden building, "same as me. By the way, Shirley Cohen, New York. We're on the dash now to get fitted for uniforms. Saks 5th Avenue merchandise, for sure. C'mon we have to hurry."

"It's in this building." Another WAAC called. We garnered a few more WAACs and headed toward a huge barracks for our clothing allotment. Presently, Fort Oglethorpe housed 10,000 soldiers who were beyond wired fences and awaiting departure orders within a week or two. Dating was forbidden.

Forget Saks, Bloomingdale's, Macy's. The uniforms were drab khakis. We tried on skirts, shirts, hats and jackets, exchanging like mad those articles that did not fit.

"Lookit this hat," a tall woman from Yonkers bellowed.

"My shirt's down to my knees," I yelled.

Belly laughs could be heard all over the place. One of us would have a hat pulled way down over the ears; or a jacket almost to the floor; a shirt that could enclose three of us. Klutzy WAAC orthopedic shoes clunked heavily about the wooden floors. Gone for the duration were my usual high style high heeled shoes. Little did we realize how grateful we would soon be for the substantial G. I. issues.

We raced back to our barracks that held more than 100 cots. I had been assigned to Company B of the 21st regiment. The whole setup was for the soldiers. Latrines were a block away. Good thing I had great bladder control. All the stalls were open, separated by a sustaining wall. I found my assigned cot. A tall brunette was sitting on the lower bed.

"Hi, I'm Evelyn Bloomfield."

"Nita Bloom." We shook hands. "I'm from Suffern, New York. And you?"

"Albany. I thought it would be easier for you, little one, if you slept on the lower bunk. Okay?"

"Sure, that's great. Thanks. We need to get over to chow pretty soon."

At five thirty sharp a large cowbell announced dinner. Chicken in thick gravy, canned corn, mashed potatoes sopped in tons of butter. Ick. I knew immediately where my extra change would go, and any care food package I received would endear the donor for life.

Orders came over the loudspeaker that anyone disobeying orders would be gigged, meaning no weekend privileges. Women were running crazy trying to meet the 9:00 P.M. curfew. WAACs shouted greetings as they raced to the toilets.

"How're ya doing?"

"Tired as hell."

"My feet are killing me."

"Marching is for the birds."

The only difficulty I foresaw was that I would have a difficult time getting used to the open public stalls. Bathroom habits had always been a private matter for me. We raced back for lights out at 10:00 P.M. I hit the sack like a bag of soggy potatoes but only slept off and on. From the tossing and turning I heard, I knew most of us wouldn't get much sleep. My mind was darting here and there. How fast my world was changing; my shoulder length hair had been cut to the regulation two and a half inches above the collar. "You're brand new," I kept thinking to myself. What fun it was going to be discovering new horizons. The only thing troubling me was my lack of domestic ability. I knew I would have to iron my shirts and I was sure most of the women would know exactly what to do. Darn, I'd probably have the most gigs but I quickly dispelled that ugly notion. Only positive thinking for this soldier. I would have to observe other WAACs in order to learn how to iron well enough to prevent a gig. No doubt I would have to perform other duties I disliked, but that was a given when I enlisted. I decided to volunteer in whatever capacity the army thought I would best serve. My resolve to become a model soldier intensified from that first night.

A bugle blasted us out of bed at the ungodly hour of 5:00 A.M. Everyone scrambled like mad to make the outdoor inspection at 5:30 A.M. One officer shouted commands while another officer

stood in front demonstrating the various poses. "Attention. Forward. At ease. About face. To the right flank. To the left flank."
Most of us were choking back our laughter.

Little Shirley muttered in back of me. "Freezing my ass off.
I don't have a goddamned thing on."

How she could stand naked in the 40 degree temperature
was beyond me. I thought I was in the south. Where were those
warm sunny days?

After a cold breakfast we were quickly brought to attention
and marched to a large stone building for our first class in map
reading. Half the class slept. March, again. Turn to the left flank.
Map reading. Army regulations (A.R.s). March. Turn to the right
flank. Getting dizzy. Another lousy meal. Tons of laughter. Sound
asleep as soon as my head hit the pillow. How would I remember
all that technical stuff?

Somehow, as the days passed, we took it all in stride, laughing until our sides ached. In fact everything I did was fun, whether
it was shoveling coal, washing the latrines, or ironing bent over
a footlocker. I was jubilant just to be a part of this incredible
operation. I was proud. I wrote to everyone: my parents, a beau
here and overseas, friends, relatives, my boss, the rabbi and The
Independent, our local newspaper.

Several of us became close chums: Big Shirley, a tall straw-
berry blond athletic type from Yonkers; Merle, rough and tough,
was a large boned good-natured gal from Macon, Georgia; Little
Shirley who stood on the scale, but not quite pushing up to the
required 5 feet, from New York, and of course, Helen. My one
disappointment was that I wasn't tall enough to join the motor-
cycle corps. My childhood chum Joey had taken me for long night
rides against my mom's orders; I sneaked out of the house and
rode with him many times. I quickly recouped from that disappointment. I knew somewhere, somehow, soon, I would find my
place and learn a new skill.

One morning while we were in formation a loud voice
shouted, "Bloom! Report to Officer's Headquarters. On the double!"

God. What did I do wrong? I raced over to the officer's
building, certain I was in for a punishment. I stood at attention,
paralyzed with fear.

"Bloom, where did you learn to march? You sure can strut."

"Marching in the Suffern High School band when I played

the clarinet," I mumbled, still wondering what was in store. To my shock, I was appointed a platoon leader of my company.

As soon as I heard the roar of the drum, my shoulders straightened, I arched my back and off I went. I could march for miles but many women could not take the long stretches. A few of them fainted. Women could be seen soaking their tired aching arches. True, it was an easy way to maneuver large groups in an orderly fashion, but in many instances it was overdone and certainly not necessary every time we went from one class to another.

One experience in basic training unnerved me. We slept in bunk beds; mine was the lower berth. Directly across from my cot was a woman from Georgia everyone called "Blondey." She hotfooted out every night to select her pick of the countless GIs waiting by the fence. She always left a pillow stuffed under the blanket for bed check and to everyone's amazement, was never caught. Late one afternoon, I was sitting on my foot locker shining my shoes. Blondey's voice became loud and screechy.

"And we wouldn't be in this Goddamned war if it weren't for the lousy Jews."

Damn, antisemitism so soon? I called out "Hey, Blondey, I didn't know we were having a religious discussion."

"Keep out of it, Bloomey. You're not even Jewish," she asserted. "I'm sick and tired of all this shit with the Jews." A long silence prevailed. "I hate this place," Blondey continued, "if it weren't for all the lousy Jews, we wouldn't have to put up with all this crap."

No one stirred. Every word went through me like a knife. I put my shoes and polishing cloth down and walked over to her bunk. "Blondey," keeping my voice low keyed, "if you want to have a religious discussion, I'll be happy to talk with you. Why are you blaming the entire Jewish population for whatever's bothering you?" My stomach was churning. "If you want to call someone a no good so and so, fine. Why blame all the Jews?"

"My father knows; he claims they're all responsible for the mess we're in."

Well, fathers knew best. Didn't mine? "Feel better, kid." I shrugged my shoulders and walked nonchalantly back to my bunk. Blondey grabbed a sweater and ran from the barracks. Later that night, someone moved my bedcovers. "Bloomey," the blond bombshell whispered nervously, "are you awake? Listen, kiddo, I just heard you're Jewish. Right?" I stiffened. "I'm so sorry. I really like you. Me and my big mouth."

"Blondey," I whispered back, "how many Jewish people do you know?"

"None 'til I met you."

"There's so much hatred based on unfounded myths. Perhaps we can talk about it over a cup of coffee."

A swift kiss on my cheek and she scooted back to her bunk. It turned out we became more than passing acquaintances. Blondey was very insecure, coming from a large family with little attention for her. Her father was bigoted toward Jews and Blacks. On the subject of bigotry I could relate to Blondey. It was a wonder that I never picked up my dad's hate signals. Perhaps I had noticed early on how inconsistent he was. He was always badmouthing other religions. My dear maternal grandfather had been the liberal in our family. He used to have coffee with many black families when he sold his wares in the hills of Hillburn, years before it was socially acceptable for a white person to socialize with a black person. Grampy always cautioned, "My child, I don't ever want you to feel you are better than any other human being." My mother was also tenderhearted; she never uttered a harsh word against anyone."If you can't say anything good about someone, be quiet," Mom advised.

The Jewish episode with Blondey evoked a whole set of feelings. Most of the time, I hadn't been conscious of being Jewish, but the first time a notice appeared for a Friday night Sabbath meal I signed up quickly. I took my friend Helen, who wasn't Jewish but was dying for some homemade chicken soup. We dined with a warm and friendly family in Chattanooga (right across the state border from Fort Oglethorpe) and ate ourselves sick from the typical Shabbos meal. I ate all the burnt crust on the garlicky roast chicken. The apple and raisin stuffing was sheer heaven, to say nothing of the mile high sponge cake. I was proud and happy to share my Jewish experience with Helen. I couldn't recall the last time I had these good feelings about my heritage even if it was mostly because of the cuisine. When the hostess asked how many Jewish girls were serving, I became uncomfortable and did not respond.

"Isn't it unusual for a Jewish girl to enlist?"

"Perhaps," I answered slowly, "but those of us who did are very dedicated."

I managed a smile. "Do tell us about the high spots in Chattanooga and what we must see while we're stationed here." Her innuendo was that nice Jewish girls stayed home, tried to get married and knit mittens for Britain. But what about Hitler? Didn't these Jewish women realize what he was doing to our people?

The following Friday I had to lead my company in a large parade drill. Hundreds of WAACs were in formation on a huge flat field. Each company received and carried out orders in one mass operation. I was leading my company in fine fettle. Over the loud speaker came the instruction. "By the left flank, march!"

Arching my shoulders, I proudly turned to the right. My whole company went to the left. I immediately came back. A few minutes later when orders were given to the companies, I had no more difficulty in knowing my right from my left.

Chapter 4

On March 1, 1943, 600 WAAC's filled a whole train with the same orders: Destination Unknown. The three day journey would have been horrendous for the average person, but not for those of us who were eagerly anticipating new experiences. We sang, laughed, told jokes and played penny poker. With beginner's luck, I was piling up pennies.

A gal with flaming red hair poked her face into mine. "Hey, you, with the dark eyes, want your fortune told?"

"No, I don't think so." I didn't want to know what my future held. The anticipation of all the grand adventures awaiting me was too intriguing to be marred by any amateur fortune teller. "Thanks, anyway."

For me, this whole experience was beyond description. It was the first time I had done any traveling; in addition, I was fulfilling my burning ambition to do something constructive for my country. Adventure was in my blood. We were having so much fun. A young handsome Captain whom we affectionately named "Daddy" was in charge. His deep blue eyes twinkled when he teased about which state would be our future home.

Finally on the morning of March 3, we arrived hot and dirty at the train depot in Nacogdoches, an east Texas town unknown to all of us. People stared; a couple of smiles, a few waves, several frowns. Everywhere we went we provoked all kinds of reactions. It was as if we'd suddenly appeared from Mars. We were strangers. People were adverse to women in uniform.

A loud raspy voice commanded, "Walk in formation," as soon as we got off the train. We marched by the side of the tracks and were soon brought to a sudden halt. This was no welcome: "Line up at once for tetanus," the woman's shrill voice ordered. In a few minutes I was eyeball to eyeball with a squatty messy looking sergeant. Her lips were tight; her short raggedly cut hair was greasy and stringy; a dirty blouse improperly buttoned exposed a fat stomach; caked dirt smudged under her fingernails; her shoes were filthy. A far cry from the Army Regulations (ARs) dress code that had prevailed at the Fort. "Name?" the sergeant asked gruffly.

"Anita Bloom."

"Bloom," she sneered, "stick out your arm."

I looked the other way. She stuck me with a vengeance. Later I remarked to my buddy Big Shirley, "That dame gives me the creeps."

"You mean Five-by-Five? Ick. I hope those damn needles were sterilized." My tall friend from Yonkers had been almost manic about health concerns at Oglethorpe. "Scuttlebutt" had it that her father was a noted physician in Yonkers, N. Y. We called her "Big Shirley" to distinguish her from our other friend "Little Shirley." Big Shirley was about five foot six with short cropped mousey blond hair, rather mannish looking, with a husky voice. She was intelligent and as pleasant a person as one might encounter.

After the shots, we piled into several large school-type buses passing through a small town similar to Suffern: a few shops, movie theatre, a drugstore, a diner, one restaurant. Shortly we came to a residential section with small white houses and bright green lawns where huge shrubbery lined the fronts of the homes. Soon the driver came to a more affluent section with elaborate landscaping displaying variations of huge cacti. When we reached the highway, the scenery became monotonous flatland.

"Here's your home," Five-by-Five snarled.

The sign "Stephen F. Austin College" elicited gleeful sounds from every WAAC. The sheer beauty of the stately pine trees that lined the driveway was breathtaking. Soon the campus appeared. What a sight after the gray dull Army barracks! Neatly pruned shrubbery gracing the well manicured lawns brought "oohs and aahs." How peaceful it looked. What a great place for walking. My new buddy Helen and I loved to take long walks after dinner when we were at Oglethorpe. We stopped at a large white dormitory and couldn't wait to grab our duffle bags from the huge pile, racing inside to see our home for the next six weeks.

We entered a long white foyer with tons of rooms lining both sides. The building wasn't a castle, but everything looked neat and clean. I met my new roommate, a fair-haired brunette whose

large boned body reminded me of my younger sister Marilyn. I
was sure she was older than me. We shook hands.

"Anita Bloom. Everyone calls me "Nita." Anita was always
used as a term of reprimand from my father or crabby school
teachers.

"Hi, Nita, I'm Katherine Brown. Kathy. You have the most
beautiful wavy hair. Is it a permanent? Mine's so damn straight.
Isn't this place the cat's meow? I'm from Pittsburgh."

"Thanks for the compliment. My hair is natural. Sure wish it
was straight jet black like my mom's. Don't we always wish for
the impossible?" Kathy nodded. "I really like our new quarters,
especially compared to the drab barracks back at Oglethorpe. I'm
from a little hick town in New York State called Suffern.
Nacodoches reminds me of my home town. Who in the world
ever heard that name before?"

The following week we adjusted to our relatively luxurious
surroundings. We also raved about the fabulous breakfasts that
included eggs, bacon, pancakes, waffles and grits, which I ate for
the first time. Usually I was a picky eater, but after the long walks
I found myself eating things I would normally refuse. I was in
high cotton. The army was everything I had dreamed about and
more. I was somewhat apprehensive about the requirements: sixty
three courses required for administrative work but I was determined to do my best and thus far I was keeping up nicely. I hated
map reading and all the ARs that I had to memorize. For the next
twelve days I adjusted to life at the college, met a few new buddies, continued taking walks with Helen and writing letters home,
to Aunt Flo and Uncle Irv.

Every so often a rumor would surface that we would soon be
entitled to franking (free mailing) privileges. Everything was coming up daisies.

Chapter 5

On March 12, I bolted from a sound sleep. A pain in my right thumb was killing me. I grabbed it, pressing as tight as I could, praying the pain would stop. My thumb throbbed as though an ice pick was constantly jabbing it. I kept swallowing to keep from screaming. Finally the pain stopped. I glanced over at the luminescent hands on the alarm clock: 4:30 A.M.

Oh, no—that awful pain again. I squeezed my thumb hard, breathing heavily, afraid any outburst might disturb Kathy. Clutching my thumb, I tiptoed into the lavatory. Sharp stabs repeatedly struck as though an angry bee were stinging relentlessly. I held my thumb under the light. All I could see was an infinitesimal red mark in the center. Was it a bite? I shuddered. God, I had read Texas was loaded with scorpions!

I caught sight of my face in the mirror and stared unbelievingly. A few hours before, I had brushed my shining hair 100 strokes: now it looked like a lusterless mop. My normally pinkish complexion looked pallid. I looked lousy. Unconsciously, I let my right hand down, but I quickly raised it again hoping the pain would abate. "Stop it." I whispered, trying to convince myself that nothing was wrong. I'll get over to the infirmary—"sick call"—as soon as it opened. Probably it was nothing more than a nasty splinter. For nearly an hour I paced back and forth cradling my thumb like a mother comforting a colicky newborn. Finally I returned to bed, only to toss and turn.

As soon as I returned to bed the alarm went off. Kathy raised her head. "Bloomey? You up already? Take a shower. Give me ten." She rolled over.

"I've been up for an hour."

Kathy sat up. "What's wrong, kid?"

"I don't know. Jeepers!" I grabbed my thumb. "It hurts something awful."

Kathy jumped out of bed. "Let me take a look." She reached for my thumb. I winced. "I'll be careful." She carefully scrutinized it. "I don't see a thing."

"See that dot in the center?"

"Oh, that," Kathy patted my head, "it's nothing. Don't worry, and the new doc'll give you a cream or something. It's time for chow. Nita."

I don't feel like it. I'll grab a candy bar soon as I get this fixed." I was struggling with a button on my shirt.

"Hey, let me. Can't you ask for any help? Good luck, kid, we'll see you in class."

At 7:15 A.M., I raced over to a large red brick building, taking the steps two at a time to the waiting room. Several WAACs were already there. Latrine Rumor (LR) had it that a new physician had arrived. I most certainly did not want any treatment from that messy Sergeant. The door across the hall opened. There she was, that filthy woman. Five-by-Five. As soon as she spotted me, she curled her bottom lip into a scowl, "What's wrong with you?"

"I don't know. I have a tiny mark on my thumb," holding it up.

The Sergeant grabbed my thumb. I thought I would die of the pain. She scowled. "You've got an infection. Open your mouth," shoving in a thermometer, and abruptly turned away to take care of the other WAAC.

I should get out of here. Where was the doctor? I hope he's inside. Within minutes I was the only one left.

"In here. Bloom, isn't it?"

That woman made me ill. I didn't trust her. I didn't get up. I didn't want her to touch me. "Where's the doctor?"

Five-by-Five grabbed my arm. "Get in here, Bloom. You have a small infection. It's nothing to make a mountain over." She pushed me into a small room sparsely outfitted with a cot, a small table and a metal cabinet. "Lie down." She went over to the table, picked up a razor blade that was lying on top and started walking over to the cot.

I froze. "What are you going to do?" starting to get up.

The woman shoved me back. "Cut out the dramatics."

I tried to push her hand away. Trying my darndest to get up, I spoke decisively, "I'll wait for the doctor."

We struggled for a minute but she shoved her knee on my

chest, holding me down. I couldn't move. "Bloom God dammit!" She wrenched my hand open. She drove the razor blade deep into the thumb.

I screamed as never before in my life but only echoes reverberated throughout the empty building.

"Stop it, stop it at once." The woman shook me. "It was nothing." I rocked back and forth moaning and hugging my thumb which was throbbing so badly I could feel my heart nearly explode. The sergeant grabbed my hand again, washing my thumb with peroxide, bandaging my finger with several layers of gauze. She went to the medicine cabinet. "Here's a bag of Epsom salts. You get boiling water from the niggers in the kitchen. Soak your thumb every few hours. Come back in a couple of days when His Highness arrives." Five-by-Five looked disgustedly at me. "What the hell are you sniveling about? Don't you know men are getting killed on the battlefield every day? You Jews are too emotional. Stop acting like a baby."

In a daze, I walked out of the room, pausing at the top of the stairs, almost afraid to step down. Why did I let that witch touch me? The painful throbbing in my thumb was unbearable. I stepped gingerly down the stairs, still weak from the shock. A few tears fell that I quickly wiped away with my left hand. "I'm not going to be a baby. It's nothing. The worst is over." I walked slowly down the hill to another large red building that housed the cafeteria, holding my thumb tenderly with my other hand.

Sounds of footsteps hustling and bustling came from the large room. Breakfast was over. Several black women in white uniforms were scurrying about carrying dishes into the kitchen. I followed them. Pots and pans were clanging; no one paid any attention to me. I walked over to a large black matronly woman, "May I ask a favor of you?"

"What is it? We's busy now, miss."

"I know. I'm sorry to trouble you." I extended my bandaged thumb."I have an infection. I was told to come here and soak my thumb in hot boiling water several times a day. If this isn't a good time, I can come back."

The woman chewed on her lower lip. She was obviously not happy. "Sure, come in. We'll get you the water. You'se can come after chow each day. Name's Liza." She headed for a steaming kettle on a huge black stove. "Let's go inside." Liza picked up a bowl, filled it with boiling water and walked over to a table, motioning for me to sit. "It's mighty hot, miss." Looking sympathetically at me.

I gingerly put the tip of my thumb on the top of the water, waited a second, took a deep breath and started to plunge it further --- yanked it out. I couldn't do it. Not for fifteen minutes! Not for a second. I lowered my head beseeching God for help. Very gradually, I forced my thumb deeper into the hot water. I closed my eyes, gritted my teeth and held the thumb there a few seconds at a time.

"What we need here," Liza shouted to one of the women, "is some music. Put on the nickelodeon." She said she'd "fetch" some breakfast for me.

I shook my head, about to refuse, then nodded, "Thanks."

The music was boogie and blues, the kind I was crazy about. It was the same jazz the black kids at Suffern High loved. I was the only white girl there who would dance with a black boy. During noontime breaks a classmate taught me the latest jitterbug. I adored dancing with him because he was a fantastic leader. Soon as I had the steps down pat, I taught them to a few friends who were hep.

Several of the women in the kitchen were dancing in the center of the cafeteria. They were terrific. When they played a sensational new song, "Cowtown Boogie," my feet began to tap. Some of the women smiled at me.

"Great," I called. They beckoned me to join and I ran into the center. The women were overjoyed when I shimmied all the way down to the floor, making a circle around me, clapping to the beat. I raised my hands high above my head, swaying my hands in the air the way they did in Harlem.

"Dance, girl, you got the beat," one woman called.

I swished and swayed my hips, wiggled my behind sliding my feet up, sideways, down and round to the tempo. I was like a woman possessed: rolling my stomach, grinding and bumping, over and over. The minute I brought my right hand down, I was overcome with pain. But for those few minutes I had forgotten.

I walked back to the table, sat down, and made a weak attempt to eat a bit of cereal, thanked Liza and blew kisses to the women who were truly my Godsend.

Chapter 6

The next two days seemed like eternity. The pain did not let up at all. I went to the cafeteria three times a day and the kitchen workers were always kind. Liza hovered over me like a mother hen. They played the music, made little jokes, and although they begged me, I never danced again.

When I returned to sick call on the third day, I heard a man's voice while I was waiting in the empty infirmary. It had to be the army doctor.

The clinic must have been a large classroom with the small office now being used as the treatment room. All the seats had been removed. Several chairs were placed in a semicircle for the WAAC patients. A WAAC came out followed by Five-by-Five who grimaced when she saw me and gave me a hitchhiker's gesture to enter.

The physician, a slim middle-aged captain with wire-rimmed glasses, was writing at the desk. He didn't raise his eyes, "What can we do for you?" acting very casual.

Before I could say a word, the Sergeant interrupted, "Captain Earheart, Bloom has a minor infection. I lanced it, gave her a bag of Epsom salts and she was told to soak it three times a day."

"Perfect. We'll have a look see." The physician asked Five-by-Five to cut the bandage. I was nauseous: My thumb looked horrible, filled with a disgusting green pus. The doctor looked puzzled for a second, and then nonchalantly stared up at the ceiling. "Change the bandage, Sergeant." He told me to keep soaking my finger and went over to the sink where he washed his hands repeatedly. "Continue the prescribed treatment. Come back in a few days." He returned to his writing.

The Sergeant put fresh dressing on my thumb. I was in agony from her rough treatment. She kept chewing on her tongue like a wad of tobacco.

"Excuse me, Sir. Why am I having so much pain? What caused this to happen?"

The physician looked up blankly. "You have an infection. I don't know how or where you incurred it. Be sure the water is hot."

"Sir, would you please tell me how long . . . ?"

"Bloom," Five-by-Five ordered, "dismissed."

God, was I frustrated. Why didn't the doctor have the decency to answer my questions? Couldn't he see what a dreadful infection I had? What did he mean by: "Where or how you incurred it"? He didn't even respond to my questions in a civil manner. I hadn't done anything! Not one darn thing. My thumb looked disgusting. It didn't appear to be any "minor infection." Yet the two of them were so darn uncaring. I couldn't wait to graduate, take my two-week furlough and see Dr. Hussey, our family physician in Suffern, but that was more than three weeks away. Slowly I descended the steep stairway.

My good buddy, Helen, was waiting. "Nita, are you going to be okay now?" Her lovely face registered deep concern. Helen and I had become very close. Closer than anyone else. She was very anxious about me and I had a hard time concealing my inner fears from her.

"I'll be okay," I responded to her question. No use worrying her.

"Nita, why don't you go home, marry that nice boy, raise beautiful children?"

My response was sharp. "I'm doing what I want to do: serve my country; release a man for active duty. Isn't that what you're doing?"

Helen wasn't Jewish. How could she understand how strongly I wanted to be part of the war effort? None of her relatives were being tortured by Hitler. How could I up and leave camp? My father had warned me: "Needala, don't be a smart aleck. You do what the army tells you." Determined not to be a smart aleck or a quitter, I said to Helen, "C'mon, gal, stop worrying. I'll race you to the dorm."

No doubt the real reason my anger flared was that I rarely got sick. I'd go to the nth degree not to display any sign of weakness. There was no way I was going to be a sicky!

However, the infection worsened: constant pain, more ugly pus. The sight of it made me ill. The next time the doctor opened my bandage, the second he lowered my hand, I saw stars and reported the pain was still severe.

"Sergeant, put her right hand in a sling. Continue the same treatment. The hot soaks."

As painful as the infection was, it did not deter me from showing up for all my classes. I didn't want to miss any of them. My fervent hope was to graduate and get out of that place, away from that awful woman, that miserable doctor. When the pain in my thumb became intolerable, I would leave the classroom, taking a long walk out to the edge of the back campus where a wall of large stones encircled an old well. I stood on my toes, looking deep within. I could barely make out my reflection. Sometimes I talked to my image, "Why did I join? Why didn't I wait until the WAAC was better organized? What was the rush?" I smothered my sobs and ruminated about the steps I had taken before joining:

I had tried to volunteer for some kind of war effort but everything interfered with the job I held, leading up to the day the WAAC had entered our store. I recalled being fascinated and observing her every move from behind my counter. When she walked out of the store, I followed for almost two blocks. Suddenly the answer had become crystal clear: that WAAC was sent to my store for a purpose. Right then and there I had made up my mind. That very night I had written to my cousin's Aunt Rose, who had previously enlisted, and she wrote back giving the pluses and minuses of the Women's Army – but I had already made my decision. The next day I took off from work. I would enlist in Newark, New Jersey where Rose did, which was not too far from where I worked.

I asked a friend if he was free to drive me to Newark and he agreed.

"Where are you going?"

"I have to look up something for my father."

I dashed into the building, and although my stomach was churning I submitted to the comprehensive physical that was at times embarrassing. The attending physician commented on my excellent health. Shortly after, I took the oath of allegiance to the Women's Auxiliary Army Corps.

My friend never knew the building I had entered was the recruiting center for the WAACs. I was a nervous wreck after enlisting. Over lunch, I continued my silence. Several days later I told him I had enlisted.

"Nita, I would have talked you out of it. The army is no place for you."

Now, looking down into the well, I cried my heart out. How impetuous I had been. I had run away without talking it over with anyone. Feeling depressed, I slowly walked back to the barracks.

The following Saturday night, several of my buddies were going to the movies and urged me to join them. We were allowed to hitch rides from the locals who were always kind and considerate but since it was a clear sixty-degree night, we chose to walk the mile and a half to the little town.

"Will you wait in the lobby, kids? I think I'll call my folks." I had called Mom and Dad only once from Oglethorpe. Since the onset of the infection I had been reluctant to call. "It's possible they haven't received my letter about our new destination," I rationalized, unable to admit I was really homesick.

Big Shirley asked, "Have you told your parents about your infection? My father's a surgeon. He always warned us about severe pain and its duration."

"Stop worrying, " I reassured my friend, "This will get better soon."

I, too, was very concerned, but I wasn't going to tell my parents, particularly my father. He'd be there the next day, raising a big hooha, embarrassing the life out of me. My father came from Poland. His booming voice could raise the dead. He could be quite boisterous and crude at times. More than once he had humiliated me. Once I came downtown with a few of my girlfriends. My father saw me and rushed over. "I'll give you one minute to take off that lipstick. You look like a street girl!" God! No way would I allow him to interfere in my army life. When I had told him I had enlisted, he said, "Only camp girls enlist."

"Needala," Dad yelled as soon as he got on the line, "are you all right?"

"Dad, I'm stationed in a little hick town just like ours."

"I got a job with the WPA. I'm doing a payroll for 200 men."

My father doing accounting work? "Hey, that's terrific." I could just picture him—proud as punch, his face all round and cherubic. My father was seldom happy. He usually was grumpy and growly. Dad was always frustrated and would lose his temper at the drop of a hat. I wondered if Mom was tending the shop all by herself now that my father had this new job.

"Mom wants to talk." He cleared his throat. "Did you go to a synagogue yet?"

"Yes, Dad, back at Oglethorpe. It's all in my letter. I was a guide for my company. You should have seen me, Dad. Remember when I was a cheerleader in high school? Well, I was the leader of more than a hundred women and marched with hundreds more in front of many commanding officers on a huge parade field accompanied by a marching band. I read WAAC poetry over the radio. Oh, yes, I sent a letter to the Rabbi, too."

"Oh, darling, you make me so happy." My dad laughed. "Did you get my package?" He spoke so lovingly in a tone I hadn't heard in years.

A package from my father? Miracles will never cease. "Not yet. It will probably take awhile to arrive here in the boonies. Thanks so much." My legs felt wobbly.

"Needala, take care. You doing everything right?"

"Yes, Dad," I mumbled. The pain in my thumb was insufferable. I struggled to keep my composure.

"Here's Mom. Take care. All right, Til, all right."

"Sweetheart, tell me about your new post." The sound of my mother's soft and gentle voice brought tears to my eyes. I was always proud of my mom. She was a petite woman with a zaftig figure, thoroughly Americanized, having come to this country when she was only six months old. She spoke softly and gently. I always cringed when my father yelled at her. She trembled with fear but always kowtowed to him. The worst time I ever had with my mother was when I was involved with my Christian boyfriend and she wouldn't defend me, even though she knew how kind and intelligent Herm was. I looked exactly like my mother and people often took us for sisters. "Have you met a lot of new friends? Are your bowels regular?"

"Mom! Yes, to everything!" Oh, gosh, I was glad no one could hear my mom. I was always embarrassed to talk about personal habits. Truth was, for the past couple of weeks, for the first time I could remember, I was constipated. "It's very scenic here with rows of beautiful pine trees and shrubbery." I had to resolve my curiosity about Dad's job. "Mom, are you taking care of the store alone?"

"Yes, darling, we're both doing our share for the war effort, just like you, baby." Her usually timid voice rang with confidence. "You would be very proud of Dad. You wouldn't believe how conscientious he is about doing his payroll each week."

"Mom, how absolutely marvelous. I'm proud of you both."

My eyes were misty. How I wanted to hop a train and go home. Three more weeks to go. Mom put Marilyn on the phone and we laughed hysterically about absolutely nothing before I hung up.

The telephone call threw me into a dither. All of a sudden I had so much to say to the family from whom I had been so eager to escape. I had not told my parents the truth that the pain in my thumb was worse than anything I had ever suffered. Tears rolled down my face in shame. Pulling myself together, I rejoined my buddies.

The war news was upsetting, showing Axis forces victorious in Europe and seeing hundreds of soldiers wounded and killed. I shuddered. My thumb again started giving me a fit. I had a splitting headache, excused myself for a minute and went to the drugstore next to the theatre to purchase some aspirin. We left in good spirits and sang all the way home. When we arrived at the gate, a sentry stopped us.

"Which one of you is Bloom? The Sergeant wants to see you in her office. On the double!"

What now?

"Bloom, where the hell were you tonight?" Five-by-Five chewed on her tongue like an old cow.

"At the movies."

"Where else did you sneak off to?"

"I called my parents."

"C'mon, you better tell me or I'll search you up and down myself."

"Oh, you mean the aspirin?" The creep had me followed.

"Stop acting so innocent. You don't fool me." She came closer. "I'm the one who dispenses medication, get it? Nobody else. I've had trouble with you ever since you came in with that lousy infection. You're too goddamned emotional. Like all Jews."

I lowered my eyes to hide my humiliation.

"Look at me, girl, and you had better pay attention. If you as much as breathe about your lousy infection until this damn mess is over, I'll have you locked up for the duration. We have a certain building where we lock up goldbrickers," Five-by-Five smirked as she held out her hand. "The aspirins," she shrieked, grabbing the bottle out of my hand. "One more thing. A famous general is inspecting our camp tomorrow. If you dare to utter one word, you know what will happen. Dismissed."

I was mortified. I might just as well have been in Nazi Germany. Running into the night, ashamed and frightened, I vowed never to mention the infection to anyone. Somehow, some way, I had to get better. I had to get out and away from that demon. Please. Please, I pleaded.

The following week, for the first time, the doctor became agitated when he saw my thumb all covered with dirty, cruddy dry sickening green pus and oozing with fresh pus. I had all I could do to keep from vomiting whenever I looked at the finger. My mouth always had an acrid taste. I was afraid to get too close to anyone. The captain ordered me to go to a civilian doctor.

I complied with his orders and went to see the recommended physician in town. Several patients were waiting in the small dark office. A receptionist greeted and beckoned me to take a seat. I tried to concentrate on the landscape pictures on the walls.

Finally a rather fatherly heavy set man peered out. "Are you the WAAC patient?" he asked in a friendly tone that was music to my ears. "Please come in."

The office was simple: a mahogany desk, a comfortable leather chair for the physician, two straight back chairs for patients. A few certificates lined the wall. Several bookshelves were filled.

"Let's see that thumb of yours." Dr. Nelson carefully unbandaged my thumb. He looked horrified. "Young lady, how did this happen?"

I gave him the history but omitted the part about the sergeant cutting my thumb with a razor blade and how she and the Captain seemed so nonchalant. If Five-by-Five ever found out, God help me, I thought.

Dr. Nelson pleaded, "Why don't you go home? This army is not for you. You need good attention to this finger."

"I can't go home yet. Please help me, Dr. Nelson. I'll be graduating soon and I want to remain with my buddies. Some of us will be going to Officer's Candidate School. We might be going overseas, too. I'll be getting a two-week furlough soon and I'll leave immediately after graduation. I promise to see my personal physician right away."

"I'll do my best but I would prefer that you went home and got this severe infection taken care of immediately."

"I can't. It's against Army Regulations. I'll be AWOL."

"Oh, hogwash. You need good medical care for yourself first. For the moment I'm going to give you a series of ex-ray treatments but if that doesn't work, I want you to promise me you'll leave."

"Oh, I know you'll be successful," I smiled cheerfully.

I saw Dr. Nelson three times. Once I heard him talking to his nurse, ". . . . That army doctor is a blockhead. He can't figure this out and dumped the kid on me. I'd feel much better if she went home."

There was no change in my thumb. The throbbing was driving me crazy but I wasn't going to run home.

Chapter 7

A few days later, Kathy answered our wall phone. "Bloomey," she yelled, " it's for you." She raced back to the room. "Kid, it's a man and it ain't your father."

Who could it be? I didn't know any men stationed in Texas. "Hello?"

"Anita, is that you? It's Jackie Dorn, your long-lost cousin, do you remember?" His cheery voice was like manna from heaven. "I heard you up and joined the WAACs. Your father gave me your address. Might have known you'd do something spunky!" Jackie was one of Tanteh Minnie's boys. My late grandfather's sister had three boys; Jackie was the oldest. He was one of my favorite cousins, full of jokes and always acting crazy. He sounded terrific.

"Of course I remember. Where are you?"

"Hon, I'm in the western part of Texas. How about meeting me this weekend?"

It was the last weekend before graduation. "I don't know. Jackie, can you come here?"

"No, it's too far. How about meeting in Dallas? Hon, bring two WAACs for my buddies. I'll line up two other guys. Hey, are you still gorgeous with those big dark brown eyes?"

Gorgeous? God forbid he should see me now. "Oh, Jackie, I was never gorgeous. How're your folks?"

"Anita, I can't talk anymore. I'm on patrol duty now and for the rest of the week. We'll meet you at the Washington Hotel, 6 P.M. on Saturday. I won't take no. Take care, lovely. Bye."

I invited Little Shirley and Ann. Little Shirley from New York City was full of fun and mischief. Ann was rather reticent and looking delicate but strong as an ox. I had asked Helen but she refused. We used every persuasion to convince one of the younger lieutenants to grant permission for the leave. Bright and early Saturday we took the bus to Dallas. We were excited beyond belief. We had packed our newly issued light tan gabardine summer uniforms that were off limits until graduation. We acted like school kids on their first holiday.

Arriving at the Washington Hotel, we took one room with two double beds and a cot, lounged in long hot baths, primped, fussed and giggled, giggled, giggled.

"Nita," Little Shirley beamed, "what a change. God, what a difference a little makeup will do."

"Thanks. We're a team of gorgeous creatures, right?" The light weight uniforms were far more becoming than the drab olive brown ones.

My freshly shampooed hair was soft and shiny. I had removed the sling despite the pain. The last thing I wanted was to alarm Jackie. All he had to do was to call my Dad. My buddies swore on the hotel's bible they wouldn't mention the infection.

We met in the lobby. Jackie swooped me off my feet for hugs and kisses. "Wow, you're even more beautiful than I remember. Those big brown eyes and you have the same knockout figure." He laughed heartily. "Hey, don't blush. It's true, right, fellas?"

"You don't look too bad yourself," I murmured, embarrassed to death. The two G.I.s were smiling at me. One was a bright redhead, skinny as a toothpick; the other towered over everyone, with brown wavy hair that looked like it was marcelled. They appeared to be a friendly group. Jackie was still handsome: about 5 feet 10, slim, with a smile that surely won many a gal's heart. I was proud.

"It's so good to see family." Jackie hugged me again, then introduced his buddies: Paul and Charley, Within minutes everyone paired off. I stayed with Jackie and caught up on family news.

My buddies and I had a ball. We were the first WAACs to hit Dallas. Everywhere we went, folks ogled, laughed, cheered. Jackie took us to a dance hall where food and non-alcoholic drinks were served since Texas was a dry state. We all ordered Texas barbeque, feasted on the best spare ribs and drank tons of cokes. Jackie and I got up to dance. Very gingerly, I laid my hand on his shoulder.

Oh, Lord, it felt wonderful to be dancing again. My cousin was a fabulous leader. I closed my eyes, letting the music permeate my body, following his every step. Jackie put his hand on my hip, twirling me away and bringing me back. Then he let go of me all together and there I was, dancing all by myself. My buddies dashed over to join me. People were clapping and whistling. All the G.I.s were grinning and cheering. Jackie's broad smile made me happy. He came over for the next dance. "Anita, you're sensational."

"You're very terrific yourself. Jackie, everyone calls me 'Nita' now." I had forgotten about my thumb but as soon as I put my hand down, I moaned. The music stopped and we walked back to our table.

"What's the matter, kid? Why are you cradling your thumb?"

"Oh, it's nothing. I have a little infection." My finger hurt terribly and I was exhausted, but I didn't want to ruin our fun. He'd call my family and everyone would get upset. In a few days I would graduate and leave shortly for home. I couldn't wait.

"Are you getting good care? I know a lot of army doctors. Some are terrific, but plenty of those medicos leave a lot to be desired." He put his arm around me. My buddies heard him and their eyes implored me to tell, but I ignored them.

"Sure. Let's not worry about it." I forced a smile. "This was a great idea. We're having a terrific time." I leaned over and planted a big kiss on my cousin's cheek.

"Cuz, what made you join the army? Did you have a broken heart or something?"

I faced my cousin squarely, praying he would accept my every word. If he started questioning me, I was sure one of my buddies might blurt out the whole business about my thumb. I looked directly into my cousin's eyes. "I felt it my duty to go when my country called for women to join so they could release a man for active duty."

Jackie's face lit up. "Proud of you, gal." He leaned over the table, "C'mon, kiddos, time to take our Cinderellas home. We need to get off the streets before the 11 o'clock curfew." Jackie led our group in formation, giving all the commands in Yiddish. It didn't matter whether or not anyone understood. Somehow we followed, laughing hysterically when, quite suddenly, Jackie spotted several officers coming toward us. "Sha, sha," he warned.

"Halt," a smartly dressed young lieutenant ordered abruptly. Everyone saluted.

A colonel marched right over to Little Shirley. "You," he growled, "what's your name?" The heavy set man's deep gray eyes glared at her. We all started to shake.

"Auxiliary Shirley Cohen."

I thought I would faint. What in the world was going on?

"You," he spewed in the same tone, "are ordered to report to the Hotel Adolphus tomorrow at 2 P.M."

My buddies and I were frantic. Jackie urged us not to worry. "Let's not spoil our holiday. Don't forget we're going to the Bicentennial Fair tomorrow. Nothing's going to stop that. You can see that jerk afterwards."

"My God, kids, we'll be AWOL but we're going to see this through, right?" I looked at the women who nodded in agreement then turned to the men. "You guys have to go back. We'll go to the fair and after we'll go with Shirl." Inwardly I was frightened to death. If we were late Five-by-Five would surely lock me in that isolated building!

"Nita," my cousin reassured, "we'll all stay."

"Listen everyone, let's stay calm," Shirley stated firmly. "I have to see the damn colonel, that's for sure. Not everyone has to be punished for whatever the hell I did."

Shy Ann spoke assertively, "We're going to be with you all the way."

I looked at the men. "We'll go to the fair but you fellas have to go back afterward. We'll stay with our pal. We're in this together."

The next day's outing was spectacular. I struggled to ignore the terrible pain in my thumb. Again we were the main focus because no one had ever seen WAACs. The red carpet was rolled out. We sat proudly in a jeep that was assigned to take us around the fairgrounds. People were taking pictures right and left. The men were eating it up, too; everyone had a marvelous time.

At 1:30 P.M., we piled into a cab. I sat on my cousin's lap. "We had a great time, kid. If we weren't cousins. . . . You know I always had a soft spot for you."

"Oh, Jackie," I giggled, "you're something else."

"I'll call you, hon. Promise me you'll take good care of yourself. Get that thumb taken care of pronto. Promise?" I nodded my head.

We said our goodbyes, hugging and kissing, thanking them for the terrific time. Jackie and I held fast to each other. I was careful to keep my right hand up to minimize the pain. I prayed he would come home safe and sound. We waved until the men faded from sight.

As we walked along the marble floors of the Adolphus Hotel, we discussed whether or not we should accompany Shirley to the colonel's room. The decision was that she would see what the problem was; if she didn't return in ten minutes, we would come up.

A receptionist brusquely gave her the number of Colonel Klein's room, adding tersely that Auxiliary Cohen was expected at 2 P.M.

Shirley later revealed the facts. When she knocked, a tall, lean, unsmiling lieutenant opened the door. He glared at her then beckoned to enter. Two officers with their backs to her huddled in a corner. The first officer announced in a loud voice, "Cohen is here." Shirley was a wreck.

The colonel strutted in, stared at her, "Cohen," he boomed, "why did you violate Army Regulations?" Our buddy was puzzled and asked the colonel what he meant.

"What do you mean?" He screamed at her, "Don't you know your ARs?"

Shirl was about to faint. "Yes, sir," she murmured, "I know my ARs, but I don't understand, Sir?"

"What do you mean you don't understand? You either know your ARs or you don't."

She said the gray haired and slightly balding man towered over her. "Why weren't you wearing your hat properly last night?"

Shirley said stomach spasms were killing her. It was then that she recalled feeling flushed last night and pushing her hat back, exposing her curls. When she raised her eyes, she was shocked. The colonel was grinning and began roaring with laughter while the three other officers were convulsing at the other end of the room. Finally Colonel Klein sputtered. "Hell, girl, none of us had ever seen a live WAAC. It was your damn hat that provided the opportunity." Relieved beyond words, Shirley burst out laughing and that's when we were invited to join the hilarity.

The men were as friendly as anyone could expect. They took us out for a lovely dinner in the neighborhood, asking tons of questions about the Women's Army. I did not put my hand down the whole evening so that the severe pain was diminished. Nor did I reveal the fact that my back had started to give me some excruciating pain also.

The colonel sent us back to Nacodoches in a limousine with an explanatory note that excused us from being AWOL. We were invited to return the next weekend if we were still at the college and the colonel promised to arrange for us to come to the air base where he was going to give us flying lessons. Oh, wouldn't it be super if my thumb healed. I had always dreamed about becoming a pilot.

Chapter 8

All the way back to the Army base I huddled in the corner because I was suffering from the pain in my spine as well as my thumb. I shifted from one side of the car to the other. I tried sitting upright but I couldn't, so I crouched way down in the seat. I couldn't get comfortable. The pain in my back intensified. I thought I'd go out of my mind until we returned to camp. I tried desperately to focus my thoughts on the next day's event; our graduation pictures. Two more days and then graduation. Finally, I'd have two whole weeks of leave before the next destination. "Oh, God, please help me," I prayed. "Please help me."

The next morning I took forever to dress. My back felt as though a heavy object had crushed it. I couldn't keep up with my buddies as they marched to the area where the photographer was waiting. Helen walked beside me, but I knew all my friends were very worried about me.

All 600 WAACs were assigned their places. "Smile pretty." Click. "One more time." Click. I fainted.

When I regained consciousness, Big Shirley was sitting on Kathy's cot.

"Hi, gal. How are you?"

I was exhausted, "Forgive me for giving you all this bother. I have to go home and stop this nonsense."

Big Shirley kissed my forehead. Her facial muscles tensed. "Kid. You're burning up. I'm going to take your temperature." A few minutes later, her voice strained, "Holy mother, it's 102 degrees! I have to call the bastard." She brought me a glass of water and placed a cool washcloth over my face. "The creep's not there," she said, "I'll call again soon."

Kathy was gently pushing on my shoulder trying to awaken me. She and Big Shirley, looking panic stricken, were standing over me. Kathy spoke quietly and firmly, "Bloomey, we have to take you to the infirmary."

"Oh, no," I pleaded, "I don't want to go. Can't I stay here?"

Big Shirley looked aghast. "Kid. You've got a high fever. We're sure you'll get good attention now. Kid, you should have gone home long ago."

"But you know the ARs . . . . "

"Goddamn the regulations." Big Shirley picked up my hand. "Kid, please understand. We don't want to send you over there, but you have to get immediate medical attention."

"Forgive me, Shirl, I don't want to cause anyone any trouble."

"Hush, that's been your prob—never mind. Be right back." Big Shirley and Kathy made a blanket stretcher and they half walked and half carried me to the infirmary. Five-by-Five was reading "True Story" when two of my buddies half carried me into the infirmary. She kept her eyes glued to the magazine. "Put her on a bed in one of the rooms." They helped me into bed. I heard Shirl say, "Sergeant, this girl needs medical attention. Fast!" The door slammed. The mean, fat slovenly woman took my temperature, mumbling to herself, "Finally worked herself up to a fever." Her lips were tight; her short unevenly cut hair was oily and stringy. Her fingernails were caked with dirt. She called the Captain, who came, examined me briefly and gave me a sedative.

"If your fever's not down in the morning, you're going over to the civilian hospital."

Sometime during the night I awoke to go to the bathroom. The infirmary was pitch dark. A small light shone from the bathroom. I was semiconscious and began praying. "Oh, God, don't do anything bad to me now." I prayed the watchword of my faith, "Sh'ma Yisrael . . ."

My legs felt like heavy weights that took every ounce of strength I could muster to move. I sat on the commode. Nothing happened. I waited a moment trying to relax. I felt faint. I could barely move. My legs weighed a ton and my back pains were ferocious. Somehow I managed to drag myself back to the cot where I fell into a coma-like-sleep.

The next morning a cold thermometer shoved in my mouth awakened me. Sergeant Five-by-Five shook it down. "Damn it! 103 degrees. Soon as we can get the truck, you're getting out of here." She threw my clothes on the bed. "Get dressed."

I reached for my clothing but I couldn't close my bra. I

struggled to put my arms through my shirt, gave up, and let it hang over my shoulders. I started to get up, but I couldn't control my legs and fell to the floor.

The Sergeant returned. "What the hell?"

"I can't get up." I barely whispered. My body was riddled with chest pains and my back was killing me.

"Brown, get in here!" A WAAC corporal flew into the room. "Finish dressing her. We'll put her in the truck." The two women carried me like a sack of potatoes, sitting me straight up in the truck.

Whatever they did, I was getting out of there. Away from that witch. I wiped tears away with my left hand. I wouldn't give her the satisfaction of showing any weakness. I was going to get better despite that dirty anti-Semite.

Five-by-Five shoved me in between herself and the corporal. I felt like a crumbled soggy dishrag; daggers pierced my spine. That mad woman drove the truck like an escaped convict, taking curves like ski slopes, zooming into the emergency entrance of the local civilian hospital, screeching the truck to a sudden stop, causing my lifeless body to fall forward and thrash hard against the seat. God, I feared, she's determined to kill me. I clenched my teeth to keep from screaming at the top of my lungs: God, help me. Someone! Anyone! Five-by-Five dashed into the hospital returning with two non-smiling orderlies who carefully lifted me onto a stretcher and strapped me securely with a leather belt.

"Push her to the nurse's station," Five by Five ordered, "this WAAC has worked herself up to a 103 degree fever."

I turned my head away. What did that woman want from me? I heard her talking to someone behind the counter.

"You people do somthin' with her. She's one of them kind from New York who's been hysterical over a little infection."

Would she ever stop? I couldn't hear the response.

The Sergeant continued, "My orders are to leave her here. See what you come up with in this fancy hospital. Good bye and good riddance."

The nurse's face was beyond my sight but I heard her respond. "No, don't leave yet. You'll have to see our administrator. I'll call him." I could hear her arguing. . . newspapers? If it's something serious we'll ship her out to the nearest army hospital . . . Her voice trailed off.

I fought back my tears. At least I was rid of the ogre. The

orderly in back of my stretcher said I was going to the third floor, where he called for assistance to lift me onto the bed. A large round faced woman kept staring at me, while she and the orderly pulled up the side bars. They left without saying a word to me.

"I don't like it any more than you. I don't approve of women acting like men."

Another female voice hissed. "They couldn't find a man at home so they joined this baloney army. Soldiers in skirts, what a laugh. They're in to service the men." I cringed.

"They don't know what to do with her so she gets dumped on us."

Dear Lord, I beseeched, let them call me whatever—if only someone can help. I squinted my eyes to see the sterile surroundings: the room was small, about 8 by 10; one white metal chair sat stiffly in the corner; a matching night table was placed next to my bed; a sink with a medicine cabinet was across the room. My tongue tasted like sawdust; my thumb was throbbing unbearably and the backaches were murder. Please, please, I prayed, let them help me. I have to get better. I have to get out of here, go home and rejoin my buddies. Please let them find out what's wrong with my legs.

Someone touched my shoulder. "Here's some soup and tea. You're to drink every drop so you can pee." A tall skinny aide with long stringy dyed blond hair stood by my bed holding a tray. She set the food on a movable table and cranked my bed up a little. I moaned from the pain when the table rubbed against my wracked body. I had forgotten: I had not voided all day. If only I could get up and void naturally. Did they think I didn't want to get up and go on my own? I raised my arm to reach for the glass. The aide caught it before it dropped.

The woman raised the bed higher. I winced and motioned to stop. She came around the bedside. "You have to drink. Do you want to be fed through a tube?" smoothing her uniform. "Why don't you cooperate? There's nothing wrong with your arms. As soon as you start moving around and peeing, you'll get better." She paused, scratched her head for a moment. "You want to go back to your Women's Army, don'tcha? Couldn'tcha get a man at home?" I reached for the glass. "No, no, no. You'll get the juice all over the bed." She brought the glass to my parched lips. I tried to sip, managed a swallow only to fall back on the pillow. My eyes were heavy with sleep. I tried to open them but the lids were too heavy. Morpheus grabbed me into oblivion.

Later a different voice summoned me to consciousness. The room had darkened and I could hardly see. "You have visitors," a woman's heavy Texas drawl informed me, "maybe they'll get you to drink. See if you can get your friend to drink and pee."

Two familiar buddies looked down at me. Helen asked gently, "Nita, please tell us if you're getting any better treatment here?" I lowered my eyes. "My God, girl, you have got to go home."

I panicked. Helen and Shirley's pale faces hovered above me. I whispered, "Please don't call my parents. They'll be shocked. It could kill them."

"Oh, Nita," Helen immediately reassured me, "we won't do anything to cause you grief." I fought back tears and struggled to stay awake. I was thankful they came. My friend brought a teaspoon of soup near my lips and I struggled to take a tiny amount. "One more for the road," she begged.

I shook my head despondently.

Shirley cleared her throat. "We have something to tell you. If we didn't, you'd feel we dropped out of this world. We're graduating tomorrow and we're leaving early the next morning."

"We hate to go without you, Bloomey."

"Where?" I whispered.

"L.R.s have it that we're going to Fort Devens, Massachusetts, then home for our furlough and possibly overseas. Although I'll fight like hell to stay in the U. S., Helen wants to go overseas. You did too, didn't you?" Shirley sounded very distressed. She paused. "Kid, you have to get well. We all love you and want you back," picking up my hand to kiss it.

I shook my head from side to side clenching my teeth to keep from crying but couldn't control my sobs. I had volunteered for overseas duty despite the promise to Mom that I wouldn't. My mother didn't understand how much I wanted to be the perfect soldier and go on to Officer's Candidate School to get as much education as possible. How I wanted to surprise my folks on my first furlough. I knew that then they would finally appreciate the wonderful decision I had made about enlisting.

Shirl cleared her throat. "Bloomey, we're AWOL. If we get caught, God knows? We have to get back but we just had to see you before we left. All the girls send their love. We'd give anything to carry you with us." Her voice cracked.

"May God be with you," Helen said gently. The two women blew kisses and left.

Their voices resounded along the walls. ". . . is our buddy going to get any better?"

"If she wasn't so stubborn and began to drink and pee, she'd be a whole lot better. I thought you was going to bring her to her senses?"

"Goddamn it," Shirley exploded, "you have an angel in there. She needs good medical attention. Fast!" Their footsteps fled down the hall. I was crying uncontrollably.

What had I done to deserve this? I had severed the relationship with my Christian boyfriend whom I had loved so much. I had worked hard to improve my lot from a salesgirl in a prestigious shoe firm to become the manager of my firm's women's department. When my country called, I felt it my duty to join the WAAC, especially because I was Jewish and because I knew our country would soon liberate all the suffering people in Europe. But for the grace of God, I might have been born in Germany. Who would believe what I had suffered? None of my best buddies knew the whole story. Suddenly I panicked. What if I died in this lonely hospital? Out in God's country—unbeknown to anyone. No, no, I mustn't allow myself to think such a thing. I mustn't. I struggled to pull the sheet over my head.

Sometime later a night nurse lifted the sheet. "Couldn't you find a boyfriend at home?" she laughed nervously.

I was mum. This night nurse wouldn't understand, any more than the rest of them. God, why did I join? I couldn't remember.

"How could your parents let you go. Yer a Jew, right? I thought they took good care of their own?" Their voices all sounded the same. Mean and uncaring. I kept my eyes closed.

"Good evening," a bespectacled man stood over me, "I'm the resident physician. I'm going to examine you."

"Do you need any help, doctor? She won't do a thing for herself."

"No, thanks. I'll ring If I do." He remained close to my bed. My rank mouth odor flowed through my nostrils. His face was a blur but I could make out a dark patch above his head. At least his tone was not irritating.

"You're one sick lady. I hear you have a problem voiding. What seems to be the matter? Were you in any trouble?" I sighed shaking my head. "Why is your thumb bandaged?"

I struggled to clear my throat. In a voice that was barely audible I whispered, "I've had an infection for several weeks."

The doctor scratched his head. He went to the door and called to the nurse. "Let's take the bandage off." I could hear the tap water running. "Did you know about this infection?"

"I saw the bandage." She unraveled the soiled gauze. "Gad."

Their voices registered shock. Squinting my eyes I could see my thumb was a mass of ugly dried pus with gobs of fresh pus still oozing. I gulped back the nausea.

"Let's clean it up." The man came closer to my bed. "Look, miss, you can tell me." He turned to the nurse, "Er, uh, when you're finished, I want to talk to this girl. I'll call if I need you." The aide bandaged my thumb and left. I was breathing heavily.

"How did this happen?" The doctor lowered his voice. "I can't help you if you're going to be stubborn."

"I don't know." Mumbling with great effort I asked, "Doctor, do I have infantile paralysis?"

"No, you don't," he attested with certainty, "and you will get better if you drink and urinate." The man cleared his throat several times. "Were you out on a toot somewhere? We've all heard about the army girls in skirts. The Catholic Church is vehement against women going into the armed services. Our lobbyists worked tirelessly to block the vote. Any time you have a woman butting into a man's job there's trouble." He pressed me again, "I need to know what happened, Miss."

"Believe me, I want to . . . " I gulped helplessly.

"I'm ordering a complete workup in the morning." The nurse reappeared. "The only advice I have for you is to make her drink, drink, drink. Good night." He pushed the aide toward the door. His whisper chilled me to the bone. "You know damn well there's monkey business in that women's army. We don't want any part of it."

I stared into nothingness. I had not taken a drop of water. I lay there helpless and knew for a certainty I was going to die in that godforsaken hospital. No one would ever find me. All my buddies were shipping out. I had been singled out and punished. I would rot and die. Five-by-Five had her wish come true. Oh, my God. Why was I punished? Why did I defy my parents? Oh, God, why had I been bad? Why, why, why, I kept asking myself over and over, crying uncontrollably until I fell into a comatose sleep.

Chapter 9

In the late morning, barely able to talk or move, I endured several examinations. One doctor poked around and asked if I felt anything from my waist down. I shook my head from side to side. He never uttered a word. I was wheeled back to my room. An eternity passed while I waited until an orderly appeared with a stretcher. I was taken down an elevator and parked in the hall where I could hear an angry male voice.

"I spoke to a damn Colonel in that Army Hospital in Longview and told him to get an ambulance here pronto. Let them figure this mess out." I could hear someone pacing back and forth. "We have a very sick WAAC here. Running 103 degrees. We're not set up to take army cases. He told me he was not set up either. He said they're not even part of the Army. I want this WAAC out of here. She's one helluva sick lady and she was dumped on us. I told him. I want her out. Pronto!" The pacing started again. "I told him I don't want anything to do with any women's army." His voice was almost shrieking. "I said she'd be ready by 5:30 P.M." The pacing stopped. ". . . records. All of them. Understand?"

My stretcher was moved.

One of the aides from my room looked down at me. "You sure worked yourself into one sick girl."

I didn't answer. Nothing mattered.

The ambulance sped 90 miles an hour, blasting the siren all the way. I could hardly breathe. Every time the driver hit a bump, I felt death was imminent. "Please, please," I whispered, motioning weakly to the medic sitting alongside my stretcher. I could barely see the soldier's face, it was a blur.

Speaking in a kindly tone he said, "He can't slow down, miss. Orders are to get you to the hospital on the double. We're almost there. Rob," his voice panicky, "hurry it up. Jesus, Joseph and Mary . . . what if?"

45

"Are you nuts in the head?" The response was sharp, "I've got my foot down to the floor."

I was in and out of consciousness, struggling to breathe. I no longer felt anything from my waist down. Mommy, I cried to myself, come and hold me, Mommy.

The ambulance came to a screeching halt.

"Don't worry miss we'll take good care of you," the young man reassured, "you'll get good care now."

"Welcome to Harmon General Army Hospital," a caring voice greeted me. My stretcher was lifted off the ambulance and wheeled into the hospital. "Page Dr. Gordon. Tell him on the double!"

The soldier pushed me into a room. Carefully I was lifted onto a bed followed by a clanking of bars and a curtain being drawn. I heard hurried footsteps.

"Miss, you're with us aren't you?" A pair of black eyes came face to face with mine. I barely nodded my head.

"Lord," he spoke to someone, "she's white. Get Ellie fast."

"Where the hell is Gordon?"

"I don't know," a woman answered nervously. "He's had his dinner. I'm still paging. He should answer any minute. Stay here. I'll go to take her temperature."

"Dear," she whispered, "can you open your mouth slightly? That's just fine. The doctor will be here in a moment." I overheard her, "Did he answer yet? Oh, God. Don't think she'll last." A phone rang. "Hurry, Captain Gordon. A WAAC was just admitted. Fever's more than 104 degrees."

Shortly someone tenderly touched my shoulder. "Hello. I'm Captain Gordon. We're going to help you. Please bear with me. I'm going to ask you a few questions. Can you hear me?" My head hurt. I tried to move it. "Good girl," the Captain spoke gently, "I understand you are having severe pains in your back?" I painfully nodded. "You can't feel your legs at all?" I shook my head. "Can't void?" I tried to shake my head again, it only wobbled. "Can you tell me how long this has been going on?" Shakily, I held up three fingers. "Three days? Three weeks? What?" The doctor cleared his throat. "Days?" Rolled my head. "Weeks?" I nodded. "You said three weeks?" He paused and repeated. "Three weeks?" sounding puzzled. "We're going to take several x-rays right away. We'll try our very best not to hurt you."

I heard him talking. "Alice, call Major Connally. At home or at the club. Emergency!"

A young man's voice whispered in my ear. "I'm Vic. You're so pretty. When you're better, I'd like to take you out dancing. Hang on. You're going for a ride." I was moving. The icy cold table was unbearable. "Hang in there, Miss. We're all here to help you."

"Hello, young lady. I'm Major Connally," a shock of white hair appeared through the blur, "We're going to operate on you tonight. A lot of pus has accumulated; it's pressing against your spine. We are going to remove it. Can you hear me?" I bobbed my head.

"Can you give me your parents' phone number?"

The room went black. When I regained consciousness, I was spiraling down, down deep into "the well." I grunted from sheer terror. A damp cloth soothed my forehead. "Hush, little one. Just a minute longer." Warm hands held mine.

". . . . If they're not home, we'll operate without permission . . ."

Moving. Moving. Down. Down. . . .

Chapter 10

Vivid purples and bursts of hot pinks emerged like fireworks. Total blackness. A strange voice, deep and strong. "You will walk a new path. You will give up evil ways. Walk in the path of the Lord. Walk in the path of the Lord. Give up evil." The voice waned, softer, softer, into nothingness.

Light footsteps. Running water. Cool washcloth on my forehead. "Good morning," the melodious voice greeted. I squinted my eyes and saw a small framed dark-skinned nurse flashing pure white teeth. She smiled down at me.

With a great deal of effort I managed to sputter, "Did they send me to Hawaii?"

The nurse's laughter was the sound of tiny bells. "No. Hawaii sent me to you." She lifted my left arm gently. It was like torture, passing a warm washcloth over it. "I'm Kay Akana. At your disposal."

It hurt to smile. I whispered haltingly, "'A kaneh' means enema in Yiddish."

"Okay, we'll get to that too."

It was difficult to keep my eyes from closing. Sleep was all I craved.

In the afternoon, the dark haired orderly who had wheeled me into the operating room last night was standing over my bed. "We're all praying for you. If there's anything you need, tell someone to call Tony." He patted my hand and left.

I couldn't see anything above the bed because something high had been placed above the sheets. When I was moved to the right, I saw a blank wall; when I was turned to the left, window blinds were drawn.

A man with two shiny bars on his epaulet spoke to me. "Young lady," his husky voice pleaded, "it is necessary for you to cough.

It will be hard as hell but you must try even harder. Kay, she has to cough. Try harder. I'm counting on you."

"Yes, Captain Porter."

Sleep overtook me again until I was awakened by the constant ringing of a telephone. A man's voice spoke loudly, "No, sir, we can't tell you. She's in a forty-eight-hour coma. Try to control yourself. We're doing all we can."

My legs were shaking uncontrollably. The call threw me into a panic as I was certain he was talking to my father. I began grunting sounds. Footsteps came running.

"Please," begged Mary, my night nurse.

"My father?" I stammered.

"Hush, child," comforted the red-haired nurse, "the doctor's talking to him."

Tears spilled on the sheet. I moaned, "Please . . . doctors tell him . . . I'll be fine. I'll be fine."

Mary scooted down the hall. I could hear her talking. "Captain, come quickly. She's responding now." She returned in a flash. "Hush, it's all right. Your father's been told you'll be fine." placing a cool cloth across my forehead.

The Captain rushed in. "Mary, the kid's got to cough." He lowered his voice but it was audible. "Mr. Bloom will be here tomorrow if he doesn't get bumped from the flight."

"How are we going to get her to cough?"

"God only knows. Try anything you can."

The morphine gave me nightmares: I was attending my father's funeral. A Nazi plane bombarded his plane. I awoke with a blinding headache.

Kay patted my forehead the next morning. I heard her rustling something. "Nita, I have a simple exercise for you." She brought a paper bag close to my mouth. "Blow into the bag as hard as you can. Come on now, let's try to blow up the bag." I huffed a little. "Harder, Nita. I know you can do it." Nothing. "C'mon, girl, you're brave. You had to be to go into the army. Show your guts. Let's see you blow."

"I'm in too much pain," I gasped, "No energy left." Tears flowed in torrents. I was exhausted.

"Don't tell me you haven't got one burst for this bag. You can't let yourself go down the drain. Think how your father will react when he comes and finds you so sick?" My father would be fainting all over this place. He could have a heart attack. I summoned all my strength. The bag expanded.

"Thank God. That did it." Kay kissed my cheek. "You're okay, honey. That was our stepping stone."

Later that afternoon I heard footsteps enter and leave my room at least five times. A familiar face, pasty white, stared at me. I choked my sobs.

"Needala," he sobbed.

I heard my voice for the first time. "Dad?"

Dad kissed my hand passionately. "Dollink, Mama sends her love. She'll come later. Aunt Jen will come first."

"Aunt Jen?" She and Aunt Min were Mom's younger twin sisters and only ten years older than me. Aunt Jen and I were great pals. When I worked in Paterson people said we looked alike. "Did Aunt Jen join the WAAC?"

"Gottenyu," Dad exclaimed flying out of the room, mumbling, "oy vay . . .mental," a loud thump, hurried footsteps.

I pushed the bell with all my strength. "Where did my father go?" I asked the new nurse.

"He went to see about a place to stay with a Jewish family in Longview."

Poor Daddy. He could not bear hospitals. Neither could I. Sickness was for the weak. For other people. Not me. Dad stayed one more day and left.

The rest of the next day I asked to be turned more than usual. I was very restless. Later that night tumultuous claps of thunder that I had never heard before crashed repeatedly like a machine gun. I took it as an omen. I'd suffered enough. With all my might I pushed the cradle that protected my legs and feet off the bed. I pulled the sheets off, yanked the intravenous from my arm, and pulled out the catheter. God, I beseeched, as I lay prostrate, take me, take me. I can't bear it anymore. Take me. Don't let me be a burden to anyone. Take me. I don't want to live. I want to die. Please, God. Please.

Nurses raced into my room from all directions. Mary cried. "What happened? You were doing so well. Oh, you poor darling. Here let me help you."

"No, no," I muttered.

Captain Porter, the ward physician spoke gently. "It will be all right. Don't be frightened. Texas storms are noisy. You'll get used to them." He patted my hand. "We're going to help you. Don't let us down now."

I turned my face away. The Captain moved quickly to the other side of the bed. "You've come too far to give up now." He patted my cheek, swollen from crying."Besides, I have good news for you. Tomorrow you'll get some broth and Jell-O. A banquet for a princess. How about that?" He hesitated for a moment, "Nita, I think it's time for you to understand what happened here at Harmon. As you must have known, when you were brought in here you had over 104 degree fever. You were paralyzed from the waist down. We had to perform a laminectomy on the 4th and 5th dorsal vertebrae to remove an epidermal abscess."

I stared incredulously and whispered. "Then you repaired my spinal cord, and I'll be able to walk when I get better?"

Captain Porter hesitated. "How I wish it were that simple."

"Nita, your spinal cord has been severed."

I gulped, "You repaired it, didn't you?"

"Can you visualize a million telephone wires going into your spine?" He asked gently, "Science hasn't found a way to reconnect them. Maybe in the future someone will discover the secret, but in the meantime, we have to concentrate on improving your condition now." He patted my hand. "Are you going to help?"

Perhaps God in his infinite wisdom has heard my prayers and will answer them. I nodded my head slowly.

Maybe the crisis has passed and soon I will recover and return to my company. Didn't the doctor tell me that they were going to help me?

Chapter 11

Several days had passed and I was gradually improving, although I had almost no appetite nor desire to engage in conversation. Mary, my red-haired evening nurse from Oklahoma, was sitting near my bed when I awoke from a nap.

"Hi, Nita. You are some lucky woman."

"Oh?"

"Captain Porter asked several of the officers on this ward who are convalescing to take turns feeding you." She looked at me and laughed heartily. "Why Nita Bloom, you're blushing."

I flustered, "What's the reason?"

"It will relieve the nurses considerably and perhaps your appetite will improve." She straightened my sheet. "The men are apprehensive about feeding you because they feel there's a possibility that you could choke."

"I assure you I'll be very kind to them."

Mary turned as footsteps were heard. "Hello Rabbi Schuster."

Two somber dark brown eyes looked down at me. "Ve must pray." The man with the yarmulke shook his head sadly. "Ve must pray," the rabbi repeated, "you are very sick."

"I'm sorry, Rabbi," biting my lower lip, "organized prayers aren't meaningful to me. I have to talk to God my way and I have already done that."

The rabbi tightened his fingers around his prayer book. "My child, you must pray the way your people have done for centuries. We have special prayers for the sick. You are very sick. You need to say these words of comfort that have helped many people to a full recovery."

"I'm sorry, Rabbi. I can't."

"All right. All right. I'll pray for you. I'll pray every day." He rocked back and forth. "Why can't you pray the way your father does?" A tear trickled down my face. "Don't worry. Shh. Just rest and get well."

In the afternoon my little plump nurse from Massachusetts, Johnny, carried a huge bouquet of flowers into the room. I was lying on my right side. Turning me every hour was important in order to prevent bed sores.

"Chickadee, let's see who sent this magnificent bouquet?"

"I have no idea."

"The card says, 'All my love, TJ.'"

No comment.

"You don't seem very interested?" Johnny cajoled, "If someone sent me these gorgeous flowers, I'd flip."

"Ordinarily, so would I, but I stopped seeing him before I went into the army. He hurt me badly. I don't need his flowers now." I was puzzled that Ted had already heard the news about me. Suddenly, I realized everyone in Suffern knew I was paralyzed.

"Gee, kid, sorry to butt in. None of my business anyhow. Is it all right to leave them? I'll be back in a little while."

"Oh, yes. They're magnificent. Please take some for yourself." I turned my head to the side, reflecting on T.J. and what he would think if he saw me now. No more legs for the tango, the rhumba, the conga. Dead weights. I strangled my sobs. I was beyond dancing.

A dark-haired attendant stood at my bedside. "Hello, beautiful. Remember me? Victor. I'm the one who promised to take you out dancing."

"Sorry."

The young soldier came closer. "You are a very lucky lady. Did anyone tell you what happened the night you had the operation?"

"What do you mean?"

"Listen, kid, I shouldn't be telling you, but I feel you should know." Victor lowered his voice. "You died on the operating table."

"What?"

"Your heart stopped beating for a few minutes. Everyone panicked. Thank God it started after the surgeon kept massaging your heart." Victor paused while the serious lines on his face eased into a beautiful smile. "Lovely lady, you have to get well. God meant for you to live. We're all pulling for you." Tears filled the young man's eyes. "I have to tell you I'm shipping out in a couple of days. I wanted to wish you all the luck in the world. I'm sorry I won't be here to dance with you at the big celebration."

I vaguely recalled that Victor promised to take me dancing just before the operation. He gallantly kissed my hand. "Just stay beautiful."

Now I knew for a certainty it must have been God's voice speaking to me that night. No one would ever believe me. It didn't matter. I knew and I believed. I looked over at the flowers and kept thinking about Ted. How did he know where I was? My father never spoke to him. My father never spoke to anyone I loved. Maybe he found out from Mom? Oh, what difference did it make? Pity was the last thing I wanted from TJ.

Johnny announced brightly, "Someone's here to see you, Nita."

"Aunt Jen!" Grateful tears flowed freely. She covered my face with kisses. "Please tell me how you got here. When I asked Dad if you had joined the army, he dashed out of my room." I held onto my aunt's hand. "Did you get fired and join the WAAC?"

"No, honey, my boss gave me permission to see my favorite niece." Aunt Jen was striking with long, thick dark auburn hair fashioned in a twirled bun at the nape of her neck. I worshiped her and was flattered when I was often taken as her younger sister.

"When is Mom coming?"

My aunt paused for a second. "She'll be here soon, dear." She kissed my cheek. "Tell you about my trip. I was bumped only once. You know soldiers have first priority on all planes. I had to wield my feminine powers this time. I can't tell you how wonderful it is to see you." She kissed my cheek again. "Did you really like the Army? Why is your thumb bandaged?"

"Oh, yes," evading any discussion about my thumb." I loved every part of it. My small town upbringing was a great asset. I took to the marching easily; unfortunately, many of the women were totally knocked out."

"I knew you would be a leader."

"Some leader," I laughed. "I almost led my company astray," and then regaled her with the story about how I marched away from my platoon. The excitement of being with Aunt Jen made the urine bottle tinkle. We continued talking but I could feel my face getting flushed.

"Were your courses difficult?"

"Not really. I found them easy but terribly boring, especially map reading. So many courses were a complete waste. What impressed me most was the spirit, the comradeship. I'm almost certain I'll be sent to OCS when I return."

"What's OCS?"

"Sorry. Officers Training School."

"I'm sure you will, sweetie."

"I'm hoping I'll qualify for a college education too," taking a deep sigh. "All I hope and pray for is that I begin to make more progress soon."

"You will. Everyone is proud of how far you've come."

"Maybe by the time Mom comes I'll be almost all better."

"That's what we all want, dear. Now, you just relax and I'll bring you up to date about the family."

The next day my aunt and I talked more intimately, "Neet, how did all this happen?" She took a brush from her purse to fix my hair.

Sooner or later I knew someone would ask. I couldn't tell her. I didn't want to remember. It was over. I was away from that awful woman. I didn't want to talk about it.

"Oh honey, I'm sorry. Believe me, and I won't ask again." Aunt Jen kept turning a little pinky ring. "I just want you to know if you ever decide to tell me, I promise I'll never repeat it to anyone in the family."

Later that evening a colonel who had been injured in England was taking his turn at feeding me. He was a tall, lean aristocratic man who walked with a slight limp. "And what do we have here?" pointing to a series of pipes alongside my bed.

"That's my coat hanger, Colonel Watkins."

"Just as you say, my dear. Now let's get to the business at hand. My, we have a lovely tomato broth tonight."

Actually the coat hanger was a makeshift irrigation system set up to flush my bladder and kidneys. I was terribly embarrassed when it tinkled in front of visitors, but somehow I managed to keep my cool. I had no sense of when I was voiding, or moving my bowels, nor did I have any sensation in my legs. The doctors were always sticking me with pins but I could only feel the pricks above my abdomen.

"You're a dear, so patient. See how you've coerced me into eating more and more." I opened my mouth for some mashed potato. "What story have you in mind for today?"

"I was thinking you might like to hear about the good old days at West Point."

The men related the most fascinating tales. Usually, I tried to entice them to talk about their personal lives. They seemed to relax when they knew that nothing would be repeated.

One afternoon toward the end of Aunt Jen's stay, she announced, "You're going to have visitors soon."

"Visitors?"

"A doctor and a WAAC from Nacogdoches are waiting to see you."

I gritted my teeth. "Is she short and squatty?"

"Yes. Nita, are you all right? Don't you want to see them? I'll tell them you're not feeling well."

I didn't utter a sound. It was a moment of terror. I motioned her to wait and closed my eyes. "Dear God, what shall I do? I don't want to cause a commotion. What's done is done. I know that You will take care of them in Your infinite ways." I looked at my aunt, "Tell them to come in. They won't stay long."

Five-by-Five, washed and scrubbed with a pure white starched collar, and Captain Earheart stood at attention as far as they could from my bed. The sergeant chewed on her lips. She didn't get to lock me up after all. He remained in the rigid position.

"How are you?"

"Fine."

"Getting there?"

"Goodbye."

Goodbye forever. Aunt Jen's arms held me close while I sobbed my heart out. "What is it? What did they do to you?" Slowly and with great effort, I blurted out the barest facts.

My aunt was horrified. "A razor blade? I must tell the person in charge of this hospital. He has to bring them to trial."

"No, no, Aunt Jen," I begged, "You promised. It's over. Finished. My thumb is still oozing with pus but not as painful as it was. The doctors have reassured me that it will heal in time. I don't have to worry about that woman. God will punish her."

"Nita, something has to be done. Let me handle it for you. If justice isn't pursued now, it will go by the wayside. You'll be just another number. I'm going to write to President Roosevelt." Aunt Jen sat on the edge of the bed still holding me. "You won't have to bother one bit. I'll take care of everything."

"No, no, no! I beg of you. No!" I was so exhausted I had to

stop talking and thinking about that terrible experience forever.

"All right. Please don't torment yourself anymore. You need all your energy to get well. I won't let anyone hurt you. I promise. If this is what you want, I'll never tell anyone."

I couldn't tolerate the mere thought of any more trouble. I never wanted to see that woman again.

The next afternoon I heard someone pacing back and forth outside my room. It was Major Connelly, the orthopedic surgeon who performed the laminectomy on my spine.

"Good afternoon. How's my star patient coming along?

"I hope it won't be long before I get walking again. The quicker I can get started the sooner I'll be able to rejoin my company."

The Major carried a chair over and placed it close to the bed. "Tell me, young lady, what do you know about your body and how it functions?"

"Not too much. My body's a stranger now. We don't speak the same language." Connelly jumped up and began pacing again. "As I see it, you have two options. One, you can be a spoiled brat. God knows you have a right to be waited on hand and foot."

I stared at the man intently, absorbing every word. "Everyone will want to help you. Help the heck out of you. Especially when you go home. They'll pamper your every whim." He opened a silver cigarette case. "Mind if I smoke?" I nodded enviously wondering when I could smoke again. Dr. Connelly offered me one.

"Not yet, thanks. My mouth still tastes like straw."

"Or," the doctor continued, "you could take this time to learn about your body. How it works. The functions of your muscles. What does it take to make one muscle work?"

The man made everything so fascinating. "Really, I never took the time to become that acquainted with my bodily functions." The only knowledge I had about muscle training was when the polio epidemic occurred and I heard how hard it was for the children to drag around heavy braces to help them walk again. "I'm sure it will take a while before I can walk again and maybe I'll have to wear braces on my legs first."

Major Connelly looked pleased. "You are certainly starting with the right attitude." He patted my hand. "You won't be seeing me anymore. Captain Porter will be assigned full-time. I must say you have a great attitude."

"How can I thank you for saving my life?"

"Just continue your beautiful spirit. I wish I could take you with me on rounds to some of the sad sacks. You would be a shot in the arm for them."

Tears of gratefulness fell freely after he left. Everyone at the hospital was helping me. Somehow, I promised myself, I'll get the strength to persevere faster than they dream possible; I'll learn all about my body. God gave me brains and I would put two and two together and make it all work just fine!

Chapter 12

Aunt Jen's stay was all too short. Despite the reason for her visit, I was certain she had enjoyed herself. Not only did she dine with several of my nurses but one or two of the officers had taken her to dinner. After each date, when she visited the next day, she would give me a blow by blow description and we giggled until I couldn't tolerate the pain. After she left I went into a slump: moody, sullen and full of despair about my future. Thoughts began spinning, mainly focusing on memories of early childhood, my first love and my guilt.

I would reflect on my rebellious childhood. My introduction to unthinking prejudice came in the third grade. A new classmate, a slight and frail looking girl named Hannah, and I were walking home from school. Margie and another girl came charging up to us. Margie, rough and tough, began taunting Hannah, calling out, "Yer nothin' but a lousy, dirty Jew. Jew broad-Jew bitch!"

I was small but I stretched to my full height to face this tall tormentor. "Stop it, Margie. Leave her alone. Pick on someone your own size."

"What are you going to do about it, runt?"

"I'll show you, if you keep it up." My buddy Joey had taught me how to fight. I had no fear of this lummox. Margie pushed my shoulders. I shoved her back. She punched me in the chin. Angered rather than frightened, I grabbed her by the shoulders and shook her until she screamed. I released my grip. "Leave us alone. We haven't done anything to you. I'm going to tell my father and he'll tell your mother." That stopped her. She knew her mom bought last season's clothes from my dad's small baby shop.

Margie yanked her friend's hand and the two of them ran off. "Let's leave the Jews alone. Save it for another day."

That day never occurred. In fact, although most of my school chums in Suffern were gentiles, I never suffered another antisemitic incident there. My father constantly railed about the pogroms that had been part of his childhood in Poland. Although I felt badly for him, I didn't relate to his fears. I was an American. Such terrors had no place in my life. Until my freshman year, Dad had allowed me to go to all my friends' parties, even though Bernie Fox and I were the only Jewish kids. But as a sophomore, when I met Herm, my father forbid me to date non-Jews.

Out of the blue, my father became adamant. "You're not a child anymore. You're to stick to your own kind."

It made no sense to me, because my father didn't confine his friendships to only Jewish people. He was very friendly to all his customers, Jewish or otherwise. He knew their names, their children's first names, and shared family stories with them. He was also a great kibitzer with the local shopkeepers. I didn't understand why he carried his anger to such extremes.

Just before my senior year in 1938, Dad's business began going downhill; he had to declare bankruptcy. One night I heard Mom consoling Dad because he was very despondent about his inability to pay his creditors, which meant he would be forced to find another means of making a living. A few of his friends lent him money to buy a small liquor store in Piermont, New York, about forty minutes from Suffern. My parents rented a house in the neighboring town of Nyack.

When Dad told me about the move that would take place before I graduated, I became hysterical. Between sobs I appealed to him. "Dad, I beg of you, please don't ask me to leave my friends now. I'm class editor for the yearbook. I'm a cheerleader. I'm in the band and orchestra. I've been with these kids since second grade. I'll die if you make me go." What I didn't say was that the thought of leaving Herm, my Dutch Protestant boyfriend, made me frantic. He was the light of my life and the thought of leaving him left me distraught. Dad finally agreed to ask a Jewish family in Suffern, the Lichts, if I could live with them until I finished high school and they agreed.

My boyfriend's parents came from Holland. His father worked for the county water works in the daytime while his wife and two sons operated their corner grocery store a few hundred feet from where my parents once lived. Herm, was four and a half years older than I. Whenever my mom sent me to buy a few items,

I would hear him practicing on the piano. I was certain that one day he would become a noted pianist.

I met Herm when I was fourteen and at first he was like an older brother. He and his younger brother invited me to play street tennis. I was totally shocked when he asked me to go ice skating at the Bear Mountain Rink. Even though I suspected another girl had turned him down, I was overjoyed that he thought to ask me. I was in the seventh grade; Herm was a senior. He was about six feet tall, sandy blond curly hair and emerald green eyes. Although I was flattered, I was very concerned about my father's insistence that I date only Jewish boys. I asked Herm if he would go down to the store and ask my father's permission, explaining to him that my dad did not want me to go out with gentile boys. I was floored when he told me that my father had granted permission for what was to be our one—the only—the last date (or so I thought).

Bear Mountain was the greatest day of my life. Herm's younger brother, Gerrit, and his girlfriend came, too. Herm was an outstanding skater and I found I had no difficulty keeping up with him. What a thrill it was when he taught me how to waltz on the ice.

At the end of the evening we took his brother's date home first. When his brother got out of the car to take his date in the house, Herm and I were listening to 'Stars Fell on Alabama.' He put his arm around me and asked if he could kiss me. I was thrilled beyond words and nodded. His lips were soft; it was like being in heaven instead of sitting on the front seat of a roadster. One kiss led to another. My heart pounded. We came home an hour after my curfew.

As soon as the car pulled up to the curb, Dad flew down the steps and yanked open the front door.

Herm immediately interjected, "Sorry, Mr. Bloom. I meant to be on time."

My father ignored him. "Aneeda," he shrieked, "get in the house." I scooted past him, my face burning with embarrassment, fearing the whole neighborhood must have heard. His accent seemed thicker and more out of place than ever before. "You lied," I heard him accuse Herm. "It doesn't matter. You are never to see her again. Do you understand? Ve are Jewish. She does not go out with Christians. Good night."

Mortified, I ran to my room slamming the door. Dad punched

it open. "Aneeda, it's for your own good. I knew I shouldn't have said yes. You don't go with Deutsches." My father seemed to have become more prejudiced since that maniac Hitler became chancellor of Germany. "I am vorrying night and day about my brother and his children and you're going to carry on with a shaygets? You know what Hitler is doing to the Jews? Don't you ever let me catch you with him again, do you hear?"

Dad's threats didn't stop me. My parents both worked in the store until late every night. I came home to an empty house. It was easy for me to see Herm. There was no way I was going to sever the relationship. My sister was flattered that I shared this confidence, vowing never to spill the beans.

Herm treated me like a queen; he was my mentor. If I didn't eat with proper manners, he didn't ridicule me. I simply learned by watching him. I had poor study habits but with his patient teaching I began to improve. When I had a problem with a report, he met me in the library and slipped me notes explaining how to go about getting the information. He was kind to Marilyn, who thought Herm was the greatest. Usually I considered my sister a pest but in this instance she was a Trojan.

Herm taught me to love classical music. We played all kinds of musical guessing games. Was it Beethoven? Tchaikovsky? Chopin? In his spare time, Herm was studying to become a concert pianist. My own piano playing improved. We were ideally matched physically; smooched for hours. Kisses left both of us breathless, yearning for more. Just when I thought I'd die if we didn't go further, he would hold me and rock me into quietness.

How I yearned to put my arms round my dad and tell him what a bright caring person Herm was, but I knew it would lead to naught. My mom concurred with everything my father said, and sadly, I began to lose respect for her, because I felt she didn't assert herself. Herm said no other girl affected him as I did but he wouldn't go all the way until we were married. In fact, Herm insisted that I continue to date others. He didn't want me to feel cheated after we were married, and in turn, I encouraged him to take out other girls, but my voice lacked conviction.

I loved to dance and I was usually invited to all the dances. During my senior year, my card was filled with a different partner for most every set. School dances usually ended early. A boy would take me to the Lichts, where I would pretend to walk up the steps, but soon as the car pulled away, I would race up the street to where Herm was waiting.

I had no trouble hiding my romance from the Lichts. They were an older European couple who had just adopted a baby boy. The poor woman was in a constant state of panic in the care of her infant. I was relieved because I wasn't there most of the time and felt more relaxed when I saw she had things under control. Of course they had promised my father they would keep tabs on me, but the truth was neither one of them ever paid any attention to my comings and goings. The only one who knew about Herm was my good friend Hannah, the same girl I had protected years ago. Hannah was a couple of years older than me. Quite shy, she rarely dated although she was beautiful. Too bad she always smelled of garlic. Hannah loved to hear about my escapades with Herm, lapping up every single word. She promised to be a witness at our wedding the following year when I turned eighteen. Religion was not a problem for us. Herm promised that if his being Jewish was important to me and would bring peace with my family, he would convert. I decided to make an appointment with our rabbi, but this produced negative results because he was on my father's side.

Thinking about my past in the hospital gave me a severe headache. How I yearned to talk to Herm now, though I knew it was impossible. I had called his mother to say goodbye when I left for the service and she told me then that he was married. For that moment I felt dead. Like the end of the world had come. The past was forever over. I gritted my teeth. I knew once and for all I would have to face my own problems.

When would my mom come? Why hadn't she been here before? I blinked my eyes to restrain the tears. I visualized Mom's beautiful face, her deep penetrating brown eyes, her jet black hair encircling a rosy complexion. Everyone said I look just like Mom and we could be taken for sisters. We had been great pals then. Mom told wonderful stories about her past. She taught me many songs that I played on the piano and we would sing together. All my parents' nieces and nephews loved to visit us. They even liked Dad, who catered to my mother's family. That was a long time ago. Poor Mom, she still suffered from depression. At least once a year she would leave home for a couple of weeks. Sometimes she would go to Atlantic City or visit Aunt Jen. I was certain that merely getting away from my father was the only medicine she needed. She always returned in good spirits. For a while my father was sweet to her but soon he would forget and resort to his normally gruff disposition and his vicious temper. I once asked my mom why she stayed with him.

"Where would I have gone? I had two children. No money. It was impossible," she said as she took a deep sigh, "besides, when your father is calm, he is caring and gentle. He performs good deeds for people in need. You can be proud of your father."

I decided a decision must have been made to keep the news of my paralysis from my fragile mother for now. There was no use. Mom had stopped being a pal because she catered to all of my father's demands. I couldn't wait to get away from my parents: it seemed everything I said caused a major calamity. My father's face would get blotchy and turn crimson; his eyes would glare and his voice would reach a terrifying pitch. Despite the fact that he never used physical violence, he was frightening. There were many occasions when Marilyn and I stood up to him, but he was hard to take. Everything was a major catastrophe. The rare moments when I had loving feelings for him were when he showered to go out for an occasion—I liked the smell of his shaving cream, his selection of clothes, his cherubic smile when anyone complimented him, but most of the time he looked and acted like a bulvan: rough and tough, sounding like an oaf who just got off the boat. When I told him I had enlisted, I almost feared for my life. I could still hear him screaming.

"You know what kind of a woman joins the army? Camp followers. Is that what you are? After Momma and I gave you such a proper upbringing!" His voice reached that crazy pitch again. My mother had stood by without uttering a sound.

How could either of my parents ever be of help now?

Chapter 13

One afternoon a strange man wearing a stiff white collar poked his face over the cradle that covered my legs on my bed. "Hey, when am I going to see you looking decent? " I turned my head and looked away. It was the first time anyone at Harmon had been nasty to me. "Okay, if you want to look like a creep. I won't be back until you're fit to be seen." I pulled the sheet over my head. The nerve of him. Who the devil was he anyway?

A new nurse, Kay, carried a basin of water for a bed bath. "I see Father McGinnis paid you a visit."

"What an ugly person! He said some pretty mean things to me."

"Father is the Catholic Chaplain. We're all crazy about him."

"I can't believe my ears. Crazy about a man like that?" I sulked while she sponged soapy water over my body.

As soon as the nurse left, I reached over to my night table fumbling for a mirror. I was shocked to see my pale drawn reflection and straggly hair. My nightclothes were government issue. I felt my yucky hair. I hadn't looked in a mirror since the morning of graduation when pictures were taken. No wonder Aunt Jen was always brushing my hair.

I began musing about other incidents for the first time. Marilyn would be graduating in June. Had my condition affected her and her ability to study for exams? She was very bright, but still . . . What was happening? She never wrote. Whatever happened to Cousin Jackie? Did he know about me? I never looked at all the hundreds of cards and letters that were sent. I knew one of the nurses had read them to me, but I had forgotten who sent them. The world bottomed out–like it never was.

"Kay, would it be possible to get a shampoo?" Kay began to whistle. "I think Mary will find the time." Mary and Kay had been assigned to special me through the critical period. They were now assigned to the full ward but they came occasionally to do little favors after they were finished with their regular work.

Two days later the Chaplain returned. His six-foot hulk loomed over the cradle. "Hey, there used to be an ugly puss in here. Well, I'll be darned if this little lady isn't mighty attractive."

"Father, it's not you I'm dressing up for. It's for all those handsome officers."

"Where did you get that sexy nightgown?"

"My WAAC buddies sent it before they shipped out."

"Well, you better be careful. Some of those men haven't seen a woman since they arrived."

"Father, the men are perfect gentlemen. Speak for yourself."

"Now this conversation is getting out of hand. I'll stop in another day when you're not such a brat."

I laughed heartily. It had been a long time since I'd bantered with anyone. "No, don't go. I was only kidding. I'm sorry."

"Okay, brat. I'll give you another chance. How about a little poetry?"

"That would be simply divine, sir."

An endearing friendship blossomed. Each sensed the other's vulnerability and the two of us developed the ability to tease without malice. I craved his visits as well as his many surprises: a milkshake, a candy bar, a few sprigs of desert spring flowers.

A week later, there was a knock on my door. Rapidity-rap-rapidity-rap-rap-rap. That could only be one person in the whole world: "Mom!" Softness and sweet scent surrounded me. "Oh, Mom, I'm so happy you're here."

I had to be careful to conceal my feelings. This time there would be no tears. I did not want my mother to become frightened. "Oh, what a darling nosegay. Mom, thanks."

We yakked about nothing and laughed about local gossip. "Mother, they're going to start me on therapy tomorrow. I'm truly happy you're here. Now I know I'll start making real progress. Mom, how is Mar doing? It must be really hard for her."

Mom placated my fears and all my concerns. She was wonderful as long as I remained calm.

Therapy consisted of light passive arm and leg exercises. The treatment lasted ten minutes. The second day I was lifted onto a large wooden wheelchair with the back inclined, and the pedals elevated. Everyone cheered when they saw me out of the stretcher.

"I told you things were going to get better." Mom smothered my face with kisses.

Several times my mother left the room. Her pain was obvious when my legs began shaking uncontrollably. The only way such a "clonus" could be stopped was when a therapist exerted a lot of pressure to the balls of my feet. Then it would take several minutes before the severe jerks and quivers ceased.

One afternoon I was sipping on a malted that Mom had brought. "Mother, what do you do when you're not visiting me?"

"Sometimes I help the nurses feed bedridden patients. I take walks. Daddy had rented a room at the Sosland's and that's where I stay. They are very considerate. Occasionally they've taken me sightseeing. Once or twice I had dinner with your nurses. Everyone is very kind."

While we were talking, the director of the hospital, Colonel Emerson walked in. "How's our star patient?"

"I'm coming along. I've been going to therapy three times a week."

"Fine. Young lady, I have a surprise for you." He paused, glancing quickly at my mother. "How would you like to be transferred closer to your home?"

The water jug tinkled as though someone hurled a hundred pennies into it. "You must be joking."

My mother cautioned, "Dear, don't get yourself upset."

"Colonel Emerson, what are you talking about?" I asked tersely.

The colonel shifted from one foot to the other. "My dear, Harmon is a hospital for emergency surgery only. You have stayed as long as Army regulations will permit. Your mother and I discussed this and we feel you'll be much happier close to your family and friends."

"No," I shrieked. Mary flew in; Emerson waved her out.

"We are going to send you to a Veteran's Hospital relatively near your home."

I was aghast! A Veteran's old age hospital? My God, they were sending me home to die. I'd been kidding myself. All the time I thought I was making progress. Going to rejoin my buddies. What a jerk. A first-class jerk. "How can you do this to me? Everyone promised I'd get well here. They believe in me. Everyone wants to help. You're sending me to an old age home to die." I turned to my mother. "You knew it all the time. That's why you finally came. So you could take me home. I'm not going. Do you hear? I'm not going!" My voice was becoming louder and louder. Mom left the room.

The colonel handed me a piece of paper. "Nita, this is your discharge paper. Please sign here."

I ripped the paper out of his hands tearing it to shreds. "Never! Never will I sign my death certificate. I want to make my progress here where everyone is kind. Everyone promised I'd get well here. I want to rejoin my buddies."

The next thing I knew Mary was giving me smelling salts and wiping my forehead.

My mother left the next day. We never said goodbye.

Three days before my 22nd birthday, I was separated from the army. Two officers signed the honorable discharge papers. I was taken by stretcher and put on a train accompanied by a physician whom I had never seen before and two strange nurses.

Destination: Bronx Veteran's Hospital.

Chapter 14

Before I left Harmon General, Captain Porter, Kay, Mary and Johnny brought a bottle of Haig and Haig Scotch to my room. I knew it was a bittersweet celebration: to my health, to the great improvement that I'd made and to more progress in the future. Somehow I maintained a cheerful disposition for these dear, dear, people and never allowed myself to become sad. I requested a sleeping pill that night.

Two days before I was discharged from Harmon, Captain Porter stopped in. "Honey, you're looking mighty good sitting up." No reaction. "Honey baby, how'd you like to try something really new?" New? Perhaps I wasn't going to be discharged after all? I perked up a little. "Let's get the hell rid of the indwelling catheter, the tidal drainage and the whole damn system."

I gasped, "What? You must be kidding?"

"There's an old European method, called *credee*. You find your bladder, push on it gently until you express all the urine. You'll have to record how many times a day and night you need to do it. In a short time I hope you'll develop a routine. There is evidence that you're getting some return of sensation."

"Wow, wow, wow, I can't believe it. Take out my catheter? Go to the bathroom like I used to?"

"Now, Honey," the Captain interrupted, "don't get carried away. Please." John Porter patted my face. "It may not work. We only have a few days. Are you willing?"

I grabbed the doctor's hand, kissing it passionately.

The Captain called Kay to assist. When they removed the catheter, the bed was soaked.

I covered my face. "I can't. Please don't make me. I can't."

Captain Porter pulled a chair close to my bedside. "Sweetie, you'll be leaving soon and we will have to insert a catheter while you're traveling. We only have a short time to practice. I don't give a goddamn if the bed has to be changed a thousand times.

Eventually you'll be successful. I know you can do it, but most of the time, especially at first, it will be a bust. You'll need the patience of a saint." I couldn't look at him. "Girl, this is your only chance. Promise me you'll give it your best try. Promise?"

The Captain had been unusually kind to me and my family, but he had not offered any positive physical recommendations. This was the first ray of optimism; the only specific directive he or anyone else had offered me. If it worked, it could change my life. I didn't want to think about my incontinence or loss of bowel control. My daily prayers were that somehow everything would all return to normal. I owed it to this wonderful man to try this system. I extended my hand. John grabbed it warmly.

Getting on the bedpan was extremely painful to the point that I felt like my back was breaking. I knew that I had to endure the suffering if I was to get rid of the disgusting catheter. I tried several times to stay on the bedpan and each time I tried my best to *credee*. The pain was intense. My efforts were unsuccessful. I could not urinate. They struggled to lift me off the bedpan and each time that they did lift me, the bed was wet. Sweat poured out of me.

"Please, I can't."

They quickly changed the wet sheets so that I could try again. This occurred over and over. Their patience was unbelievable.

Once more they struggled to lift me on the bedpan and once more I pressed with all the strength I had on my bladder. At last the first sound of urine was heard. One would have thought the Messiah had come, the way everyone cheered. How would I ever persuade the VA staff to allow me to remove the catheter that had to be inserted for the trip?

The next morning two orderlies carried me by stretcher on to the train. How different this would be from the trips to Fort Oglethorpe and Texas. Accompanying me were two strange nurses and a doctor I had never seen before. The nurses performed their duties in an offhand manner and the doctor scarcely paid any attention to me. I was strapped to the bed in a private compartment and left alone for long periods of time. The constant droning of the wheels intensified the rawness of my back surgery. It was just like the shivers that went through my body when a piece of chalk scraped against a blackboard.

"Will you take some broth?" one of the nurses asked.

"Thank you." Drink, drink, Captain Porter's last pleading instruction had urged. That's the name of the game. At least ten glasses of water a day!

As soon as the nurse left, I began mulling over every detail of my last week at the hospital. I felt guilty about how I treated Mom. I prayed that she wouldn't go into a deep depression. I had to force myself to concentrate on the good aspects of being closer to home. I would see Marilyn. I would see all my relatives and friends—but the thought of them seeing me in this horrible condition made me sick. Everyone would pity me.

God had deserted me. He had been playing tricks. Flashing a light, then snuffing it out. All the loving care, the excellent medical attention—all the good at Harmon—down the drain. Why didn't they just let me die? Why the torment?

Every week Captain Porter had examined me. He would stick my legs with pins and ask if I felt anything. He tapped my knees for the knee jerk spasm; he ran his finger up the back of my feet and my big toe would jump back: the bobinski, indicative of a spinal cord injury. I had almost normal sensations to the waist but from there on down, feelings became sketchy and less and less definable. I felt nothing on my tush. If anyone accidently put their hands on my legs, I cringed as though an emery board was filing a hangnail. The slightest pressure to my legs caused involuntary spasms that lasted several minutes almost driving me crazy. The bed would shake and cause my bladder to expel fluid. The urine bottle underneath the bed jangled endlessly. The only progress I made was when three pillows were propped behind my back and I could sit up for 15 minutes, three times a day.

The staff at the hospital lied to me. They wanted me out of there. They knew I was going to the veteran's hospital — to die.

The three day train ride seemed endless. The meals were horrible, endless miles of boring scenery, nurses who were merely doing their duty and an indifferent doctor who had about as much interest in me as he would in a stuffed pig. I never said a word to the nurses except to thank them when they brought a meal or to say good night when they finished their nightly duties. Finally we arrived in New York.

A VA ambulance awaited the train at Penn station. The medical team left saying they would meet me at the hospital. The ride to the Bronx was maddening; the blasted siren screeched as the driver sped through the city streets; he drove like I was about to die, and because of him I was sure I would.

"Guys," I pleaded, "my back surgery has not healed and the ride is causing me great pain. There's no emergency. The worst is over. Please don't drive so fast."

"Okay, lady. Sorry," slowing down maybe 5 miles an hour. About an hour later several large red brick buildings outlined the horizon and the ambulance soon came to a stop. My stretcher was lifted out of the ambulance and rolled through the emergency entrance, passing patients in the halls, then on to an elevator which stopped on the 6th floor where I was pushed into an office.

"Good luck, miss," the driver said.

"Thanks and much appreciation for slowing down."

After an endless wait, I heard the doctor and the two nurses who had accompanied me, talking to someone in subdued tones. Shortly, a man in a white coat with a chubby round face and dark wavy hair poked his head over my stretcher.

"Hello," he greeted with a half smile, "I'm Dr. Kessler. You'll be sharing a room with another woman."

Another patient? Probably someone from the World War I. "Oh, please, sir, may I have a single room?"

"Now, Bloom," the army doctor interrupted, "these are the VA rules."

Dr. Kessler looked very uncomfortable and began fidgeting with his pencil. "I'm sorry. . ." He seemed embarrassed and avoided looking directly at me.

"Dr. Kessler, please, I'm learning a new technique to empty my bladder. I just have to have privacy," I pleaded, trying to keep from crying. I felt faint and summoned every ounce of strength to beg. "Doctor, it would mean everything to me. I have to strengthen my bladder or I'll have this horrible catheter for the rest of my life."

Dr. Kessler took a deep breath. "All right. We'll try, but I can tell you that the nurses won't like changing your bed one bit." He cleared his throat. "Mrs. Wright, please take this patient to Room 611."

I kept shaking my head in gratitude. The Texas contingent said their goodbyes and left. The VA nurse was silent as she pushed me all the way down the hall. A couple of white-haired elderly women stood in the doorway. No one smiled or said a word. I learned that most of the patients were from World War I and even a few from the Spanish American War. Some of them would glare at me when my door was open, even though I smiled and said "Hello."

The next day, May 30, 1943, would be my 22nd birthday. Suffern was now incredibly close. "Nurse, may I call my parents to tell them I've arrived?"

The response was short. "Let's get you to bed."

Imposing solid steel bars across the window verified that I was securely locked in the veteran's hospital. My immediate thought was, "Don't worry, I won't escape; but you can bet your bottom dollar I would, if I could!" The decor consisted of a twin size gray hospital bed, a gray steel dresser with a matching night-table and one chair.

"I'll have to get someone to help me put you in bed. Oh, Jesus, your catheter fell out," and out she ran. She returned with another unsmiling nurse. In a jiffy they got me into bed and to my shock, did not insert the catheter. It really felt good to get on to a comfortable mattress.

"Give me the change and I'll call."

My eyes filled again, "I'm afraid I don't have any money yet. My parents will bring some tomorrow." The nurse stiffened. I waited. She added grumpily, "I'll see what I can do."

"Thank you so much. It's my birthday tomorrow. I have to let my folks know I'm here." I knew I was groveling. "Would you please bring me a bedpan." A strange nurse went to fetch it.

"How're you going to get on the pan?" she glared when she returned.

"Please help me. I'm sure I'll be able to do it myself soon."

I stayed on that cold piece of steel for an hour, but no matter how hard I pushed I couldn't express my bladder.

"Just don't make it a habit," the nurse said sternly. The air was as cold as the metal in the room.

Dr. Kessler reappeared. "You look exhausted. I'll examine you on Monday." He turned to go.

"Sir, I would like to discuss my bladder condition," praying he was unaware that I was still on the bedpan.

The man shifted from one foot to another. "I'm sure it can wait until Monday."

"Dr. Kessler," I persisted, "a few days before I left the Army Hospital, I was taught how to *credee* my bladder." Kessler's nose twitched. "My army physician begged me to have patience." I detailed the instructions taking great care not to offend the doctor.

Dr. Kessler's eyes lit up, "I have a great idea. You should keep the catheter. You can water the daisies just below your window. They could certainly use daily watering." He laughed and his belly was jiggling. The man was ridiculing me.

I knew I would always have a difficult time with him whenever a hard decision had to be made. I winced. God, how could he? "Doctor, I beg of you to give me this chance. I gave the Captain my word." My legs were shaking badly.

"Do you have any idea what havoc this is going to cause the nursing staff?"

The expression of fright on my face must have alarmed him. "Wait until Monday when our neurologist examines you."

"Oh, please, I can't bear for my parents to see the bottle one more time. Tomorrow is my birthday. Please?" The spasms in my legs were pulling so hard I thought I would fall out of the bed. The bedpan was killing me.

"All right," the ward physician said wearily as he mopped his brow, "we'll give it a try. Have a good night. Happy Birthday."

I closed my eyes saying over and over to myself, "Don't think. Don't think." Kay had cautioned me to proceed very tenuously. I'll never last, I feared, I'll never last.

I pondered tomorrow. Who would come? What did the family think about my being in a veteran's hospital? They must all know I'm going to die soon. Die in a soaking wet bed. Maybe I should keep the catheter? No fights. To heck with a Captain who gave an order he knew was impossible to keep. If I was going to die soon why should I torture myself and everyone else?

Chapter 15

My parents visited the next day after my VA arrival. Mom came over to kiss me. Dad sat down across the room, teary eyed. All he had to do was come near me; hold me and I would have let my guard down and opened up all the pent up emotions. I really wanted to tell him about everything that had happened. . . . but he didn't and I didn't. . . . I never told my parents the truth about what took place while I was in the WAAC.

However, I was more than thankful to see Mom looking alert and cheerful. Dad brought me a box of bittersweet chocolates — the kind he loved and I hated. My father gobbled one piece after the other, his eyes filled with tears, but no words were uttered.

Mom smiled broadly, "Sweetheart, Happy Birthday. Everyone is asking about you. Next week the family will be here."

"Oh, great, but just a few at a time, please. When is Aunt Jen coming?" I was anxious to tell her how the army railroaded me out of the hospital. My father wiped his eyes, jumped up and dashed out of the room.

The two of us sat quietly. "Mom, Daddy can't stand the sight of me, can he?"

"Oh, honey, don't say things like that. Daddy loves you."

There she went again, always defending Dad. Never a word of criticism. Always making excuses for his behavior. I knew my parents were hurting but I was hurting more. Mom was smiling, but I suddenly became aware of the dullness in her eyes. No, I had never been sure of my father's love. The only time I thought he cared for me was when I dated a Jewish boy of his choice. Well, he wouldn't have to worry about any of my dates any more.

I wanted to tell my parents about the *credee* method but I knew that was a lost cause. They weren't capable of understanding, we simply could not communicate. I knew they must have questioned my doctors and nurses; my curiosity was aroused as to what kind of questions they had asked.

Suddenly I had to use the bedpan. "Mom, could you please ask the nurse to get me a bedpan. In a hurry. Please."

"Where do I go?"

"You may have to go to the office. Only please, hurry." My legs shook. It embarrassed me to ask for a potty like a child. I felt underneath the covers. The bed was wet. Oh, God, I predicted another fight with the afternoon nurse.

The darned captain had asked an impossible task of me and the VA staff. The catheter would have been much easier. All I was good for was watering the daisies. The nurse gave me a drop dead look. What a great homecoming. My parents didn't stay long. I waited over an hour for someone to change my bed. I knew I was in for the fight of the century.

On Monday morning, the doctor told me he would allow me to *credee* my bladder but if I didn't show any progress soon, I would have to submit to VA rules. What rules? They had rules about peeing? I learned that day that I was to receive physical therapy (PT) three times a week for ten minutes at a time in my room.

Two weeks later I heard muted voices outside my door. Each word stung like a dagger.

A woman's voice said unequivocally, "She's not going to make it. Even ten minutes of passive exercise three times a week will be too exhausting for her. The WAAC's obsessed with this *credee* nonsense and she's continually incontinent."

A man responded, "The nerve damage is too severe." I recognized Dr. Kessler's voice, "It's too much of a problem. Dr. Flowers, may I suggest that you talk to her parents." He lowered his voice but my ears were extra sensitive. "The poor thing does not have long to live. It's in her best interest to go home."

With those words I pulled the covers over my head. It was over. Finished. Go home and die. No wonder I was discharged from Harmon. Their enthusiasm about my progress was all phony. They knew I was going to die and they wanted me out . . . OUT. The VA wanted me to die at home. Home, where I would be a terrible burden to my parents. Mom would fall apart; Dad would go completely wacko. The next day Dr. Flowers, the chief neurologist examined me briefly and left. That afternoon I was probed, stuck and x-rayed.

My body was wracked in misery, all of which I directed at God. "I hate you, God. I hate you. You have no forgiveness. God, how I hate you. Go ahead and take me but please, I beg of you, don't send me home. Take me soon and be done with it."

For the next few days I starved myself. I refused physical therapy and insisted that my door be shut most of the time. For hours I lay in my urine. For the first time I developed a bed sore. Someone must have called my father. I had nothing to say to him.

"Dollink," he said, wiping his eyes, "you can't stay like this. You'll get sick."

"Dad," I sobbed mournfully, "I'm going to die. They're giving up on me. Don't you know?" I turned away from him.

"Vat do you mean? You're wrong. They're sending you home to be more comfortable. I'll buy you art supplies."

"Dad, you don't understand," forcing myself to be sensitive to his feelings. "Home is not for me now. I have to make progress first. I have to learn how to walk again. They're getting rid of me. Face it." I summoned all my strength not to tell my father about that mean rotten Five-by-Five.

"Give up? You're a healthy young girl. We'll see about that. Goodbye, dollink" He bent down to kiss me."Your papa will fix everything—only promise me you'll eat and drink and be a good girl."

What could my father do? I leaned over and kissed him warmly. He picked up my hand kissing it passionately. I knew he was happy that for once he might be able to do something positive for me.

The following week, to my amazement, Dad brought an eminent neurosurgeon to examine me: Dr. William Masters. How he managed I never knew. Dr. Masters was tall and personable. Every once in a while he would nod his head up and down. When he was finished with the examination he excused himself, saying he'd be back shortly.

"Thanks, Daddy. How in the world—?"

"It's always good to have a second opinion. Nothing but the best for my child," he said, wiping his eyes as I feigned agreement —while in total shock.

Dr. Masters returned with Dr. Flowers. ". . .You understand? As much as she can stand. Every single day." He smiled at me. "You're too young to stay in bed, young lady." He turned to Dr. Flowers, "Does Anita run any fevers?" Flowers shook his head

negatively. " I'm ordering PT daily. A few minutes in the beginning, gradually increased as she gets stronger. Also a new drug
"curare," a venom extracted from snakes, has been discovered in
South America and has been tested successfully in humans to lessen
spasms. I have a supply and I will send it over for you to give her
daily doses." Dr. Masters towered over Dr. Flowers. "You'll send
me a report in three months."

Dr. Flowers did not move a muscle. "Yes, William, certainly."

My father looked like he'd swallowed a canary. He was beaming at Dr. Flowers, who never reacted.

"Yes, my girl," Dr. Masters assured me, "the sooner you move
around, the less pain you will have. We don't know too much
about nerve regeneration and as long as we don't know, we have
to continue exercising and assume there will be more progress."

I extended my hand. "Dr. Masters, you have answered my
prayers. I'm not ready to throw in the towel yet."

"Give up?" the big burly man bellowed. "You've just begun.
I never want to hear you take that attitude. A girl your age. No
siree." He shook hands with my father. "You are a very persistent
father. I think your daughter will take after you and I have every
confidence that with hard work, Anita will do just fine."

"Doctor, if I were a rich man I would give you a fortune."
The two men shook hands.

Dad and I embraced. Quite suddenly I wanted to go to the
hospital services to implore God's forgiveness for all the nasty
things that were in my mind about Him and my father. I decided
I would ask if I could be taken to the chapel Friday night.

From then on, each morning at 10:30 A.M., an aide would
come with a stretcher that had wheels to take me to physical
therapy. A few weeks later I was transported down to the PT room
in a large wooden wheelchair. I was delighted to see other patients, all male, several young paraplegics and a few quadriplegics. A new therapist was assigned, a slim Irishman with powerfully strong arms. First, Shawn massaged my legs without too
much pressure and followed with light passive exercises. A few
minutes were spent strengthening my arms where he gave me a
little resistance after which he increased the pressure which made
it more difficult for me to push against him. By that time I was
getting very tired, but he urged me on, and the last part of PT was
spent trying to see if I could produce any voluntary movement

with my legs. Nothing was accomplished. I would return to my room thoroughly spent. Although the PT sessions were painful and fatiguing, I never complained. I knew what was at stake: my life. The intensive exercises did give me one problem: they played havoc with my bladder. Thankfully one of the unusually kind evening nurses brought a large piece of plastic which she tied like panties and inserted Kotex pads. I was so grateful for her help. She spared me a lot of embarrassment.

All the experimental drug curare did was make me feel drunk and within a week it was canceled, but I was eternally grateful to Dr. Masters for all he had done for me. He had opened the door for me to receive physical therapy more than ten minutes a day. I was confident I would walk again if I persevered.

One afternoon, one of the VA orthopedists was sent to examine my right thumb. It was messy with dead skin and still oozed pus. He said emphatically, "It looks like we're going to have to amputate your thumb."

I was stunned. "No, doctor, you're not. There's nothing wrong with my thumb. I can feel it, and move it. In time it will heal, and if time is essential I have plenty of it." I stared the doctor down. "End of discussion, Sir."

The following Saturday a nurse carried in a dozen or more red American Beauty roses. "You have a visitor," she announced coyly, "a man." It was the first time this nurse had shown me any friendliness.

"Oh, gee, I have to comb my hair first. Please shut the door. What does he look like?"

"I think he looks just like Lloyd Nolan."

"I know who he is. An old beau, T.J. Friedman." I panicked. Why did he have to come into my life again?

He was thirteen years my senior, very sophisticated and a fantastic dancer. Although he was Jewish, my father did not care for him. Dad thought he was too old for me, that he ran around and never honored any commitment. He was right. After several months of dating, T.J. stood me up one New Year's Eve to go skiing with a group of men. That finished the relationship for me.

"Hello." T.J. wore an enlisted soldier's uniform tailored to look exactly like an officer's dress uniform. I suspected this was simply to impress the women. He walked briskly to my bed, bending over for a kiss.

I turned the other way, extending my cheek. "Hi, Ted. Thanks for the flowers and the camera I received in basic training. These are breathtaking."

"You look wonderful. How are you, really?"

No denying he looked like the actor with those squinty eyes. "What do you mean – really?"

TJ shifted from one leg to another. "Rumor has it you had spinal meningitis and looked horrible." He tried to kiss me again but I moved out of his reach. "You look like a picture. Same beautiful doll." He reached for my hand which I quickly withdrew. "Honey, are you still angry with me?"

"Ted, I'm not mad at anyone. I'm struggling to walk again. Maybe one day I can go back to my company." I smiled at him. "Thanks for telling me the rumor. At least I'll be prepared if anyone looks at me peculiarly."

Ted looked uneasy. "Tell me about you and your army career."

We talked casually for several minutes and I was careful to keep the conversation light. I asked about the experimental surgery, a sympathectomy, he had undergone to eliminate high blood pressure. He had not been accepted in the Army because of that condition but after the successful operation, he was granted permission to enlist. He became a corporal and was stationed at Camp Edwards, Massachusetts.

"Hon," Ted smiled confidently, "when this God awful war is over, I want you to marry me." He came closer to the bed, leaned down and picked up my face.

A whiff of whiskey almost suffocated me. I flared. "I told you I'd never marry you if you were the last man in the world." He was shocked. "You had to have a drink before you faced me." I ranted."You don't have to face me ever again. Please leave. I have to rest."

"God almighty, Nita. Oh, it's no use. I don't want to make you feel sad. Please." He put his hand on the bed. It was soaking wet. He looked stricken.

I lowered my eyes and whispered, "Please go."

I waited until I heard the elevator bell and then rang for the nurse. "I'm sorry, Maria, my bed is soaking. That man never fails to upset me."

"You always have an excuse, don't you?"she snapped."What you've gotten away with is murder."

I lost my temper again. "Get out. Get out. I'll manage myself. You purposely make me wait forever for the bed pan." The nurse stormed out.

I stared at the enemy—my wheelchair. How in the world could I get into the john by myself? I strained my body until I could pull the chair close to my bed. I locked the chair; put my feet on the floor and carefully transferred my body onto the chair, covering my soaking wet body with the top sheet. I raced down the hall to the lavatory, using the wheelchair pedals to force the door open. I wheeled over to a stall facing the commode.

"This is it, Johnny. You or me." The toilet tissue container would have to be my grab bar.

Maria had seen me and raced back, poking her head inside the lavatory. "Nita, come back. It's impossible. You can't do it. You'll hurt yourself. Face up to it girl. You need a catheter."

"Leave me alone. Please!" The door closed. I threw the top sheet off, opened the foot pedals, placed my feet on the floor, placing one hand on my wheelchair, the other on the metal toilet-paper holder, praying it would not pull out from the wall. My legs were shaking, I crashed down in my chair exhausted, taking several deep breaths, and started again. I pressed down on the arms of my chair, held the holder, wobbled and crashed onto the commode sideways. Oh, blessed Lord. I've done it. Oh, thank you. Thank you. I pushed hard on my bladder until I expressed it completely using the *credee* technique. Oh John Porter, what a genius you are.

The bed was neatly made when I returned. I had won my first major battle with the VA.

Chapter 16

On a dreary Wednesday morning, a chubby little man walked into my room. "Jacob Friedman from the Jewish Welfare Board," he said extending his hand. "I came to see you about your army records and your request for compensation from the U. S. Employee Compensation Commission."

Someone had advised me that the WAACs were entitled to this compensation and I had written to the Jewish Welfare Board to investigate the matter.

"Hi, Nita Bloom."

"I have some concern about your file. Do you mind if I sit down?" The slightly balding middle-aged man took a chair far from my bed. "Err- ahhh," he sputtered clearing his throat. "Miss Bloom, I have to ask a lot of personal questions. Do you mind?"

"Not at all." My curiosity was aroused.

Mr. Friedman, looked around the room, fidgeting with a pencil between his fingers.

"What is it? What's wrong?"

"Can you tell me how you became injured?"

His tone was insinuating. "Mr. Friedman, what exactly are you talking about?"

The man cleared his throat several times. "Miss Bloom, were you off duty when you became paralyzed?"

"What?"

"I saw your records when I searched through the files of our Jewish patients in the VA. Your records show that you were off on a toot when your incident took place and, if true, you will not be entitled to any employees' compensation."

"I don't care what my records state," I retorted angrily, taking several deep breaths to control my temper. "Mr. Friedman, terrible things happened to me in the service. I never told anyone the whole truth about what happened to me in the WAACs. Perhaps it's about time I did." I proceeded to tell him about the thumb infection and the possibility that it was caused by the unsanitary conditions under which the tetanus shot was given at the very beginning. "I heard that I was entitled to a pension and I should write to the Jewish Welfare Board for their assistance." I clenched my teeth. "Exactly what does my record state? Please, Mr. Friedman, I need to know."

The adjutant sat quietly for a minute, then got up and closed the door. He opened his briefcase. "My job is finished if I ever get caught showing you this record." He lowered his voice. "You are one of us and we are bonded to help each other. Right?" Not waiting for my response, Mr. Friedman took out a file, searched through several papers while I sat on pins and needles until finally, he handed me one of them.

There it was in bold English: ". . . the WAAC was on leave when she became paralyzed and had to be brought back to camp in an ambulance. Request for compensation denied."

My breathing was labored. I felt washed out. "That is not true. Not a word. They have really punished me. What can I do?"

"Nothing. You can't do one thing. It was signed by the Army physician at the Steven F. Austin WAAC base." Friedman kept tugging at his nose. "Let me think about it."

"It's not fair." I began clasping and unclasping my hands.

"Whoever said life was fair—especially for a Jew?"

Two weeks later Jacob Friedman came back to see me. He rapped on my door, calling cheerfully, "Somebody's here to see a pretty lady."

My heart beat faster. "It's okay. I'm decent."

He entered, closed the door, motioning for me to be quiet. "A goy is a goy. You ply him with a few drinks and the picture changes."

I hated prejudice, but I knew it was the wrong time to argue. "Tell me, tell me."

Jacob pulled up a chair. "My mazel, the supervisor of the U.S. Employees' Compensation Commission, was in New York. I met him for lunch and ordered a couple of martinis. Mine I hardly touched. Oy, it's like sickening medicine. What do they care, as long as they can drink."

I couldn't wait until he got to the point.

"I convinced him that the statement about your having been brought back to the Steven Austin College in an ambulance was false and that he should eliminate it from the file."

I looked adoringly at Mr. Friedman.

"Oy, if only I weren't married. I would carry you off like a Princess into the wilds."

I squealed happily. "Did he do it? Did he do it?" I thought the man would never stop nodding his head.

"Yes," he said proudly, "right in front of me, he scratched the statement from the record. You'll be getting a letter from the Commission requesting that you file a claim on Form GA 4. You are now service connected as far as the Commission is concerned." Until this moment I had not been concentrating on any money matters, but I was more than thankful that the false records had been righted.

"Bless you, my good man." I reached for Mr. Friedman's hand, bringing it slowly to my lips. "For the rest of my life, I will never forget your good deed. God bless you."

Chapter 17

In July of 1943, through the inter-hospital mail, I received an invitation to attend a Chinese dinner on the male paraplegic ward. I had met some of the men in PT: young men, some mere boys, many embittered by the war. I was longing to visit but I was forbidden to go in their ward.

I decided it was time to see Dr. Flowers, who was the only one who could reverse that decision. I told him about the invitation. "I would really like to attend their dinner party."

"Nita, what in the world would you have in common with those men?" asked the neurologist. "You won't be able to tolerate that ward with its stench from the urine bottles under the beds or some of their horrendous deformities. The men run high fevers. Believe me, it's a miserable situation. Most of them talk about life in the most abject terms. They use filthy cuss words. Nita, it could be very damaging to you."

Another battle. I swallowed hard. "I have been sheltered long enough. Life is real. I'm well aware that these men have suffered. I want to be with them. We have a lot to learn from each other. There's no one else with whom I can discuss bladder and bowel problems." I clasped my hands tightly. "Dr. Flowers, I promise, if I become overly depressed by the men, I won't go back. I've come too far to do myself any harm."

Dr. Flowers searched my face. "I have your word. No depression, you hear?" He reached for his pipe. "Do you mind?"

"Not at all. Do you mind if I join you?"

The doctor lit my cigarette first. "My dear, you've been here long enough. It's about time we began to think seriously about your future. A girl as bright as you surely doesn't want to remain in the Veteran's Hospital forever."

"Oh, my goodness no. I have every intention of leaving. But, first, I have to become independent."

The doctor frowned. "Tell me what you mean by 'independent.'"

"Well, for one thing I'm working very hard in PT. Right now I couldn't go anywhere. I'm not independent in the sense that I can take care of myself completely. My arms are strong but they need to be stronger. I'm working hard on the mats but I have to achieve super strength. I need to be so strong that when I leave this hospital I won't have to worry about who will care for me. I'll be able to do it myself. That's the goal I want to achieve before I leave this hospital. When I become sufficiently independent, then I will find a job, get an apartment and, later on, perhaps go to college."

"What can you do? What are you trained to do?"

I began to drum my fingers on my thigh. "I don't know yet."

An expansive smile broke out on the doctor's face. "I have an answer. The VA has had a request from the Bulova Watch Company. They will train our paraplegics to work in their factory and guarantee every graduate a job when they leave the hospital. We can arrange for your training immediately."

A factory worker? That might have been a possibility once upon a time, for the war effort. Not for my vocation. "Dr. Flowers, you are most kind, but that's not exactly what I had in mind. At the moment I'm not quite sure about my future, but I promise I'll start thinking about it and you'll be the first to know when I make a decision." I extended my hand. "Thanks for allowing me to visit the boys."

In mid-afternoon I pinned an artificial flower in my hair for the dinner party. I wore the white blouse and navy skirt that Aunt Mary, Mom's unmarried sister, had sent. I took the elevator down to the third floor and wheeled past the shocked nurses at the entrance of the infamous ward: 3C.

"Well, whaddya know, here comes Crip. Fellas, look who's here. The lady of the house, Miss Crip, herself."

Although I hated the demeaning title, I smiled and waved as I went past each bed. I almost passed out: the stench was worse than Dr. Flowers had described. It was suffocating. I tried to appear nonchalant and maneuvered slowly toward them. On one bed a pair of haunting eyes peered at me. In others, drunken stares. The mixture of alcohol and urine was blinding. I was getting sick to my stomach and kept swallowing so I wouldn't vomit all over the place.

"Nita, it's about time." The greeting came from Chen, a handsome Chinese paraplegic I had met in PT. "Have a drink before we eat."

"Sounds good." I'd only had those shots of whiskey back at Harmon and wine at Passover since I enlisted. Chen handed me a glass half filled with whiskey. Some of the men were watching me intently. I took a large swig that almost knocked me out but I took a few deep breaths to regain my composure. Chen introduced me to the guys sitting around and then he led me to the foot of each bed to meet those who were bedridden. All in all there were thirty-five men in the room. I was horrified by many of the quadriplegia who couldn't even turn their heads, let alone move their arms or legs.

"Chow time," someone called.

How would I ever choke down a mouthful of food? I wanted to leave but I knew I had to stay even if it was just for that one evening. I didn't even have the strength to propel my chair back to the ward. I maintained a fixed smile and made small conversation.

Those of us who could manage wheeled over to a long table. Chen's father owned a restaurant in Chinatown and had catered a sumptuous meal for the entire ward. Surprisingly, as soon as I saw the food, I became ravenous. I tasted everything: spring rolls, egg rolls, various shrimp dishes, beef dishes, fried rice, ice cream and of course, fortune cookies. We all read our fortunes out loud laughing until our sides hurt. Many of the guys were witty and had a sense of humor that almost had me half out of my chair. I began to relax and I knew the crisis had passed.

A pair of dark brown eyes from a bed across the room haunted me. After dinner I wheeled back to the young boy's bed. He appeared to be about eighteen.

"Hi, I'm Nita."

"Hi, Ralph," he uttered weakly. Ralph was a quadriplegic, paralyzed from the neck down. He told me he had been shot in the South Pacific. He was painfully thin and had to be fed and turned constantly just as I had been back at Harmon. Ralph's tormented expression was pitiful. If for no other reason, I knew I would return to 3C to see this lad from upstate New York as often as possible. Many a night I would read the comics in the Sunday papers to Ralph. Sometimes I would sit by his bed holding his hand and we would talk about the good old times. Some of the fellows teased me about ignoring them and I reminded myself to stop by their beds, but I felt I had to spend more time with Ralph, who always seemed calmer after one of my visits. On one occasion he gave me his class high school ring, begging me to wear it, because he said I was his friend and he thought the ring was attractive and should be displayed. I wore the ring proudly.

Ward 3C was like a magnet. Soon I was totally accepted by the men and it didn't take long before I was taking two and three drinks during an evening. Sometimes I returned to my ward not quite sure where my room was. I enjoyed the light feeling, a devil-may-care-to-heck-with-the-world attitude.

One afternoon one of the guys beckoned to me.

"What's up, Lou?"

Lowering his voice, the young man from Rochester whispered excitedly, "My uncle's visiting. He's sound asleep and guess what?"

"What?'

"I stole his car keys. He usually takes a nap for about an hour. Can you steer a car?"

"What, are you nuts?" I whispered.

"Stevie wants to go, too."

"Oh, my God." And off we went, down the elevator, out the emergency door and over to his uncle's car in the VA parking lot. I stood up and sat in the front seat behind the wheel. Lou pushed my wheelchair out of the way against a brick wall then transferred into the front and got on the floor where he could control the gas and the brake. Stevie somehow managed to get into the back seat. I started the car and I yelled to Lou, "Don't go too fast! I haven't driven since I've been paralyzed."

Stevie directed us. We were shrieking like lunatics, weaving around, and then we went out of the hospital grounds and into Bronx traffic. Wow, I thought, this is for real.

About half an hour later, Stevie shouted, "Hey, Crip, I'm hungry. Pull up to the curb in front of that deli, Lou, put the brake on and I'll hail some kind soul." Lou and I were screaming with laughter. Stevie called out to a young woman, "Hey doll, how'd you like to buy a few starving crippled veterans a couple of sandwiches?" The lady simply glared and walked on.

"Allow me," Lou volunteered and waited until he saw a middle-aged man. "Sir we're three crippled veterans and we're starving from the lousy food the VA hospital feeds us. Would you kindly buy us some sandwiches? None of us can walk and we're very hungry. We'll give you a good tip." He held out a twenty-dollar bill.

The stranger agreed and brought us three out-of-this-world corned beef sandwiches, pickles and three cokes. We gobbled them down like we never ate before and quickly drove back to the hospital where Lou's uncle was calmly reading the paper. No questions. We'd had the time of our lives.

The next day I went back down to ward 3C because I was concerned about Ralph. I didn't like his dull yellow green coloring.

Usually I never asked questions about a patient's condition because I simply didn't want to know the gruesome details. When the doctors were going to give a patient a spinal tap, they would send for me to put the patient at ease. I'd hold the man's hand but I had to avert my eyes. When the physician inserted the long needle, I couldn't watch; I could not bear to see anyone in pain or look at a scar or an open wound. A nurse I would never be.

"How's my boy tonight?"

Ralph's eyes were dull without the usual spark whenever I visited. I patted his cheek and felt his forehead. The kid was burning up.

"Be right back, hon." I rolled over to the nurse's station. "When I felt Ralph's forehead, it was unusually hot tonight."

"He has a high fever. Nita, he's not doing well. We've sent for his parents."

I spent as much time as I could with Ralph. As soon as I was finished with PT, I dashed back to 3C. Ralph was becoming weaker and weaker. When I paid an early visit one morning, his mother was there. She asked me to stay with Ralph while she went to get a paper.

The kid looked painfully weak and white as a sheet. "I'm with you, hon," I murmured.

Ralph gave a faint smile. His eyes were closed. He was very still; his breathing was faint. I leaned over, gently brushing my lips across his. A morbid stare appeared on his face. His eyes were glazed. I saw that he had died. I eased myself away to reach for the buzzer.

I sat there sobbing quietly. His mother returned and we cried together. Sadly I took off Ralph's ring and returned it to her.

That night there was more drinking than usual on 3C. I

guzzled a lot of scotch with the men and a couple of hours later headed for the elevator. I couldn't see the numbers, rode to the top floor back down to the first floor, until I finally found the sixth floor, wheeling very slowly to my room. I closed the door and tried to transfer onto my bed but fell to the floor. My shorts were soaking wet. I sat in a drunken stupor for a while, sobbing until I almost passed out. "Oh, God, forgive me," I whispered. "I know you didn't save my life so I would end up a lush." After that I never took more than one drink no matter how much badgering I took from the men.

Chapter 18

The summer of 1943, I read the news that members of the Woman's Auxiliary Army Corp (WAAC) could re-enlist in the Woman's Army Corp (WAC). Now they would have the same benefits as all the GIs. My heart was broken because I knew that I would have been the first to re-enlist had I not been paralyzed. I was blinded by tears to realize that it was only a few months after my forced discharge. Of course I was incredibly happy for all those WAACs who now had the opportunity to be part of the armed forces. It never occured to me that I was not part of the regular army since I was in the VA Hosptial receiving the same medical benefits as all the other paralyzed veterans. I did not think about what might have been. It was too late for recriminations. I had to go on with what was.

Also during the summer penicillin was discovered and I knew this new antibiotic would have been much more beneficial for curing my infection than sulfa. Those were the facts and I did not allow myself to dwell on them.

My sister Marilyn graduated from high school and visited me with Mom and Dad. We never talked about her graduation. We really didn't have much to say to each other but I was elated when I heard that she had been accepted in the Cadet Corps nursing program and would be leaving for her training in September. She had wanted to be a nurse ever since she was four years old and had asked for a stethoscope. Their stay was very brief.

Soon after, Dad surprised me with an unexpected visit and a pronouncement: "Aneeda, ve are going to the Brooklyn Jewish Hospital to see a specialist. I already made arrangements with the VA for you to leave next Monday. Dr. Leo Davidoff is one of the country's leading neurologists. Please God, he vil help you."

"Oh, Dad thanks. You're so wonderful. I hope so too." Dad

told me that a son of one his friends, knew this doctor and was able to get the appointment for us.

The following Monday morning my father drove me to the hospital. I was put in a room with a woman who had asthma, was constantly coughing, and forbade me to smoke. Dad informed me I would have to submit to many tests that would take three days before the noted physician would give his prognosis. I was very nervous and never so bored in my life: I wasn't allowed to get out of bed to use my wheelchair and my craving for a cigarette was unbearable—not that I was a heavy smoker, but when I wanted a cigarette I could not control my craving—it was a compulsion. I was more than thankful when Dad arrived about nine-thirty in the morning to await Dr. Davidoff.

"Dollink, I couldn't sleep last night. If any person can help it vil be this man."

"I hope so. God, how I hope and pray."

A half hour later, Dr. Davidoff, with eight fellows following on his coattail entered my room. He was probably in his late forties, slender in stature. He barely nodded at me and Dad, turning immediately to address his entourage. "This girl has transverse myelitis, T4 level—spastic. . . which she will never overcome. . . no treatment. . . "

Shocked beyond belief, "Sir." I interrupted, noting Dad's shaken expression. "If you'll excuse me, I think I have heard enough. My father and I are fully cognizant of your esteemed reputation, but I don't want to hear another word. In my estimation you have failed to learn a few basic things. Your patient is a human being and not some piece of stone lying here. Furthermore, I don't want to hear anymore. I've heard enough. Please be so kind as to write my discharge papers. Thank you."

Dr. Davidoff shrugged his shoulders. "As you say, Miss Bloom." Dad wiped his tears, staring angrily at the man. And that was the story of the Brooklyn Jewish Hospital.

In January of 1944, while I was doing passive exercises in PT, Dr. Flowers, Dr. Kessler, Mrs. Berber the head of the PT department, and a slim bespectacled man watched as a therapist was putting me through a series of passive motions on an exercise table. I was introduced to Dr. George Deaver, Director of the Hospital for the Crippled and Chronically Ill in New York.

"Miss Bloom, how would you like to stand on your feet

again?" Dr. Deaver asked. I gasped, unable to utter a sound. "We have been bracing several of our spinal cord cases and they have become weight bearing for the first time in years."

I could not restrain my tears. "Dr. Deaver, please, I'd be ever so grateful." I kept shaking my head in disbelief, looking from Dr. Flowers to Dr. Kessler.

"We're going to measure you today and have the braces in several weeks."

Every day was like a year. I continued to work even harder in PT to prepare myself for the braces. On a sunny afternoon in mid February after a vigorous hour in PT, I returned to my room, propelling my large wooden wheelchair, and was surprised to find Connie waiting for me. On his first visit, I was bedridden.

"Nita, you are something else. What kind of potion have you imbibed? Your face is rosy red like a country girl's." The young man leaned over and kissed me on the cheek.

Aunt Mary had sent me a light-blue polo shirt that I was wearing with my navy shorts —I was happy I had worn the outfit. "You're making me blush. Good to see you Connie." He held out a beautiful rose. "Oh, how exquisite. You're spoiling me and I love it."

Connie took my right hand, bringing it to his lips. "Why don't we go outside? Do they have a sun deck?"

"Yes and I love it."

"Take a sweater. You'll need it. But first let me show you what I brought for Suzy and Betsy." (On a previous visit he had named my legs.) He opened a package that contained a pair of handsomely designed moccasins.

"They're really nifty." Connie bent down to remove my saddle shoes, replacing them with the softer ones.

"These will be my vanity shoes. I'm sure they'll fall off my feet when I stand," I casually remarked.

"Stand? Suzy and Betsy can stand? Show me, show me."

I opened the pedals of my chair and placed each hand on the arm rest. Gradually I pushed myself to a standing position for a minute. "It's not much, but there's a bonus: it allows me to stand in the bathroom; I don't require any assistance to get out of bed. I practice standing for a minute in the parallel bars in PT."

Connie was ebullient. "It's the beginning. Right?"

"Right." We shook hands enthusiastically.

"May I push you to the sundeck, princess?"

"Sure, Prince Charming."

Connie whizzed down the hallway, pausing to open the door to the veranda. The large stone sun deck was protected by high walls.

"You were a dear to send the sketch pad and water colors. I'm a dud when it comes to art but I'll give it a whirl." After I caught up with Connie's activities, I exclaimed. "I have another great surprise. A renowned orthopedist Dr. George Deaver examined me last week. He prescribed braces and crutches so I can begin to get out of this clumsy wheelchair. I'm going to be fitted next week. I want to ambulate well enough to go home for Passover."

"Colossal! I'm sure your whole family will be there for the holiday."

"Not everyone but I'm certain we'll have a crowd."

I wanted to invite Connie who had been thoughtful and considerate beyond words, but I knew how that would sit with my father. Every time I thought about his unfounded prejudices, it infuriated me. After all, Passover was the holiday where an extra plate was set for the stranger. I felt like telling Connie to arrive at the point in the Seder where someone has to open the door for Elijah.

"The next time I visit, I'm going to take you to my home. Mumscha wants to meet you and fix a Russian meal. Will you come?"

"You mean you would take the responsibility of taking me out of the hospital all by yourself?"

"It will be my pleasure, Princess."

I crossed my fingers. "Sounds wonderful." We chatted for another hour.

Connie checked his watch. "Doll Baby, it's that time. I'll see you anon." We looked at each other for a long time. For the first time in ages I felt warm and cuddly, but I pulled back when he reached forward to kiss my lips. Connie was a "goy" as my father demeaningly put it and besides, I had taken an oath. I thrust my cheek forward and he covered it with lots of kisses.

The following week my motivation was at an all-time peak. My braces arrived. When I tried on the long-legged braces, it felt like I was dragging a hundred pounds. The braces were attached to a pelvic band, heavy and impossible for me to put on by myself. At first I was only allowed to stand in the parallel bars. My legs shook until I thought I'd faint. I grabbed the bars so tight my fingers and wrists turned ruby red. The feeling I had standing on my two feet in one position was like heaven. I practiced shuffling from the beginning of the bars to the end.

After two weeks with the aid of three therapists, I moved outside of the bars, petrified that I would crash to the floor. Shawn held on to the pelvic band around my waist, the other two stood right next to me as I shakily tried to shuffle using the crutches navigating just a few steps. In the beginning I would stand in one position and shake until my body got used to being in an upright position.

After a couple of weeks. I learned how to "bunny hop" with my braces and crutches but I always had to keep my eyes focused on my feet to see the placement of my legs because of the poor sensation in my lower extremities. My clothes and sometimes my pad would be soaking wet when I returned to my room.

In mid-March I asked Shawn "Do you think I'll be ready to go home for Passover next month?"

Shawn hemmed and hawed. "Not yet. It's too dangerous. The spasticity in your legs causes those involuntary jerks, which could throw you off balance." The man sensed my disappointment. "Patience pet. First you have to learn how to control your spasms."

"I don't understand."

"You can learn to use your extensor spasms effectively in order to keep you in an upright position."

My eyes filled. "Shawn, it means everything in the world for me to go home this holiday. My sister's in training to become a nurse and she'll be there to help. Please, I beg of you. I'll work harder." Marilyn was at Adelphi College taking her nursing training and had not been able to visit again.

"Nita, if anyone can do it, you will. Let's see how we progress."

A month later on April 10th, an attendant wheeled me to my father's car. The entire PT Department came out to wish me a good vacation.

"Take it easy."

"Watch where you're bunny hopping."

"Bring back some matzoh ball soup for me."

When Dad picked me out of my wheelchair, he looked as though he would faint. I saw him whispering to Shawn; the two men went inside, and when my father returned, he was smiling at me. He'd brought his crony, Mr. Honig to keep him company. I sat in the front seat, but the two men kept a running dialogue for the hour it took to get to Suffern.

I was content to gape at the stores, sidewalks, cars and all the people scampering hither and yon. How good it was to be away from the iron bars. It took great effort to restrain my tears when we approached Suffern. I knew every street, who lived there and every familiar landmark. Dad drove directly to the house. We had not exchanged one word.

Home. My parents lived in the same two-family dwelling where I had spent my last year of high school, the house the Lichts owned, but Mom and Dad lived on the first level. I was terrified. Gosh, I was coming home like a basket case. I couldn't dress myself; I kept a bedpan under the bed; I never knew when I might have an accident. Why had I pushed? Shawn had allowed me to leave but with many misgivings. Why couldn't I have accepted his good judgment? What did I want to prove? Did I think I could shock my parents into reality?

Dad pulled into the driveway. Then I remembered the steps. Oh my God, I was a wreck: my father would have to carry me up, braces and all. Maybe it was for the best that he had brought his crony along. With a prayer and hope they could both lift me.

"Dad, you'll have to carry me."

"Don't you think I know?" His voice was starting to rise "Shawn showed me how to do everything."

"That's great Dad." I sat stiffly on the edge of the seat. My father reached out to grab me and pulled me toward him. I quickly retreated.

"No, no, no. I'll fall!" I had to control myself. "Dad," I said more patiently, "you have to put both hands under my legs."

"I told you I know how," my father shouted angrily, "let me do it my way." He pulled me around the waist and tugged me toward him. "Julius, grab her legs." Together they lugged me like a heavy sack across the driveway. The two men were huffing and puffing. My father forgot to open the front door. They had to carry me back to the car, then back again to drag me up the steps and into the house where they plunked me on a living room chair.

My father mopped his brow; his crony looked like he was going to drop dead. "You see, Dollink, (my father tried to pacify me), I told you I could do everything." Then he phoned my mother in the store, "Til, everything is fine, just like I told you." The two men walked to the kitchen door to leave.

I managed a weak smile. "Please, Dad, let Mom come home soon." Mom worked with my father in the store. As far as I was concerned, too many times she was alone while my father either went fishing or was busy with synagogue work.

"Dollink, today's Friday. Momma has to go to the bank first. She'll come home as soon as she can."

My skirt was soaking wet. I knew I had messed the old up-holstered chair. God. I prayed my mother wouldn't go into a de-pression when she realized I couldn't control my bladder. Once I was on the john, I would have to stay there until my mother came home.

"Please, Dad, tell her to make it soon."

After he left, I sobbed my heart out. I had never practiced getting up from a chair. How would I get to the bathroom? I should never have come home!

I sat for a long time planning my strategy. Slowly, I used my crutches to help me stand but I fell backwards into the chair. I tried again. Sweat poured down my cheeks. I used my shirt to wipe it away; then I tried again. And a second time—a third time. I gritted my teeth and yay, success—up. I carefully leaned to lock my braces and started bunny hopping like a snail across the living room floor, through the short area in the kitchen and, thank the good Lord, into the bathroom. I was darn grateful the apartment was small. I glanced at the commode, scared to death. What would I grab to pull my panties down? Ah, I'd have to reach over, lean on the sink, use one hand to undress and then quickly hold the rim of the bathtub to get my balance and sit down. After several attempts, I finally crashed down on the toilet seat and sobbed. Once I was on the seat, I stayed there until my mother came home. The wait gave me the opportunity to calm myself. Finally I heard the car.

"Mom, Mom," I called frantically.

My mother flew in, took one look at me sitting on the toilet, and turned white. "Mom, if you listen to me carefully, we can remedy this mess soon." For the next hour we struggled with the washing, dressing, and changing into a new skirt. I hugged and kissed Mom and was on my feet and into the kitchen for a cup of coffee.

I was getting paranoid about drinking. I knew I had to drink the eight glasses of water the VA required each day, but how I would manage was a mystery. Only by the grace of God would I be able to accomplish that feat. In the VA where I had my wheelchair I would fly to the john, but there was no wheelchair now!

Mom had been very patient during the crisis. Once it was over, she hovered over me like a mother hen. I wanted to talk to her openly, but I noticed how drawn her face was and I was afraid to cause any undue pressure. I had to make light of my problems. Ever since I became paralyzed, and my mother didn't come until I was well over the critical period, I took care to spare her any further worry on my behalf. Uppermost in my mind was always the fear something I said about my condition might cause her to have another nervous breakdown and become very depressed.

The few days I spent at home were frustrating. My father never spoke to me when I was using my crutches. The first time Mom left for work I became overwrought; she forgot to leave the lights on and the switch was way out of my reach. If the phone rang, every time I struggled to get to it, it stopped. If I didn't get up before 8:00 A.M. so Mom could help with my braces, I had to remain in bed until noon. My friends wanted to visit, but I told my mother to give me time to get adjusted. In addition to finding my way about, I had to drink tons of fluid to keep my bladder free of infection and that necessitated a lot of exercise back and forth to the bathroom. One thing I didn't lack was exercise.

There was someone I desperately wanted to talk to: Dr. Carl Hussey. He was our family physician I'd been so frantic to see when I was sick as a WAAC. He was kind enough to come over one afternoon and his eyes filled as soon as he saw me. Dr. Hussey was a typical country doctor who had been our family physician for years. I was unaware that he was considered one of this country's ten best diagnosticians.

After several minutes of small talk, I came to the point. "Doctor, I want to share something with you but I must have your promise never to tell my folks." He reminded me that he had never told my parents when I went motorcycling with my pal, Joey. We shared a good laugh, then I told him about my thumb infection from the beginning. "Ironically, I was sound asleep in bed not motorcycling and not on a binge!"

Dr. Hussey patted my hand. "Anita, I'm truly sorry. Your suspicions were correct. When that sergeant used the razor blade on your thumb, she drove the infection further into the blood stream. First, she should have had you soak your finger to bring the infection to the surface. Then it should have been incised by a doctor or nurse, not an x-ray technician."

When I heard his words, I was stunned to silence but actually, I'd known the answer all the time. "Thank you. When I had the infection, all I wanted was to get home and see you. I didn't make it, and I've been wondering ever since, if God pulled me through for some reason."

"Keep your courage. That's half the battle. Be patient with your parents, my child. This has been a difficult time for them, too."

"I wish I could get through to them. My father only talks to me when I'm sitting down. Even then, he won't discuss my condition."

"Give it time, Anita. Your Dad is overwhelmed by what happened to you. Mother is too. I was very concerned about her in the beginning but she seems much better now. Both of your parents are taking this very hard. I'm proud of you that you seem so well adjusted. Try to be patient with them."

The next couple of days a few friends visited with me. They were understanding; some were shocked; one woman turned everything into a joke. One of my friends royally disappointed me by not coming at all. Weeks passed until she told me every time she went to open the door, she started crying so hard that her eyes were bloodshot and she just couldn't visit me.

On Passover morning I heard my mother and dad rustling pots and pans in the kitchen; they were starting to make ready the preparations for the evening Seder. First Mom had to empty all her closets to get rid of any food that was not "pasedich" (suitable to eat during Passover). Dad helped with the cooking until it was time for him to open the store. I could hardly wait to eat all the marvelous Passover delicacies. I helped Mom clean the silver. I couldn't wait to see my sister. As soon as Mar came home from the Nurse's Cadet Corps that afternoon, I began to relax for the first time since my visit home. She looked spiffy in her gray uniform with red epaulets on the shoulders. She didn't look like my kid sister any more, and I was proud of her.

Aunt Min, Uncle Jules, six-year-old Larry, and one-year-old Debby arrived just before sundown. I was seated at the dinner table. Dad conducted the Seder and as always, never skipped a paragraph. Over the years, he condescended to have everyone read a passage in English before he would spin off in rapid Hebrew, which no one understood. Marilyn noticed me shifting and immediately brought me a pillow as well as one for Dad and one for my uncle, since it is the custom on Passover, according to the Haggadah, that "on this night everyone should recline."

At long last the meal was served. Mom and Dad had fixed all the goodies: the best gefilte fish in the world, feather weight matzoh balls, tender brisket, oven paprika potatoes and our favorite: an eight-inch high lemon-orange sponge cake that Mom made. How she accomplished all the fixings and worked in the store was beyond me. Dad, who had made the gefilte fish and grated the horseradish was beaming but continually asked over and over how everyone liked the meal. The Manischewitz grape wine never tasted sweeter.

All of a sudden, Larry jumped up and grabbed my crutches, "I'm a cripple," he cried, swinging through them, "I'm a cripple." My father's face contorted, turning tomato red. "Sit down, you rotten little kid," he bellowed. The frightened child immediately dropped the crutches. Dad sneered at his brother-in-law. "You couldn't stop him?"

"Dad," I pleaded, mortified out of my mind, "He's only six. Larry doesn't mean anything. Let's go on with the singing. Please."

Larry began to cry. I had to go to the bathroom. Everything stopped. Not a breath stirred. Like a swift deer, my sister brought over my crutches, she extended and locked my braces and hoisted me to an upright position. Very unsteadily, with Marilyn at my side, I proceeded to bunny hop.

The baby began to laugh pointing to me."Da, da, da."

"Min?" my father implored my aunt.

"Stop it, everybody," Mar yelled. "Leave the children alone. It's hard enough for Neet." She remained close to me. "Easy, Nita. You're doing fine." I looked at my sister gratefully.

In my heart of hearts I knew this was the real world, where I would have to do battle—without my sister. Or anyone else.

Chapter 19

One afternoon in late April I was relaxing in my room. I had crutch walked in PT, eaten lunch, and extended my legs on my bed to keep the swelling down, when a slim young woman swung through her crutches into the open door of my room. "Anita Bloom?" she asked smiling.

"Nita, hi," flabbergasted to see another woman in a similar condition.

"I'm Betsy Barton. Dr. Deaver asked me to visit you. He thought you and I might have a lot in common."

"Please sit down." I pulled over a chair and marveled at how deft she was as she unlocked her braces, held on to the chair and eased herself on to it. I knew I was staring but I was so intrigued and couldn't control myself.

"Oh, yes, I'm sure we have a lot to talk about. You don't know how happy I am to meet you. We don't have any women spinal cord patients in the hospital and I've been dying to meet another woman to talk about mutual problems. You are spectacular in the way you manage your braces and crutches."

"Thank you. I've been practicing for years. I'm not a spinal cord victim. I 've had infantile paralysis ever since I was a young girl. George Deaver is the Director of the Hospital for the Crippled and Disabled where I learned how to crutch walk.

"He's a wonderful man. I'm very grateful to Dr. Deaver for getting me on my feet but I have a long way to go before I'm as independent as you are."

"Well, Nita, the first thing I have to do for you, is to give you the name of my tailor."

"What for?"

"You certainly don't want to wear skirts anymore. You want to cover up those awful steel braces, don't you?"

Wow, Betsy didn't pull any punches. "Oh, no, I'm proud to

101

wear them. They'll be my ticket to independence." Then I smiled, "Besides, I know one day I'll walk again without these braces, but for now, I'm grateful I have them. I couldn't afford to have clothes tailor-made anyway. Betsy, please tell me more about yourself."

We talked for another half hour and she invited me to have lunch at her home the following week. "Don't worry about transportation. I'll send my chauffeur for you."

The next Friday Betsy's chauffeur drove me to an enormous stone home in an obviously wealthy New York City area I had never seen before. He did not say one word to me. The house was dark with bare wood floors and massive furniture. We had lunch in a small room that was more casual and had some sunlight. Lunch consisted of tiny cucumber watercress sandwiches that did not satisfy me one bit. I learned Betsy was the daughter of Mr. Barton of the famous Batton, Barton, Durstine and Osborne advertising firm in the city. Betsy was very fortunate in that her bladder and bowel were not at all affected. She and I came from two different worlds and really didn't have much in common other than the fact that we both used braces. I felt she was a poor little rich girl living in this monstrous home and longing to have friends of her own. The visit did one thing for me: it made me anxious to learn how to become more independent on my braces and crutches. The following year Betsy wrote a book and sent me an autographed copy, telling me to be sure to look on a certain page where she wrote that she had met a "beautiful young woman in the Bronx VA Hospital who dreamed about walking one day." Although I thanked her for the book and wished her well, I never saw or heard from her again.

On May First of 1944, Dr. Kessler jauntily bounced into my room. "Nita, come with me. I have a big surprise for you." I was stunned by how fast he maneuvered my chair down the long hall into his office. "Close your eyes."

I waited with bated breath.

"Now open them."

I squealed, "Wow! I don't believe it." In front of me was a wheelchair, much smaller than mine, with dark-green vinyl upholstery and stainless steel wheels.

"Do you want to know the most fantastic thing about it?" the good doctor's eyes sparkled merrily. I shook my head unbelievingly. "It's collapsible and can easily fit into a car. It was invented by an engineer and patented by the VA for our paraplegics, quadriplegics and double amputees."

"Wow, golly gee, I can hardly wait to use it," I cheered.

The collapsible wheelchair opened doors to all kinds of invitations for me and the male paraplegics. Suddenly we were being wined and dined by many organizations. We took New York by storm. Whenever we went out in public, we were on display. Either people were oversolicitous, or eyed us with sadness and shock, or shunned us completely. I was repulsed by anyone's display of pity. Country clubs were hosting dinner parties; philanthropic groups bought blocs of free orchestra theatre tickets; major organizations planned trips to the baseball games. I was the only woman and I had a ball.

In June 1944, I received a letter that buoyed my spirits considerably. My cousin's Aunt Rose, the same woman I had written to before I enlisted, wrote from Camp Edwards, Massachusetts where she was stationed, that she had met a Captain Matheny who was in charge of the rehabilitation program there. Rose, now a Captain in the WAC, inquired about this man's work and discovered that his program included spinal cord patients. Rose told him about me and inquired if he would consent to a visit. He agreed.

Ten days later Rose, accompanied by Captain Matheny, came to visit. I shook hands with the powerfully built man and he asked if he could examine my legs. I found myself almost hypnotized by his azure blue eyes. When I demonstrated my ability to stand for a few seconds, he became jubilant.

"Gal, that's wonderful! You have to come up to Camp Edwards on Cape Cod, where my wife and I have a cottage, to spend a few days. I want to work with you and I know I can help you." His eyes glistened. "Gal, you are going to walk on those legs. Don't bother bringing your braces when you visit me. We're going to work without those cumbersome pieces of steel."

Tears filled my eyes—Rose's too. Adrenalin charged through my body. I knew God was going to send someone to help me. No matter how hard I worked in PT very little had been accomplished in two years. I could bunny hop with my crutches but I couldn't swing through by myself. The PT personnel were focusing on difficult maneuvers such as jumping a curb, which

was far beyond my capabilities. I was always frustrated after PT.
What this captain promised just might become a reality one day.

In late June Captain Matheny invited me to spend a few days
at his home. My anticipation heightened as I thought of all the
progress I would make under his direction. Dad picked me up at
the hospital with Mr. Honig and of all people, my former friend
Hannah, who my father thought would be good company for the
ride. She was the same girl I had befriended when we were youngsters. I had severed our friendship ever since high school because
she had eagerly proffered friendship when I was dating my Christian boyfriend, craving to know about our secret trysts, our plans
and dreams. Unknown to me she and her father confronted my
father, feeding him every detail I had confided. I had no love for
her. I had not seen her ever since that dreadful experience. I was
forced to sit next to her on the back seat and somehow managed
to engage in trite conversation. Nothing was going to interfere
with the awesome meeting with Captain Matheny.

We arrived in the late afternoon and drove down a long dirt
road leading to a small, charming New England-style, white clap-
board cottage. The Captain, looking well tanned, strutted across
the grass to greet us enthusiastically. "Mr. Bloom, I assume, Nita,
gal, welcome."

"Dad, this is Captain Matheny."

"Nice to meet you."

"Never mind the Captain. It's Walt," extending his hand,
which Dad shook.

"Bill," Dad responded. "This is Mr. Honig and Hannah Weiss."

"Pleased to know you—Bill, is it? Same as my brother." Walt
shook hands with everyone, coming over to kiss me on the cheek.
"We're going to work on your daughter here and get her back in
shape."

Dad's eyes filled. He grabbed the Captain's hand again. "Oy,
I can't begin to tell you how grateful ve vould be."

A little boy about three years old was lying on a blanket
smiling up at us. I tried not to show any emotion but I thought I
was going to faint. The child's arms and legs were flailing in all
directions and drool was slurping out of his mouth.

"Say hi, Chucky," a young, rather manly looking woman,
kindly said to her son, who grunted unintelligibly.

Walt introduced his family. "My wife Marguerite and my
son."

Somehow I smiled, but I thought, God, help me, I can't stay here. Every time I'd look at that child I would die. Chucky was beautiful, but when that sloppy drool was running down his cheeks and his legs and arms were throwing themselves around like strong weeds on a windy day, it made me ill. In fact, I was nauseous. I dared not look at my father who I was sure was having a worse reaction, let alone Hannah or Mr. Honig. "Hi Chucky." Then I turned to his wife. "I didn't get your name."

"Marguerite. We're pleased you could come."

The Captain invited us to come on the porch for a glass of iced tea. Marguerite made her "famous" lemon tea cookies. He came over to assist me and maneuvered my wheelchair like a pro, taking me up the steps easily. Marguerite carried Chucky. I didn't look at my father. Hannah looked like a zombie. Mr. Honig wore his usual blank stare. After tea and cookies and small conversation, I could see my dad was getting edgy and ready to start home.

Dad extended his hand to the Captain. "It's time for me to go. I have a long trip back and my wife is tending the store alone. God should only give you strength to help my daughter. I'll send you clothing for Chucky for the rest of his life." He looked at me. I couldn't believe my ears and smiled proudly.

Walt shook his hand, sending his regards to my mother. Dad's eyes were blurred.

I whispered to my father, "Be happy for me," brushing his wet face with my lips.

"You can pick Nita up on Monday, Bill," the captain instructed, "We'll have something to tell you, I'm sure." He extended his hand to my father.

"Good luck," Dad said to me. "Momma and I will be praying for you." He came over to kiss me.

"Thanks, Dad, thanks for everything. Have a safe trip home."

"We'll be praying too," Hannah chirped. She started walking toward me but I had moved my chair back.

"Thanks for keeping Dad company and you too, Mr. Honig."

For the next couple of days, I literally did nothing but talk to Marguerite and play with Chucky. He and I became great pals and in a short time, I didn't notice the drooling or the involuntary spasms. Marguerite told me about Chucky and the difficult pregnancy she had when he was born. Tragically there weren't many institutions that offered much help for him. The responsibility of caring for him was overwhelming for his parents. It was apparent from Chucky's reaction to adult conversations that he was very intelligent, lovable and full of personality. I watched his mother faithfully put him through a series of physical exercises and work with him on his speech.

Walt came home in the late afternoons. Marguerite had a blanket on the grass and Walt would exercise my legs, asking me to contract and relax my leg muscles and push and pull. Nothing happened. Not a twitch of a muscle. I was beginning to regret the visit. Late Friday afternoon Walt came home. As usual we went out on the grass. "Walt, I'm getting discouraged. Same exercises, same results. No movements."

"Now, now, you can't let yourself become depressed. Discouragement leads to tension, but relaxation leads to progress. No tension, promise? Let's try again."

I inhaled deeply and followed Walt's commands.

All of a sudden, the man exclaimed excitedly, "Gal, your right leg moved. God, your leg moved. Marguerite," Walt shouted, "come here, come right here!" I did not feel it, nor could I see it move from the position I was in.

As his wife walked down the steps, he called out, "Nita moved her right leg." Marguerite smiled broadly. Walt stared long and hard at me. "Gal, remember, you can stand. You are weight bearing. We have to strengthen the quadriceps to allow you to stand for longer periods and we will also concentrate only on active motion." Walt cleared his throat. "But tonight, we're going to celebrate. We're going out for a special dinner." He began to sing in a soothing Midwestern drawl, 'You tell me your dreams, I'll tell you mine.' We were exuberant.

Walt made reservations at a charming inn, picked up a sitter for Chucky and off we went. We celebrated with a round of drinks to my first successful attempt at moving my leg and drank to more progress. The food was excellent: clam chowder, broiled large tender shrimp, baked stuffed potatoes, salad and homemade apple pie. All of us returned on a happy note. Walt drove the baby sitter home.

I sat on the porch musing about the progress I had made, so grateful to Walt for the opportunity he had given me. Within several minutes I heard the car followed by his footsteps.

"Hi, Walt."

"What are you doing out here by yourself?"

"Oh, just dreaming. You and Marguerite have been wonderful to me."

"Young lady, you are about to enter another phase of your life and I'm the one who is going to lead you."

"I'm so grateful to have had these few days."

He reached down for one of my hands, holding it gently in between his. "Nita, sure as that moon is in the sky, that's how certain I am that I can help you."

"Oh, God, do you really think so?" This whole experience was beyond belief. I looked toward the heavens gratefully and as I did, I felt his hand tenderly stroke my hair. Instinctively, I backed my chair away.

"Goodnight, Walt, thanks for a marvelous evening. See you tomorrow."

"Tomorrow is another surprise for Nita. Sweet dreams."

"Same to you." I wheeled to my room turning on a small lamp, hesitated for a minute and for the first time, I locked the door very quietly. Probably acting like an idiot, I thought, he didn't mean a thing by stroking my hair. I sure hoped he didn't, because come hell or high water, I desperately wanted his help.

About ten thirty the next morning, Walt announced we were on our way to a surprise outing. "Oh by the way, Nita, did you bring a bathing suit?"

My heart began to pound. "Golly no. I had no idea." It never occurred to me that I would ever go swimming since I became paralyzed.

"Don't worry, Marguerite has an extra one, even though she doesn't swim. Mugs," he called, "bring a swim suit for Nita."

It was a tremendous ordeal for Marguerite and me to put on the bathing suit. My feet became spastic, kicking uncontrollably, making it impossible to get the suit on. It wasn't easy and after half an hour we succeeded. I hugged her and thanked her.

Walt shouted, "What took you so long?"

I did not respond. Marguerite said,"We were taking care of 'girls' affairs.'"

I said, "We are ready now. Let's go."

We drove several miles until Walt came to a dirt road, steering the car down the narrow strip until we came to a clearing with a tremendous lake before us.

"Here we are. C'mon gal, this is your day."

My heart was racing non stop. I got in my wheelchair and Walt wheeled me down to the water's edge.

"Are you ready, gal?"

"Oh yes, oh yes," My heart was beating a mile a minute, and I was quivering with fear.

Walt picked me up, walked a few steps into the water and threw me in.

I was terrified. I couldn't catch my breath. I couldn't see a thing in the deep dark water. I struggled to come up but didn't have the strength. I thought I would drown when I felt Walt's strong arms lifting me out of the water and carrying me to my wheelchair, still sputtering and coughing, totally distressed.

"Are you okay?"

I nodded my head. I did not trust myself to say anything. I was careful not to offend him in any way, but I could not bring myself to talk to him.

Walt knelt in front of me, looking squarely into my eyes. "Listen gal, we have just begun. I wasn't going to say anything until I was sure, but I can't wait any longer to tell you my plans. As soon as I'm discharged at the end of this summer, I'm going to open a school where I can help disabled people like you and Chucky. Would you like that?" His eyes dazzled in the sunlight. I had a sense of being hypnotized. "The first thing on my agenda is to look for a school, probably in the New York or New Jersey area. I'll notify you as soon as possible. You sit tight. Don't take any wooden nickels."

Once again I became aware that this man was going to help me, not harm me.

"You mean I could leave the VA hospital?" Walt nodded his head with certainty. "I'm so grateful I met you." I kissed Matheny's hand. We looked at each other and I laughed for sheer joy. Walt asked me not to mention the plan until it was firm. How quickly I forgot the swimming episode.

"Well gal, looks like you're going to walk before you swim."

"Oh, Walt, you make everything sound so easy." I quickly forgot the awful scare. After all, I was going to walk again.

A few weeks after I returned to the VA, to my delight, I was told that those paraplegics who wanted to learn how to swim would be taken to the YMCA in the Bronx for lessons. The day I arrived, I was so nervous I was trembling and certain I would drown. Very gently Jim, the instructor, put me in the water. I was petrified. My legs were pulling dreadfully from spasms. "Nita, I am going to lay you on your back. I'm right here with you. Take deep breaths and try to relax." I felt his hand under my back. My spasms stopped and my legs extended and he said, "I'm now holding you with only one finger." I remained afloat. Then he continued, "I'm letting you go and will stay right along side of you while you float. I did just that for a couple of minutes. Then Jim said, "When you're ready, turn on your stomach, take a deep breath, keep your head in the water, come up for air, and continue that same way to stay afloat. If you allow your head to remain in the water too long, your legs will pull you under. I followed his instructions and to my amazement I swam across the pool and back to the edge and began screaming, "I did it, I did it, I can swim again! Thank you, thank you, thank you!" Most of the boys enjoyed the same thrill. We went back to the VA and that night we all celebrated down at Ward 3C with a nightcap.

One Saturday lazing on my bed I was enthralled listening to a particularly beautiful aria of Tosca from the Metropolitan Opera's weekly performances, when I heard footsteps. Looking up there was Marilyn. "Oh, what a lovely surprise," as we hugged each other. "Mar, you look terrific." My sister always had a tendency to be heavy. Seeing her today was a miracle, the way she had slimmed down. She had taken off her Cadet Corps hat and her gorgeous dark brown hair was long and pulled back in a bun. "I just can't get over how wonderful you look."

My sister beamed. "Thanks, Neet. Sorry I haven't written. Been crazy busy." She immediately noticed my new wheelchair. "Hey, what's this?"

"My new collapsible wheelchair that fits easily into a trunk of a car and is so much easier to propel."

"Neet, that's wonderful."

"You bet it is. Tell me everything"

I reached over to turn off my radio.

"Oh, I hate to interrupt you. I know how you love the opera."

"Mar, for heaven's sake. I'm all ears. Tell me every single thing. What department are you in now?"

"Pediatrics. I'm really excited working with all the youngsters. You would never believe all the expressions I've heard about BMs."

"Tell me," even though I detested talking about it.

"How about dropping a bomb or filling a load or here comes a stink bomb." We both laughed.

"Enough. What a riot."

"I'll be there for three months and then on to obstetrics. I'm very excited about that."

"I know you'll be wonderful with all those babies. Have you made a lot of friends?"

"Yes. I'm anxious to complete the courses and get my B.S. degree. I wonder where I'll be assigned?"

"I hope it's not too far away. I had a great day today. I found out I could swim again."

Her face broke out into a broad grin. "How wonderful. Your legs are buoyant in the water, right?" I nodded. Suddenly her expression changed and her face became serious and drawn. "Neet, I have to tell you something. I simply can't take care of you when you come home. I have my career and my own life."

I gulped hard. "Mar, what ever gave you the idea . . .? Listen, Sis, I never expected you to take care of me. Ever! I'm staying right here until I become completely independent and then I'll figure out how I'm going to get out, where I'll live and go about finding a new career. Don't you worry for one minute about me." Her eyes filled. "Mar, the greatest joy will be seeing you make something of yourself. Getting away from Mom and Dad was the best thing you ever did and I know you'll go on to become the best nurse in the whole world."

We chatted for a while, kissed each other and then she left.

Yes, the battle was mine and mine alone.

Chapter 20

Occasionally when I went to PT and had to wait until Shawn was ready to work with me, I would get up from my wheelchair, stand in the parallel bars for a minute or two and sit down. Most of the time I had my braces on ready to crutch walk but one day I was exhausted and decided to skip the braces. I was wearing a pair of short shorts and had just sat down to rest. One of the paras was across the room and he and I were talking. All of a sudden I began to shriek. Therapists came flying from all directions. I was gasping and sputtering but couldn't make myself understood.

"Nita, what's wrong? Get a doctor at once," someone ordered.

I shook my head no but still couldn't speak. After several minutes I began to yell, "A fly. A fly. A fly. Oh, my God, I felt a fly on my leg. Oh, my God. What a wonderful birthday present."

Everyone cheered and clapped. It was so great. I knew I had sensation on my thighs but I had never felt anything as light as a tiny fly on my leg before.

In early July of 1944 the exclusive Westchester Country Club in Rye extended an invitation to the disabled veterans at the Bronx VA. Aunt Mary, bless her heart, brought me a gorgeous black and white halter type two piece silk jersey Janzten swim suit for the occasion. I was lucky. Aunt Mary and I wore the same size. She always lent me a dress for a special occasion. She was working at Blackton's Lingerie shop in the bathing suit department. "Neet," she teased, "you have to look glamorous at all times. You never know. . . ." Sure, I said to myself, like any man would notice me.

Wednesday was a glorious warm summer day with a pink-purple sky bursting with huge cotton candy clouds. Aides lifted fifteen men and me into the VA bus. The men had lots of comments.

"Who would think I would be going to a swanky millionaire's club?"

"Who cares, as long as they serve good drinks and plenty of food?"

"As long as they have gorgeous dames with big boobs and fat asses."

Another whispered, "Hey Crip, we get a chance to see what's under . . .?"

"That's enough," Pete, my dearest friend, yelled.

"Sorry gorgeous." I smiled appreciatively.

Acres and acres of forest green grass bordered with assorted pansies graced the entrance to the impressive Country Club. Men in white waiters' uniforms were waiting to assist us through the grounds and led us directly to an enormous swimming pool, surrounded with hundreds of white wrought iron lounge chairs with colorful foam cushions. Baskets of fresh fruit were placed all around the pool. Waiters were taking orders for drinks and sandwiches. One of the matrons assisted me to a large dressing room equipped with every imaginable toiletry and a huge mirror. I managed to use the bathroom and change into my new bathing suit. I had tied a bright red bandanna around my head. The attendant smiled approvingly then wheeled me back to the pool where one of the aides lifted me on to a comfortable chaise where we were waited on like royalty.

A handsome well-built man in his early thirties came over and stood in front of me. "You're not just going to lie there and look beautiful, are you? Hi, I'm Roger Simons."

"Relaxation is the order of the day, isn't it? Nita Bloom." Extending my hand.

"Would you like to swim?"

"Yes, sir. I can hardly wait."

"Did you ever swim before?"

"Oh yes, thanks to a wonderful Red Cross instructor from the YMCA a short time ago. Next to tennis, it was my favorite sport."

"Hey, if you're game, I used to be a hell of a life guard."

"That's very kind of you. I'm game."

Roger easily carried me to the pool, placing me on the edge while he jumped in, then gradually lifted me into the water putting me on my back. As soon as the cool water touched my legs, they went into severe involuntary spasms. I began to laugh. "Suzy and Betsy are misbehaving."

"Who?"

"My legs." Soon the muscles became accustomed to the water, the spasms ceased and I swam like a gazelle across the pool. After several minutes I swam to the edge of the pool holding on to the sides. Roger was right beside me and placed his hand over mine. "You are fabulous."

"Thanks. You have no idea how much it meant to be able to swim again. I love to do anything that allows me to be independent. What a gift your club gave the veterans. This is indeed a day of wonders."

The young man kissed my hand. "Just call me when you're ready to come out. No rush."

I swam luxuriously for another fifteen minutes then motioned to Roger for his assistance. "Oh it was wonderful. Thanks, thanks, thanks."

He lifted me out of the pool carrying me back to a lounge chair. "I'm happy for you, Nita. I called my wife while you were swimming. We'd love you to come to dinner Wednesday night. Can I pick you up at the hospital?"

"Thanks. I'd love to meet your wife." I was flattered. Shortly Roger bid me goodbye, saying he and Louise had an early engagement.

The rest of the day and night were perfect: we dined on hot cross buns, barbeque ribs, french fries the likes of which I had never tasted before, baked beans, salads, all the drinks one desired and desserts that were out of sight. One of the fellows strummed on his guitar while everyone sang. We left the Country Club feeling like millionaires for a day.

For the first time in ages, I became aware of my limited wardrobe. If not for the good graces of Aunt Mary, I wouldn't have had any clothes. Finally I called my father who was banking my monthly stipend from the U.S. Compensation Commission, supposedly for the day when I would need it.

"Dad, please send me some money. I'm going out a lot these days and I really need a few things."

My dad's voice boomed. "Isn't Aunt Mary buying you clothes? I send her all the money she asks for." I was quiet. "Tell me what you want. I'll get it for you." Dad quickly gained control of himself lowering his voice. "Needala, you know the aides. They would steal your money. Whatever you want, I'll make a special trip and bring you on Sunday. Needala, you like my taste, don't you, Dollink?"

"Sure, Dad." My father had good taste. He had the smartest looking children's clothes in Suffern. Maybe he was right about keeping too much money on the ward. I never knew he paid Aunt Mary. She always made it sound as though the clothes were gifts from her. I asked for a shirt waist dress, a navy blouse, white skirt, and a pair of white sandals. My father never asked where I was going or with whom.

The following Wednesday Roger picked me up outside the emergency entrance in a light-blue Buick convertible with the top down. Before I could get out of my wheelchair he had swooped me up and lifted me into the front seat. I was thrilled out of my mind to be going out of the hospital in such grand style. We talked easily while he drove down the East River Parkway to the east side of Manhattan, parking in front of an elegant apartment house overlooking the river. We went up to the 10th floor and as soon as Roger unlocked the door a stunning blond hurried over to kiss Roger.

Louise held out her hand, "Nita, it's so nice to meet you."

"Thanks for having me. Roger was most considerate of me at the Club."

"I'm sure it was because of your charming personality. Not that he isn't polite to everyone!"

"I'm certain of that but thanks for the compliment."

Louise was the epitome of a beautiful American society lady. She was about 5 feet 8 inches tall, svelte, with shapely legs and natural ash blond shoulder length hair pulled back into a pony tail. She was wearing a long pale green bare-backed linen summer dress with white open toe sandals.

Roger started to propel my chair into the living quarters. A white tiled floor lined the foyer, with natural straw-colored wallpaper, opening onto a slate floor to the large living room that included an area for dining. Modern pictures adorned the walls; the furniture was white with pale yellow pillows. An off-white floor length drape opened to a splendid view of the East River. I was spellbound. I had never in my life seen anything so spectacular.

"Louise decorated the apartment by herself," said Roger

proudly. "She came to one of our stores and ravaged the design books until she found exactly what she wanted."

"You did a wonderful job, Louise."

"Roger's talking about the family empire."

"Stop bragging, my love," Roger protested jokingly.

Louise kissed her husband on the nose. "I'm very proud of you, darling. You worked hard to become a VP. Nita, let's make you comfy. Can you manage to get on the couch? I'll serve dinner on the snack tables."

Roger went for my wheelchair. "Thanks, Roger, I'll be okay," I said, hoisting myself onto the couch. Roger took my chair out of the room and returned to make oversized cocktails, serving them with shelled pistachio nuts. We made small talk about how they met, fell in love and were married two and a half years ago. A half hour later Louise brought out a tray consisting of a huge caesar salad and tons of rare slices of sirloin steak on toast points.

Louise said gaily, "We'll have dessert later. Let's get comfy and listen to some good music."

"Louise, the dinner was scrumptious. Really delicious. I never tasted anything as tender as that steak in my life." It couldn't compare with the kosher steak my mother always burned to a crisp.

Roger asked, "Nita, do you like Sibelius?"

"I'm not sure I've ever heard him."

"You're in for a treat."

The door bell rang. Louise's warm welcome was met by a jovial male voice. I was introduced to Martin Wortman, a tall well tanned handsome young man. Southern comfort cordials were served. I sipped my drink slowly and soon I felt myself slowly seduced by the enticing first movement of Sibelius's Second Symphony. I found Martin's gypsy dark eyes staring at me whenever I looked up. When the theme was repeated for the third time, my heart was pounding. Sparks flew back and forth between Martin and me. I was thankful when the symphony came to an end and Roger served dessert from a glass teacart.

"Louise, my very favorite," Martin complimented. He spoke to me for the first time. "She makes the best blueberry pie. Louise, you shouldn't have gone to all the bother. But, um, it is good."

After a while, Roger looked at me. "I think it's that time." I nodded.

"Where are you going?" Martin asked.

"Cinderella's going back to her castle," Roger chided. He left the room, returning with my wheelchair.

Martin was visibly shocked but quickly composed himself. "Mind if I go along?"

I thanked Louise profusely. Roger kissed her, saying he'd be back in about an hour. Martin studiously watched how Roger collapsed the wheelchair and put it in the trunk. We all sat in front. Martin had to put his arm around my shoulder for comfort; I tried to squeeze closer to Roger and did not look at Martin. We chatted on a light vein, but it seemed ages until we pulled into the Veteran's Hospital.

"You were in the service?" Martin questioned.

"Yes."

"So was I. You must tell me all about it. How about dinner Saturday night?"

I looked at Roger who remained expressionless. The young man persisted, "Believe me, I'll take good care of you."

I hesitated, well aware these people were out of my social strata. "Can you call me tomorrow night? Sometimes I go home for the weekend." Roger went for my chair. I stood up, pivoted and sat down.

"I'll go in by myself." I did not want either of them to see the drab halls or my meager room. "Good night and thanks for a special evening."

Slowly I wheeled myself through the empty halls. The only sounds were the reverberations of my wheels moving along the shiny floors. I was overwhelmed with all kinds of feelings. I waved to the night nurse who ran out to greet me.

"Nita, you look starry eyed. You must have had a grand time."

"Yes. I was entertained royally. I'm kind of tired though. Night, night."

I couldn't wait to get to the safety of my bed. I hadn't been to the bathroom all night and miracle of miracles, I was dry. I went into the bathroom, washed and hurried back to my room. Getting in bed quickly and burying my face deep in my pillow, I hugged it, treasuring the delicious warm sensations shooting from one end of my body to the other. It was not like being with Connie. I turned on my stomach and slowly began rolling my torso grinding and grinding, faster and faster, until I was limp. Oh, God, I didn't think I'd ever feel sexy any more. I wasn't dead after all. By any means! But what good would it do? How could I let him make love to me? He'd vomit if he knew I wore pads and plastic bloomers. I vowed not to see Martin again but I was still haunted by his magnetic stare. What did he want from me? Surely he could have any woman. I wouldn't see him again—but I wanted to—thinking of him disturbed my whole night.

The next day I phoned Louise. "Martin asked me to have dinner with him Saturday night. I don't know what to do."

Louise spoke frankly. "Martin's a great guy, but he is a lady's man. He was discharged from the service and he's making up for lost time. I don't want him to hurt you, Nita."

"I understand."

Louise sensed my disappointment. "Martin is fun, Nita, he's a sensational date. If you feel you can handle him with a grain of salt, then by all means, go and enjoy yourself."

I tried to appear nonchalant, "I can never say I wasn't warned. Thanks, Louise. Thanks again for that most delightful evening."

A dozen roses were delivered early Saturday. 'I can't wait until tonight. Martin'.

Martin's white Cadillac convertible was parked outside the VA emergency entrance when I came out a few minutes after 6:00 P.M. I wore an aqua flowered print shirt dress, thanks to Aunt Mary. Martin swooped me into the car before I could stand.

"I can do that myself."

"I'm at your service, madam."

We talked as though we had been life long friends. Martin had recently been appointed manager of his family's large department store and he related several incidents concerning various clients and their idiosyncrasies without mentioning their names. It was my first trek into Manhattan since I went into the service and I couldn't control my "oohing and aahing' causing Martin's joyous bursts of laughter. He stopped in front of a small French restaurant, dashed out of the car, opened the door to carry me down six steps announcing to the gaping staff, "She's drunk again."

"Your table, Mr. Wortman?" Martin nodded and carefully set me on a plush red velvet love seat that was separate from the dining area. He ordered Haig and Haig on the rocks for both of us. We dined on roast beef au jus accompanied by a whipped cream horseradish sauce, oven browned potatoes, and white asparagus served in a silver dish wrapped in a white linen napkin. I was in another world, captivated by an adoring Martin.

"I have a pair of tickets for a concert at the Aeolian Hall tonight. Are you interested?"

"Oh, yes, but, please, right now I must go to the ladies room."

"Think nothing about it. I'll carry you."

"No thanks, I'll go in my chair." He had the ladies' room cleared—I almost passed out: there was nothing for me to grab except a not too sturdy toilet paper roller. I said a prayer, then quickly pulled up my dress, pulled down my pants and banged onto the john.

Martin called, "Can you manage or shall I call for someone?"

"I'm fine, thanks," adding a few extra prayers, and to my surprise, I was.

After a delightful piano concert, Martin put the top up and drove to the Cloisters, overlooking the Hudson. Stars flickered brilliantly; while birds softly serenaded us. Martin turned on the radio to some dance music then turned toward me.

"Did you have a nice evening?"

"Perfect." Louise's admonition to take everything with a grain of salt, flashed before my eyes. Oh, God, I begged, please don't put me to the test.

Martin came closer putting his arm around me. I withdrew. "Is anything wrong?" he asked.

"No. We really don't know each other. I don't want to get too cozy."

"I just want to be close to you." Martin put his arm around me again. "You smell so good." He touched my hair tenderly, gently caressing my ears. "You have such tiny ears, Nita." I was struggling with the moment. "Only diamond earrings for you." My heart was racing. Slowly he kissed one cheek, then the other, turning my face toward his and gentle as a feather, brushed my lips with his. "Your lips are like rubies," Martin whispered, kissing with a little more pressure until I relented. The kisses became more and more passionate. When Martin rolled his tongue around my lips, I thrust him away with all my force.

"Please," I said breathlessly, "I beg of you. I don't want to go on. Please take me back to the hospital."

Martin picked up my hand, stroking his fingers along my palm. "I'm crazy about you, Nita. Ever since the night I met you, I can't get you out of my mind."

"Martin, I like you, too, but I hardly know you. Besides, I'm a patient in the hospital. I can't allow myself to become involved with anyone. Please take me back."

"Only if you promise we can go out again."

The next day Louise called. "Nita, are you okay?" I did not respond. "You were smitten?" Louise was agitated. "If that son of a gun hurts you, I'll kill him."

I managed to keep cool. "I told you I wouldn't take him seriously. If he becomes too salty, I'll stop seeing him but I have to agree, he's a lot of fun."

The next time I had a date with Martin we had a two-hour lunch at the Russian Tea Room in Manhattan and once again he placed me in a booth. I marveled over the samovars and the waiters in their Russian tunics. We had wine, their special blintzes and two cups of coffee. The door to the ladies' room was too narrow for my chair. When he picked me up to put me in my wheelchair, the seat cover was wet. I was mortified.

"God, I'm so embarrassed," I said as soon as we got outside.

"Hey, don't think a thing about it," Martin said reassuringly. "Let's go and buy you a new outfit. May I help you select it?"

We had so much fun shopping and found a gorgeous London brown linen suit with a silk beige shirtwaist blouse, shoes, and a beige leather pocketbook.

"Wow, some gorgeous doll," Martin raved.

I thanked him profusely but he was nonchalant about the whole episode. We were going to a movie; thankfully I managed all the necessary changes in the fairly large bathroom. Later we had a luscious Chinese dinner and talked about war happenings, music, and art, laughed about nothing in particular.

Martin drove to the Cloisters again. I didn't stop him this time. His tender kisses led to thrilling soul kisses that left me panting. He put his hand inside my blouse slowly massaging my breast, then reached around to unfasten my bra. He slowly started sucking my nipple, rolling his tongue around until I was faint. I yearned for more and more, but I stopped him when I felt the pressure of his hand on my thigh.

"Sorry," he whispered withdrawing his hand, "I got carried away."

"I think it's time to go." We both laughed.

Marty and I dated several times, always delighting in each other's company, always leaving when things got too hot. He sent me a book of poetry by the English poet A. E. Housman. I was floating on cloud nine. One evening he called, "Nita, I would like you to meet my sister and her family who live in South Carolina. I told her all about you and she'd like us to come down next weekend. Please say yes."

"Marty, I'll have to let you know." I had to think. I had to think about a lot of things.

"If you're worried about her house, my sister assured me there won't be any problem for you in navigating your wheelchair. Please say yes. I'll call you tomorrow, my dearest."

I was shaking. I had to get off by myself. I called my parents Sunday feigning a headache. After lunch I wheeled down to one of my favorite doctors' office, which I knew would be empty, and closed the door.

Think, girl, think. Martin Wortman was the epitome of every girl's dream: handsome, intelligent, considerate, attentive and wealthy. He was too wonderful to be true. I would have everything a girl desired. He would carry me all over the world. The word "carry" stuck like a sharp knife. He would pamper me like a baby and yes, face it, he would soon tire of me. A man in his position would think nothing about straying. Face it, girl, you're a novelty now. You're not educated. You're still incontinent. How can you travel, meet his family? I knew too, that I would become more intimate with him. I had to get on with my life. Make something of myself. I sat for an hour staring into the wall. My eyes were wet when I left the office. I transferred from my chair to the pay phone and called Louise.

"I've been seeing a lot of Martin."

"I know, Nita, he's crazy about you. I've never seen him like this before."

"Louise, I'm not going to see him again. He asked me to go to South Carolina this weekend to meet his sister but I've decided against it."

There was a long silence. "I hope I didn't say anything to dissuade you."

"No, I thought about the situation long and hard. He's a dear man and I care for him very much but I'm not ready for a serious involvement. Do you understand? I would appreciate it if you didn't say anything to him yet."

"I understand," she said compassionately.

"Please give my warmest regards to Roger. It was a pleasure meeting you and thanks for your warm hospitality."

"Our very best to you, Nita. You deserve the best in life."

"Thank you."

Late that afternoon I was called to the phone. I knew who it was. "Hi lovely, it's I. Will you come?"

"Marty," I barely whispered, "I can't see you anymore. I'm still a hospital patient. I have to make more progress and get on with my life."

"What? Nita, I'll help. . . ."

"Martin, please listen. I want to become independent. Go to college. Make something of myself. I need to do it alone. Please understand. I can't complicate my life now." My stomach churned. "Please, I beg of you." I whispered, "Please don't call again." Slowly I replaced the receiver, staring into the phone. Yes, I thought, it would be lonely again but I had to be grateful. If nothing else, Martin had given me a wonderful gift—the return of my sexuality.

Chapter 21

In late September of 1944, Tommy, a bright red headed para yelled over to me in the PT department, "Hey Crip, over here."

"What's up?" I was still not comfortable with the moniker, but no way was I going to jeopardize my friendship with the boys.

"Five of us, including you, were selected to perform on our braces at Madison Square Garden in the beginning of October."

"Hey, that's neat. I'll really have to work on swinging through my braces and crutches." A couple of months had passed since I began struggling with braces and crutches.

"You're good, Crip, you're better than any one of us at getting out of a chair. You'll knock 'em dead."

"Thanks, Tommy. You're not so bad yourself. Should be fun, eh?"

"Get us out of this nuthouse for a while. We're going to have dinner there and see a show at night. A lot of show people are going to entertain us."

"Wow."

In mid-October, the VA ambulance took a group of five of us to the Garden. Many professionals: doctors, social workers, physical therapists and other interested medical people watched our performance. We were introduced to the audience as model war veterans who had worked hard to demonstrate the proper way to crutch walk, and get in and out of chairs. All of us performed like champs and received a standing ovation. We were served dinner in one of the private dining rooms. By the time we returned to the Garden, it was filled to capacity for a charity performance. We were ushered along the side wall fairly close to the tremendous stage to watch the evening's festivities. Among the entertainers were Milton Berle, Bill Robinson, Joey Bishop, Dean Martin, Danny Thomas and many others. I was thrilled to death and laughed until my sides split. One aspect of the gala night made me very sad: a couple of the men didn't laugh at all. Laughter had been snuffed out of them on some battlefield.

After the show, several of the performers came over to thank us for our gallantry. Lo and behold, I found myself looking into the incredible eyes of Bill Robinson.

I beamed. "Hi, Bill Robinson; I'm Nita Bloom."

"Young Lady, what are you doing two weeks from tonight?"

I laughed. "I'm free as a bird."

"I'm opening a new nightclub called 'The Club Zanzibar.' I'd love you to be my guest. The guys are invited, too."

Oh, my golly. "Thanks, so much," The same echoed down the line.

"Aunt Mary, you've got to help me," I begged on the telephone the next night. I told her about the invitation, frantic about not having something special to wear.

"Don't worry. I have just the thing. You'll love it. I'll bring it with me Sunday."

"Oh, you're an angel."

Every day was eternity but then all of a sudden it was November 5th. In the afternoon, a florist delivered a box from Bill Robinson.

Oh, my God. I called over to a patient who suffered from muscular dystrophy, "I just received two magnificent white gardenias on a comb for my hair." Later I put on the deep red skirt with the paisley chiffon blouse that Aunt Mary had brought.

"Crip, you're a knockout!" Whistles shrilled from the other guys.

I smiled, enjoying every single bit of their flattery.

At Club Zanzibar, we were royally greeted and led to a table directly in front of the stage. The nightclub was filled to capacity; there was an air of excitement bouncing off the walls. I could hardly contain myself. Finally the curtain parted and Mr. Bojangles himself came to the front of the stage.

"Good evening and welcome to Club Zanzibar." He stopped for a second to give me a broad smile. "Tonight I will start the evening off with a dance tribute to Nita. I'll start with a few slow steps, just as Nita will do one day and gradually get into the jive, just as she will."

I felt faint. My breathing was slow and heavy. For sure, I was in fairyland or floating somewhere in heaven. Bill Robinson did exactly as he promised: dancing slow and easy, picking up gradually and then, dancing all over the stage as only the inimitable Bojangles could. I was radiant, thrilled beyond words, out of my mind with excitement. After his performance, he came over and a photographer followed. I leaned over to kiss him, shaking my head over and over.

"How can I ever thank you?"

"By keeping up what you did a couple of weeks ago and proving me right." He was grinning from ear to ear "Are you getting enough to drink and eat?"

"Oh, yes, thank you." My voice was almost hoarse.

Then, a tall woman stood in front of me. It was a strain for me to look up at her. She sat down on the low stage. My God, it was Eleanor Roosevelt! I opened my mouth but not a word came out.

"Don't say a word," she said sympathetically. "I understand you were a WAC and became injured."

I nodded, tears in my eyes from embarassment. I would have loved to have talked to her. "With your spirit I know you will conquer your problems just as Bill predicted."

"Thanks," I finally whispered. I had my address book and a pen, and asked for her autograph.

I still look at that litle book and the picture of Bill Robinson and me with all the signatures of the famous entertainers on that memorable night.

Chapter 22

In March of 1945 as I was going into the PT Department, I found a group of paras talking to a stranger. Chen called, "Nita come here, I'd like you to meet Chris." I smiled at the good looking young man whose bright eyes acknowledged mine. Chen went on. "Guess what? We're going to get our driver's licenses. We've been waiting for you. You're going to be the first woman to learn how to drive with hand controls and Chris is our driving instructor."

"Oh, my God! Drive again? Chen, it's a miracle. It will be the happiest day of my life."

Chris was laughing. "We will start next week."

When I was notified that Chris was in the emergency entrance waiting to give me driving lessons, I wheeled down as fast as I could. Chris beckoned me over to a two door sedan. My heart was pounding. Before he allowed me to drive, I had to stand up and pivot into the front seat, collapse my wheelchair and pull it into the car between the back of the front seat and in front of the back seat. Then Chris explained what I had to do. I had a hard time at first, learning to push up on an extended arm in order to drive and push down on the same gadget, for the brake. I was petrified as soon as the car moved, but it didn't take long to catch on. What a phenomenal feeling it was to get behind the wheel again and drive by myself. I went up the hills of the VA, down the hills, to every niche and corner, to places I never knew existed. I had to turn around in the narrowest places. It was the hardest training I ever experienced.

Chris told me that an amputee patient had constructed a pair of hand controls which the government had improved considerably. I passed easily on the day of the test and received my license. This also meant real independence for the paraplegic community.

Photographers were all over the place. My face was publicized in many newspapers throughout the country.

Then I applied to the VA for the car allotment to which all service connected spinal cord injured veterans were entitled.

Shortly after I got my license, I called my parents to tell them the good news. My father came in during the week bringing me of all things, a box of my favorite Fanny Farmer chocolates. He pulled a chair close to my bed. "Dollink, vould you like to drive a new car?"

"Dad, what are you talking about?"

"I vouldn't vant you to take a chance with the old Hudson. Ve'll get a new one. An Oldsmobile."

"Dad," I laughed happily. "you amaze me. You'd better believe I'd like to drive a new car, or any car for that matter, as long as it has wheels and can move. Dad, don't forget, you have to install hand controls."

"I know, I know. I have to buy the car in your name. Here's a piece of paper to sign. Ven you come home, you can drive it anytime you vant."

"Don't forget I'll be receiving money from the VA to help you pay for it."

"Vonderful, Dollink."

Waiting for the answer to my request for the allotment from the VA was interminable. Finally, a reply came: ". . .because you did not serve in the United States Army, you are not entitled to receive any GI benefits." I was in total shock. Where was I? Wasn't I being treated in a Veterans Hospital? I was livid. I slammed the door of my room and remained there for two days without eating. *What is it with me, God? Why is everything a nightmare? Every time I think you're on my side, I find out it's quite different. Why are You punishing me? One of your own children. How am I ever going to get out of here?*

There were no answers. Only the facts: I was not a veteran because I had enlisted in the WAAC and had been discharged before that organization became a regular part of the Army. Shortly after I was discharged, the WAAC became the WAC, which was part of the regular Army. I was determined that if it was to be my only accomplishment, I would find a way to become a full-fledged veteran of the United States Army.

The anticipation of driving again pacified me somewhat, but it took eight interminable weeks until my father called to say he was coming for me with the brand new Olds. I immediately got a weekend pass. I waited impatiently outside the VA emergency driveway. The smashing, shiny black automobile with whitewall tires that pulled into the emergency driveway had to be mine. I zoomed over to the driver's side. "Dad it's terrific! Can I drive home?"

"Dollink," he said as he got out of the car. "Have a little patience." His crony, Mr. Honig, sat in the back seat. Dad opened the door for the suitcase. "Oy, I'll have to put your wheelchair in the trunk as well. You haven't driven in the city in a long time. Tomorrow you can drive in Suffern.

"Dad," I persisted, "I can drive when we cross the George Washington Bridge. I know the way like the back of my hand."

My father's face reddened. "Needala, please, I will tell you when you can drive." He came around and opened the door. The interior was beautiful. The dashboard was all bright and shiny. Something was missing. "Dad, where are the hand controls?"

"Get in the car, Aneeda. Don't raise your voice to me."

"Where are the hand controls?" I frantically repeated raising my voice to a higher pitch. Dad's crony got out of the car and took a walk. People going into the hospital gaped at us.

"Get in the car, you are not going to drive."

I raced around to the back of the car, grabbed my suitcase and shouted, "I don't want to go home!" Embarrassed to tears, I wheeled back to my room as fast as I could and closed the door and cried my heart out.

It was unusual for my door to be closed. Someone knocked, but I did not respond. The person knocked again and opened the door. I was sitting in my chair with my head down.

"Nita, what's wrong?" Dr. Zane asked. He was a young psychiatrist who became friendly with me although I had never talked to him professionally. He knew how much I loved music and whenever he was on duty he would come down to my room and we would go up to the waiting room where I would sit enthralled while he played the piano for an hour or more. "Whatever happened, I want to help you." He paused. I covered my face with my hands. "Girl, what is it? Did someone hurt you?"

"My father promised to put hand controls in our new car," I said in a monotone without looking up. "When he came today to take me home, there was a beautiful new Olds but no hand controls."

"How did your father acquire a new car?"

"I'm not sure about all the details, but I know the car is in my name because he needed my signature."

"Nita, there's a ban on buying new cars. You can only get one in an emergency." Dr. Zane spoke slowly, "The only way your father could get a new car was to put it in your name and tell the Commissioner you needed it." Lowering my eyes, I held my stomach tightly, trying to control the grabbing spasms. I looked up at the doctor. "Nita, you know what you have to do if you want the hand controls?"

"No," I whispered.

"Your father broke the law. You have to call him and tell him that if he refuses to put hand controls in your car, you will call the authorities."

"No," I whispered.

"I'll say it again. Your father broke the law. You have to call him and tell him that if he refuses to put hand controls on your car, you will report him."

"I can't."

"Then I guess you really don't want the hand controls."

"If I thought pleading with my father would do any good, I would get on my knees. I know Dad. When he gets stubborn about something, he won't change." I was silent for a minute. "You're right, Dr. Zane. If I do battle with my father I have to be absolutely certain of the facts."

My friend patted my hand, "It's difficult for you, isn't it?"

"Yes," I sighed, "everything is difficult. I have to grovel. I'm not independent anymore. I have to accept food and clothing. I have to ask for things like a baby. I gave up all my independence when I became paralyzed."

"And now you have to accept the good graces of your father so that you can drive your own car which remains in his possession." The psychiatrist never took his eyes off me.

"I know it's really not my car because my father paid for it. I'd be satisfied if he kept his promise."

I smiled sheepishly. "Will you wait until I make the call, please?"

I wheeled up to the phone booth and transferred on to the seat. "Hi Mom, how are you doing? I'm fine, too. Will you please put Dad on." I waited a minute. "Hi Dad, I'm calling about the hand controls."

A voice I had not heard in a long, long time was cold and precise. "Aneeda, don't get upset. I'm doing it for your own good."

"Dad, you bought that car under false pretenses."

"Vat are you talking about?" His voice was rising.

"You told the Commissioner that you were buying the car in my name. It's really my car, isn't it?"

"Aneeda, stop carrying on like this. I'm doing this for your own good." He repeated. I sat there stunned at his last statement. All of a sudden it was clear that, although my father was able to purchase a car, he was never going to put hand controls on because he thought I would dirty the white wall tires or some other silly thing.

"And you said anytime that I came home I could drive, didn't you?" Sweat was pouring out of me. "If you don't have the hand controls installed immediately I will report you to the authorities." I grabbed my stomach with my free hand, taking long deep breaths.

"All right," my father raved, "I'll get them. I'll get them."

Battle was as hard as ever, but victory was sweet.

Chapter 23

In July of '45, during rest hour, while I was engrossed in reading the book *Homeward Bound*, a stunning brunette Red Cross volunteer stood at my door. "Mind if I come in?" Her sexy, sophisticated tone piqued my interest.

I looked up and smiled. "Hi. Nita Bloom. Have a seat. You match my decor."

The woman smiled as she lowered her gray uniformed body on to the gray metal chair across from my bed. "Ruth Drexler."

Usually I was unimpressed with average Red Cross women, who always treated me like a pathetic helpless creature, with their, "Oh, my goodness, such a young girl like you in bed?" or, "You must try harder in PT, dearie." I sensed that Ruth was of a different sort: cultured, well groomed, intelligent. Her sleek black hair was pulled back into a bun at the back of her neck. Her long red polished nails were perfectly manicured. No, she didn't look at all like the typical mollycoddles with their cloying "How do you bear it?" Grrrr.

Ruth smiled admiringly at me. "Nita, your hair is most attractive. It's the new page boy style isn't it?"

"Yes. My beautician from New Jersey stopped in a few weeks ago to give me instructions with curlers, brushes and setting lotion."

"How considerate." Ruth paused for a minute then asked delicately, "Would it be presumptuous of me to ask what happened to you?"

I folded and unfolded my hands. Well, I guessed wrong. These Red Cross women must take a course on how to "rile patients."

"Oh, I'm sorry. I didn't mean to upset you. How stupid of me." Her eyes were downcast. She looked absolutely appalled.

"It's okay. Ordinarily I don't like prying." Something about Ruth's openness didn't offend me. "I had an infection in my right

thumb. Three weeks later I became paralyzed and had a laminectomy performed on my spine. Although the operation saved my
life, I became a paraplegic." Short and not so sweet.

The woman was obviously disturbed.

"I need time to digest what you said. What kind of medical
attention did you get? I know the women's army wasn't part of the
regular army until a few years ago."

"Believe me, it wasn't the best," I said, struggling to sound
casual.

"That's horrible. I hope you're getting all the GI benefits."

"No, I'm not," I mumbled.

"My God, why not?"

"It's a long story. From the moment that I arrived at Fort
Ogelthorpe in 1943 all of the WAACs were led to believe that any
day we would become part of the regular army. By the time the
WAAC did become part of the regular army I was already paralyzed, although it had always been my intention to rejoin my company and possibly be sent overseas. So you see it is a mere technicality that I do not receive veteran's rights." I was feeling nauseous.
It was hard to drag up the horror.

Ruth took a long breath. Her eyes never left my face. "Nita,
my husband Paul Gumbinner and I have a friend, a prominent
attorney in New York who has a lot of political connections in
Washington. Is it possible for you to come out to our home in New
Rochelle? I will invite Dick Monfried, and you can give him all the
details. If anyone can help, it's this man."

I nodded my head up and down. Tears of joy drenched my
face. This woman was sent from heaven. "Of course I'll come. You
are most kind. I've been floundering about the situation, not knowing where to begin. Thank you for the opportunity."

The following Saturday morning, a black Lincoln convertible
with the top down waited outside the emergency entrance. A well
groomed middle aged man wearing dark sunglasses and casually
dressed in a dark shirt and white pants waited alongside the automobile.

"Hi, you must be Mr. Gumbinner."

"Paul. And you're, Nita," extending his hand. "Can I help
you?"

"No, thanks, I can manage. I'll show you how to put my chair
in your trunk." I stood up proudly, pivoted and sat down on the

leather seat. "Just fold the center, *et voila*! You don't have any problems with your back, do you?"

"No." Paul opened the trunk; the chair fit in perfectly and off we went.

Was I ever excited. My hair was blowing in the mild July breeze. What a thrill to be riding in a convertible again. "This is just great. I love it." Paul smiled.

"Your wife is gorgeous, but she also has an inner beauty that is even more admirable."

Paul absolutely concurred. "We're pleased you're going to spend the day with us. The children can't wait to meet you. They'll have all kinds of questions. I hope you won't mind?"

"Heck, no."

The Gumbinners lived in a sprawling white colonial in New Rochelle. Ruth looked dazzling in a navy and white linen dress. Nancy, age 7, and Paul, Jr., age 4, immediately surrounded me.

"Show me how your wheelchair works?"

"Can I have a ride?"

"How did you get sick?"

"Can I help you by moving your legs?"

"When will you get better?"

"Children . . ." Ruth reprimanded.

"Let them be. I can handle it." Interrogation from innocent children didn't affect me. I was sitting in a chaise longue sipping a bloody Mary and daydreaming that this kind of life wouldn't be hard to take.

At one o'clock Ruth announced lunch would be served. Paul brought my wheelchair over and took me to a white glass table on the patio where a friendly Martha, to whom everyone spoke affectionately, served an elegant luncheon of cold poached salmon, red potato salad, and Belgium endive salad with warm french bread. A super raspberry pie and iced coffee ended the splendiferous repast. I interacted easily with the Gumbinners, learning how they met, and how a "simple" experiment led to Paul's dynasty of the Faberge perfume company and why they sent their children to public schools instead of private ones. Obviously Ruth was concerned about the accessibility of her bathroom and had rearranged everything to make it easy for me. I felt blessed to meet this caring family.

At about five thirty, a tremendously heavy set man, at least 6 foot 4, joined us and from the squeals of the children I knew it was someone they dearly loved. "Uncle Dick, oh, come meet Nita. She can't walk." The kids practically dragged him over, and the big man towered over me. "Hi, Nita, I'm Dick Monfried." His smile was genuine, his handshake firm. "First I have something for my favorite little people," he said, handing each child a wrapped package that elicited "Oh, what a pretty doll" and "Wowie, a Mack truck."

Ruth arched her eyebrows. "Well?"

"Thanks, thanks, Uncle Dick." They exclaimed vigorously.

Almost magically, within a few minutes, everyone disappeared, leaving the two of us to chat. I gave the lawyer a summary of the pertinent facts regarding my army career. Several times his lower lip tightened, as though he was about to interrupt, but he remained silent until I finished.

"You mean to tell me the army hospital was only 70 miles away from Nacogdoches and you were never sent there until you were paralyzed?"

"That's correct."

Dick mopped his sweaty brow. "It's totally unfair. Preposterous. We have to do something about this."

"I would be eternally grateful." I stammered, "but I have to tell you, Dick, I don't have much money."

"Did you hear me mention money?"

"No, but. . ."

"No buts. If I can do one thing for someone who's been screwed by the Army, that's payment enough. It kills me to think a person who enlisted in all good faith received such outrageous treatment from the U. S. government. Horrible." He mopped his brow again. "It will take time. Don't think it's going to happen next week or next month."

"However long it takes. I really don't know how to thank you."

"Nita, I want you to send me a written report of everything you told me today. It will be completely confidential, I promise. I need to have it for many reasons."

"I'll get it out to you immediately."

"By the way, how would you like to go to the trotters in Yonkers next week?"

"Sounds neat. I've never been to a horse race."

"You'll probably have beginners' luck. I'll pick you up at six and we'll have dinner at the clubhouse. The VA hospital, right?"

I nodded enthusiastically.

I left the Gumbinner's, smiling all the way back to the red brick fortress. Someone believed in me. One day justice would be done. One day.

Chapter 24

The summer and fall passed slowly. I prayed every night for a letter from Matheny telling me that he was scouting for a school. He had written several letters imploring me not to lose faith and once sent an old book of his, entitled *It Can Be Done*. Of course I responded to say I would wait. I continued working hard on my braces and crutches but I had reached a plateau and didn't make any real progress. Several of the paras and quads had been discharged. Dick Monfried took me to the trotters again and told me that he had contacted several Congressmen on my behalf but had nothing positive to report. I went home for the Jewish holidays and surprisingly, found them very pleasant. The rest of the year was uneventful and I would have been depressed but for the thought of going to Matheny's and the hope that lay ahead.

During the end of 1945 and early part of 1946, several new, young physicians came to the VA. They had been in the service and were spending a year or two in this hospital before going on to open their own practices. I became friendly with three of them: Drs. Weiss, Falluti, and Leder. Johnny Weiss and I hit it off immediately. He would come down to my room for a sherry, tell me about his war experiences in Europe and we would listen to music on my new record player that the National Council of Jewish Women had given me the previous Chanukah. Harold Leder was an internist, and he and I shared many hours talking about his army life and problems of life in general. I didn't know Dr. Falluti very well. The young neurologist had just recently come to Ward 3C.

Ever since Passover of 1944 Marilyn and I had became closer. She came to see me one day looking even more radiant than ever. She told me that she was seeing the same man and we talked about the difficulty she would encounter with my father. "Are you really serious about him, Mar?"

"I like him a lot. Ed's been a nurse for a few years and he's

134

at Adelphi to get his Bachelor's. We have a wonderful time together." I had never seen her eyes shining so brilliantly. "Neet, I
never understood how you could give up Herm. He loved you so
much. You liked him a lot, didn't you?"

"I loved him with all my heart, Mar. It was the hardest thing
I ever did, the day I parted with him."

"Why did you do it? Dad would have gotten over his anger."

"I had spoken to Gramps about Herm. He said he knew
without even meeting him he must be someone special. But he
also said it would change the tenor of our whole family forever.
You know, Mar, I have many non-Jewish friends that I truly love
but I can't deny there is a special, almost a different quality, call
it a spirit, if you will, that exists among our own, and it's not to
be tossed off lightly." My sister was staring at me intently without
uttering a sound. "I have enough confidence in you that, whom-
ever you decide to marry, he will be a person of high morals and
convictions. Someone who loves you and will treat you as you
deserve. You're entitled to your own life and whatever you decide, you know I'm with you 100%."

Mar came over to hug me. "Herm was going to convert, but
Gramps hit the nail on the head when he emphasized the impact
on the family. But it's long been over, my life has changed and I
live with my decisions that I make today. The same as you Mar,
because you will have to live with yours."

A few months later John Price's newsletter evolved into a
national magazine as part of a new organization called Paralyzed
Veterans of America (PVA) that began with a few veterans who
served in the armed forces and who had incurred an injury affecting the spinal cord, causing paraplegia or quadriplegia. It was
formed "to deal with the unique problems and challenges facing
them."

In October 1946 I received a letter from Captain Matheny . .
. "Nita, I'm sure this will be your best Christmas present. I found
an old building, a former hotel, with a rambling porch that I know
you'll love when you practice your walking. As soon as we repair
major problems, I'll send for you." I read repeatedly until each
word became a photograph.

Soon the reality of leaving the VA began to focus. How would
I pay for my board and tuition? Would the VA approve? My only
means of support was the small pension from the U.S.
Employment's Compensation Commission. I gave the money to

my father each month who was keeping it for a rainy day but this small amount would never cover those expenses. Thus far my effort to become a veteran was a mere dream. After several sleepless nights, I decided to test the waters and asked to see Dr. Flowers.

The neurosurgeon smiled sympathetically. "My dear woman, I fully understand that you want to leave. You could go home. But, in all honesty, we cannot permit you to go to a quack."

"Why are you denying me this opportunity before you hear all the man's plans? Captain Matheny is the only person besides Dr. Masters who has held out any hope for me. You have to give me this chance. I'll die here."

Flowers straightened to his full height. "You wouldn't die here if you had gone to Bulova as I suggested. You would be earning a nice sum of money. Quite possibly you might be living outside of this hospital by now."

"That's not what I want—to work in a factory. I want to be physically independent. I want a college education. The Captain is offering the first opportunity to gain my independence."

Dr. Flower's lips were taut. "The man is a fraud. There is no doctor in the world who can restore nerve damage from T4 spinal cord injury. It would be an insult to your intelligence if we permitted such an outrage and you can be certain, we won't." He walked over to me and patted me on the head. "Forget wild promises. You're too smart for trickery. Anita, I hope you come to your senses."

I clenched my fists. I didn't think he was fair. I turned my chair around to face the bars on the windows. How much longer would I have to remain a prisoner?

A week later I was deeply touched to receive a letter from the director of the Bronx VA: "You have been chosen to receive the VA's highest award for outstanding valor and courage in the face of adversity." He invited me to attend a ceremony the following week where General DeVoe would present me with a magnificent Hamilton gold watch inscribed with the words: "Christmas 1946 Anita Bloom for Valor Bronx VAH." Several physicians were in attendance including Dr. Kessler, Dr. Flowers, Dr. Zane and Dr. Weiss. After the ceremony, General DeVoe asked me to remain.

The tall man spoke succinctly. "Nita, your performance with other veterans has been outstanding. How would you like to be an example for all the other disabled veterans all across our nation?"

"I really haven't done anything. Most of the men should receive this honor."

"My dear, you are modest." He smiled benevolently. "We have created a job expressly for you. We want you to demonstrate to our paraplegics in every VA facility, how to take care of themselves, how to ambulate, how to go about the business of living." The white-haired gentleman shook his head confidently. "We will give you a nice salary and pay all your expenses."

This was indeed a fine offer. "General DeVoe, I don't know how to thank you. You are very generous. May I have a few days before I give you my decision?" We clasped hands warmly.

Yippee, the gateway to freedom! I always wanted to travel and I would be of service to many veterans. It was a wonderful opportunity. I wheeled like a demon back to my ward, feeling like I had won a million dollars. Everyone congratulated me.

Dr. Zane was on duty that evening. Although I never had the need to see him professionally, we had become friends and I always knew he was interested in me as a person. He usually came down to my room and we would go up to the waiting room where he'd play the piano. Before he sat down to play, I enthusiastically repeated the general's offer. His expression was somber.

"Hey, you don't look happy for me. Is something wrong?"

The psychiatrist sat down to where he was at eye level with me. "You do understand that once you make this commitment, you will live as a handicapped person all your life. You will live in VA hospitals, you'll think VA and breathe VA."

"I guess I wasn't aware of that aspect," I said meekly, but then quickly perked up. "I'll be traveling, seeing the country, getting better and better at ambulating. Most important I'll be helping other veterans."

"I repeat. You will be forever a handicapped person."

"Isn't that what I am?"

"Only if you believe it. You haven't found out yet. And you will never find out if you give up so easily."

"But I'll be totally independent. I won't be a burden to anyone. I can pay my way again."

Emanuel Zane sat back and pulled his pipe from his jacket pocket. He took a long time puffing, finally lighting it. "Nita, you're not the typical paraplegic. You instinctively refused the factory offer." Zane took a deep draw on his pipe. "There's another world out there for you. It isn't in the VA."

"But the only other option I have is with Captain Matheny and the VA powers that be insist he's a quack."

"Do you think he is? You were with him."

"No, I saw the eagerness in his eyes when I stood. I know he believes I can walk again."

"Then don't give up." The young doctor looked at me thoughtfully. "I'm going to help you. At the very least you'll get out of this hell hole. One of the higher ups at the VA in Washington owes me. If I can get my friend Bert to persuade the VA, they will cover your stay at Matheny's school."

I brought my hands to a prayer position. "You're sensational."

"No, my love, you are. That's why you must have your chance."

"I'd better make an appointment with General DeVoe."

The next day the VA director's secretary opened his door for me to enter. I went in, aware of how busy he was. I squared my shoulders and got right to the point. "General De Voe, I can't tell you how flattered I am that you offered me a job as a demonstrator."

"Then you'll take it," the General's smiled to pacify me. "Enough of that quack in New Jersey?"

I squeezed my left thumb staring straight into the older man's eyes. "No sir. I've decided not to accept the job."

DeVoe's eyes appeared hard as steel. "You're making a mistake young lady. Flowers concurred, it was the perfect job for you in—er—ah, in your condition. How can you turn it down? You refused work at Bulova. What will become of you wasting away in a hospital? The tall spindly man rose to approach me, lowering his voice. "My dear, we can no longer justify a single room for you. You had better think long and hard about your decision to leave."

I had thought about it a lot. "I understand, sir. Thank you again."

The next morning before therapy; eight thirty in the morning, Dad appeared. "Needala, dollink, we're so proud of you."

I pursed my lips. What now?

"Such a wonderful thing the general did for you?"

My God, they were really putting on the pressure. Stay calm,

I reminded myself, stay calm. "Dad," I kept my voice deliberately low articulating slowly, "I do appreciate the offer but it isn't the job for me. I would always live in a Veteran's Hospital. I would always be an invalid."

"Dollink, you're forgetting something very important. How many people in your . . ." He stopped, unable to say the awfulness. Tears dripped down his cheeks.

"Dad, please listen. The Captain bought a school in New Jersey. He is going to help me to walk again. No one here has ever encouraged me to walk. I'm still young. If I don't take this chance, maybe it will never happen again. I have to go. God will help me. When Walt sends for me . . .

"How will you pay for all this?" Dad shouted, "I can't afford . . ."

"Dad, I'll find a way. One thing I know for sure. I can't live in a hospital all my life."

"Don't forget, Aneeda, they will pay you. They will take care of all your medical bills." Dad wrung his hands. "You can't afford to say no."

"When I become a veteran, I'll have money and I'll find work to support myself."

Dad yelled, "You are making a mistake. You have to take this job." He lowered his voice. "Dollink, think about it, you might find a doctor in the VA who will help you to walk."

I shook my head slowly. I refused to discuss it further. He became frustrated and left shortly. I refused to go down to PT.

I thought about the situation before I went into the WAAC, how I had tried to explain to Dad how much I wanted to do something for the war effort. He had raged and screamed when I had suggested that I give up my job and work in a defense factory.

"No daughter of mine is going to work in a factory. You're earning a good salary. I have bills to pay," his voice reached a high pitch, "vot do you vant, I should go bankrupt?"

Lord, I had been frustrated. I simply couldn't explain to him how I felt. What if I had been in Germany? I wouldn't have had any choices. He wouldn't listen. My head was spinning in circles. The need to do something for my country was becoming more powerful every day. When that woman in the uniform of the Women's Auxiliary Army Corps came in the shoe store I knew what I had to do. After I enlisted, I came home to tell my parents. "Dad, you know how anxious I am to serve my country."

"Men are doing the fighting. Women stay home. You stay right where you are. Do you hear?"

I swallowed hard. "Dad, I enlisted in the Women's Army."

My father crashed his left hand with his right fist—again and again. "You'll be like a whore. A camp follower . . ."

I ran out of the room, grabbed my suitcase with Mom moaning behind me, "Nita, he doesn't mean it. It's for your own good. Don't go, darling, don't go." I ran all the way to the station and waited an interminable hour for the train. The next time I saw my folks was the night before I left for the army—when we all went to the station. It was the loneliest day of my life.

The telegram from the Captain said, "Come." I called Dr. Zane, who promised he would speak to powerful people on my behalf. Dr. Zane brought me to the day room and gave me a blow by blow description of what had transpired: "The two of them, General DeVoe and Dr. Flowers were stupefied, 'Emanuel,' the General said, 'surely you know your request is ridiculous. Everyone knows Nita has put you in an embarrassing position.' I reassured him that I was well aware of his generous offer for you to become a demonstrator for the VA spinal cord cases all over the country. However upon much reflection, I told him I was sorry to disagree. Nita, you should have seen their deadly looks. 'This young lady,' I continued, 'has to make a different decision, one that would not limit her activities to the VA. She needs a chance to explore every possible potential.' DeVoe sat with his hands across his chest. 'Zane, you realize she's rejecting this great opportunity for some quack's proposal?' Flowers was even more outraged. 'No patient of mine would be allowed to venture into a fool's paradise.'

"Now, Nita," my friend went on, "here's the clincher, Flowers said, 'Who will pick up the pieces once she's out of here? She can't come back and have things the way they were. We have catered to her every whim. She had her own radio, which was strictly against army regulations.' Can you imagine them still resenting the fact you have a radio? But I kept my composure and persisted, 'This Captain has offered help. He was the director of rehabilitation at Camp Edwards. Maybe he can do more for her than we have. She's ready to go out and face the world. Let's give her the chance. If she fails, the VA will know without a doubt that we gave her that one big chance.' DeVoe stroked his chin, 'Emanuel, my boy, maybe you're right although I think it's preposterous. On the other hand, this girl is unusual. She's not the run of the mill average veteran. Talking about being a veteran, which the poor kid is not. All right, Zane, let's give her a break. Let's do it.'"

I put my head down sobbing tears of gratitude. "I'll make you proud of me, Dr. Zane. One day . . ."

"There, there, you already have. You deserve your dreams."

The boys on ward 3C gave me a bang up farewell party. I saw envy in many of their eyes. "Crip, come back to show us how you walk." It broke my heart to leave them.

Connie came on Friday. I didn't want to leave the hospital grounds, and he went out for deli sandwiches and cream sodas that we ate in my room.

"You're going out of my life," Connie sadly prophesied.

"It would have happened sooner or later. You know our situation. I never tried to deceive you." My eyes were wet. "I will always love you. You brought tenderness and love into my life. If things were different—another world . . ."

Connie patted my hand. "Nita, this is the real world. Why are you so afraid?"

"I can't hurt my parents again. I can't." I covered Connie's hand. "I tried once and I couldn't go through with it." I pressed his hand gently. "Take care of yourself."

"I have to hear from you how Susie and Betsy are doing. How will I know when they're walking?"

"I'll keep your sister posted."

Connie's face looked like a wrung out washcloth. "Sure. Okay." He got up. "Stay sweet. Don't take any wooden nickels." He saluted and left.

I looked at the bars on my window, but this time I saw through them to the bright blue sky beyond. Freedom "is a-coming."

I was off to a new world—new opportunities—walking to freedom!

Chapter 25

February 1, 1947 was the day I left the VA for Matheny's school. As usual I sat in the back seat. I didn't insist on driving, although my father had finally had the hand controls installed, because my father always brought Mr. Honig, not only to keep him company, but in my opinion, to keep a certain distance between the two of us.

The long drive to Pluckemin, New Jersey, allowed me time to reflect on the awesome decision I had made. I knew my life was going to change drastically. If I had any doubts, I quickly dispelled them. My mind had to be clear about this awesome decision. I knew hard work was the name of the game; it was the one, and only necessity in learning how to walk again. The mere thought of walking was mind boggling. My heart raced like a dynamo. *Walking!* Oh, dear Lord.

Dad took one turn after another along curvy route 202, where I drove many times before I went into the service, passing gigantic oak trees all stripped of their foliage by the brisk weather, passing the Catholic seminary where I used to see the handsome young seminarians take their daily stroll. An hour later we passed Morristown and I recalled that Walt Matheny had written it wasn't too much further. We were now driving in horse country where I had read about the rich and their famous foxhunts.

I thought of how generous Dick Monfried had been to me. During the late summer he had taken me twice to the races, to several concerts and two nights ago, he hosted a small dinner party in honor of my new life, with the Gumbinners and a few friends at a plush restaurant in New Rochelle.

The still heavyset and very imposing Dick Monfried raised his glass in a dramatic toast to my future: "Here's to your sojourn at the Matheny school." He bowed to me, "All I ask for is the first dance." Everyone was moved to tears. Reminiscing about the unforgettable evening made me weepy.

"Aneeda, how much further do ve have to go?"

"Not too much, Dad. When you pass the next school, it's a mile from there. I'm getting excited."

We were passing acres of desolate brown farm land.

"Oi, Needala, I hope you're right about this whole business. To turn down such a vonderful job from the VA."

"Dad," I shrieked, "here we are!" The sign "Burnt Mills School" hung proudly on the left side of the road. My stomach was doing flip flops. My father drove slowly down the long bumpy dirt driveway until we came to a large ramshackle dilapidated dark brown wooden building.

"Needala," Dad said emphatically, "I don't vant you to go there. It looks like a run down nothing place. Do you hear me? I don't vant you to go there." His voice started to rise. "Ve're going back to the hospital."

My stomach flip flopped again. "Dad, please try to understand. It's the Captain's first venture. He probably has a lot of painting and construction work to do but that's immaterial to me. What matters is his goal, his desire to help me and those less fortunate—like Chucky. I have to take this chance. Please help me." God, I had been discharged from the VA. There was no returning. 'The sprawling porch' that Walt had written about . . . "Dad, see that porch? It goes all the way around the front of the building. Walt said I'll be practicing my walking there."

"All right, Dollink. But if there's anything wrong you'll call me right away. Promise?" He parked on the grass in front of the building. Mr. Honig did not budge from the car.

"Yes, Dad." My heart was thumping away. I could hardly wait to see Walter, Marguerite and Chucky. "Dad, please go in and tell them I'm here. I'm sure someone will help with my luggage."

"Okay, Dollink." I rolled down my window.

Matheny raced down the steps followed by a large heavy set man. "Nita, gal, here you are. Welcome. Meet my assistant, John Muller. John, this is Nita; her dad, Mr. Bloom and oh, yes, I remember, Mr. Honig. John, will you please take Nita's luggage to her room? Her 'special' room," giving me a wink. Walt reached into the back of the car, pulling me toward him, his hypnotizing eyes ever commanding me to do his bidding, lifted me like a butterfly and whisked me up the steps through an open door passing through a large sitting room, and into his office where he placed me on a chair. "Gal, you look terrific. Are you all set for hard work?"

"I can hardly wait. Where's Marguerite and Chucky?"

"Marguerite went into town. Chucky's in school. You'll see them soon." Walt turned to my father, who had followed us inside. "Bill, I don't want you to worry. Nita's in good hands. I just hired another assistant, an Army man who worked in a rehabilitation clinic in Italy; Nita won't lose one minute if I have to be away," Walt tapped his pencil methodically. "Listen, Bill, I've thought about what's best for Nita here. I think you should give her a trial period. A time to get adjusted. Plan to have the family visit, say, in three months. I don't think you should even telephone." Dad's face looked pathetically dismal. "Bill, think about my philosophy: it's the motions that count, not the emotions."

That man is a genius, I thought. A simple but loaded concept. My father wiped his eyes a few times but he didn't protest.

"Come, let's see Nita's room." Walt whisked me into my wheelchair. "This will be the last time anyone carries or pushes you anywhere," winking at Dad.

We went down a long dark hall passing two closed doors on either side until we came to the last room. The captain opened the door. "Surprise."

"Wow. This is really nice." I was truly pleased, even more so, for my father who could appreciate all the work that had gone into decorating this charming room for me. Cheery yellow curtains graced the windows, a newly painted dresser with a large mirror was placed against the far wall on the left, there was a double bed with a small oak night table beside it and a ladder back chair sat in the corner. The front view overlooked the porch and the driveway. I rolled over to the side window where a stream flowed gustily in the background. "Beautiful. No bars. No darn bars."

John came in with my suitcases, setting them on the bed. "I'll be back with your braces and hatbox after I take care of a few children."

"Don't you worry, Nita, you won't need those braces much longer," Walt said confidently. "Hey, you haven't seen the best."

Marguerite hurried into the room and we greeted each other warmly. "I know you did all the decorating and the sewing. It was dear of you to put that gorgeous handmade quilt you had on your bed at the Cape on this one. I'll be very careful. Thanks."

Marguerite was a slender, rather masculine looking woman whose cold reticent attitude had been intimidating when I first met her. There simply couldn't be two strongly outgoing personalities in the family—the gift was, without a doubt, Walt's. I got along with his wife, which was all that mattered. She was very competent and loving to Chucky. Marguerite must have been a big help to her husband in the undertaking of the Burnt Mills School. In addition, she functioned as the school's speech therapist.

"Bet you thought this door was just another closet," Walt boasted, "take a gander."

"My own bathroom," I raved. "You both thought of everything. Wow." There was a john right next to the sink and a tub along the side wall. Yellow wallpaper with tiny blue and yellow flowers; the sink was adorned with a light-blue soap dish and glass. "I know all the decor was yours, Marguerite. Thank you so much. The rooms are large enough for me to turn around easily." I looked at Dad, "I can tell you right now that you and Mom are going to be proud."

"I forgot something in the car." Dad dashed out, returning with a package. "This is for Chucky."

I beamed.

Walt undid the wrapping, holding up an attractive sailor suit for his child. "You didn't have to do this. Thanks."

Suddenly a shrill eerie laugh frightened the wits out of me. Dad stood stiff as a statue.

"Don't worry," Walt explained, "that's Pete in the next room. He's harmless." He looked at my father. "Well Bill, it's that time. I'll walk you to the car."

"Needala . . ." Dad hugged me. I was grateful there were no more tears. "Take good care. God should only be with you." I leaned up and kissed him. He was fumbling for words that stuck in his throat.

"Now Bill, I'm sure you feel better. Nita, take today off."

Suddenly Dad broke away, running out the door. "Ve'll see you . . . take care. God should only help you."

I choked back tears as I sat by the window watching Dad's car pull out of the Burnt Mills School driveway. Why in the world had I acted like a big shot again? Here I was stuck out in no man's land away from family and friends. No one could get in touch with me for three whole months. Who was I kidding? Who really cared? I was out of their sight. I wasn't a burden to anyone. I chastised myself for being an ingrate, knowing beyond a doubt that everyone wished the best for me. More than anything in the world, I dreaded being a burden. Somewhere in this world there had to be a place for me. The Captain had to find a way to help me walk again.

Dad's car was long out of view. I wheeled around to admire my room. My very own room. The nicest one I ever had in my life. I could back up, go forward, turn completely around without banging into anything. The dresser looked familiar. I had admired it in Marguerite's bedroom when I was up at the Cape. How thoughtful of her. I plugged in my radio to hear Truman's droning voice and flicked it off. I was much too excited right now. All I could think about was what Walter told my father. "Sixty days and I would be walking!" How was that possible? What would the man do for me? He couldn't have lied to my father. My father could sue him. But what if he was a quack like the VA predicted . . .? Where would I go? I had to put all those ugly thoughts out of my mind. My job was to work hard and that I promised I would do a thousand times over.

The large windows facing south would bring in the warmth and sunshine I adored. Would I ever walk down that long driveway? Hey, I told myself, give yourself a chance. I stopped daydreaming and regained my senses. I knew it would take a lot of work before I could take one little step by myself. Wow, that wide, wooden veranda is fantastic. Will I ever . . . stop the torture. Captain said I had to relax.

I inhaled and exhaled deeply then decided to unpack. John had put my suitcases on the bed. My clothes fit easily in the large dresser and I hung my blouses in the closet where the bar had been lowered for my chair height. I wheeled into the bathroom. How perfect. When I had to go—I could go. No problem closing the door for complete privacy. I felt as if I was off to the most exciting venture of my life. 'Life is just a bowl of cherries,' I sang gaily and as I came out of the bathroom, John Muller was about to leave my room.

"Hi, are you settled?"

"Yes. Isn't this a lovely room? I'm delighted."

"Sorry we didn't get the ramp ready in front of the entrance. We were gonna build it last week but didn't get around doin' it. I seen your hand controls. Never seen them before. Pretty nifty.

Your door was open. Left your fancy hat-box on the bed but I doubt if you'll have many occasions to go to tea parties."

Looking straight into his brownish-green know-it-all eyes, I quipped, "Never let it be said I'm not prepared for any occasion, Mr. Muller."

The idiot. If he only knew. The hat—was my bedpan! I started to unpack a few more things, smiling as I opened the hat-box and put my bedpan under the bed. Then suddenly I stopped. I wanted to see the children.

I opened the door, peering down the long corridor. Not a sound. Voices echoed in the beyond. Slowly, I propelled myself into the hallway, passed the closed door next to mine, passed the Captain's office and wheeled into the large entrance room with spiral steps that came from the floor above. Late afternoon cast zig zag blotches along the side of the wall. A hard thud followed by another one scared me half to death. I pulled the rims on my chair to a sudden stop. Around the curve of the spiral steep steps, a woman appeared. She looked like a skeleton apparition with one bony hand straight out in front.

"No, don't," I screamed. "Help, somebody."

A woman ran in from somewhere. "What's the matter?"

The thing stood positioned in the center of the landing. I pointed to the upstairs, "She's going to fall."

"No she's not. Emma knows how to take the steps. Take it easy, Miss." She scurried away.

I was angry at myself for staring. I pushed on straight ahead into what must once have been a sun porch. I could hear the thud of that woman going down each step but I didn't look back. Several small chairs were arranged underneath the windows. Suddenly thumps, clumps, rolling wheels and heavy steps stampeded past me. I flew to the opposite side of the room, turning my chair sideways against a pair of double glass doors. The aide I had just seen was carrying a small child and lowered her into one of the seats. Her head was bobbing back and forth against the back of the chair uncontrollably. The child's knuckles were sore from banging on the wooden tray that locked her in securely. She cocked her head to look at me. I managed a weak smile. Back went the little girl's head, hitting hard on the wood. I continued to wheel.

"I'm Nita," my strange voice whispered to an adorable blond child with gentle blue eyes sitting in another chair.

"I'm Baarbra. I'm Baarbra. I'm Baarbra."

Dear Lord.

"Look at her," an older boy accosted me. "You're crippled, you're crippled."

John Muller held a child about two years old with huge jet black eyes and hands and legs jerking in all directions. Muller carefully placed him in a chair and tied a sash around his waist to keep him from falling out.

"Butch, this is Nita."

"Hi," and I turned my chair around, almost knocking down the wraithlike woman who had come down the stairs. Her color was pale as death; her hands pathetically deformed; her boyish hair was done by some jokester. She wobbled unsteadily toward me.

"ImmEmma" she repeated over and over.

"I'm Nita," I whispered. Emma extended her hand and grabbed mine. God help me, I beseeched. I felt I was going to faint. "Excuse me," I took a deep breath, about faced my chair and flew like lightning down the hall to my room.

I had to get out of there. God, it was not the place for me. I hated it. Why did I leave the hospital? Why did I fight the whole Veterans' Administration? I'd call Dr. Zane to find a way to get me reinstated. I struggled to get out of my chair onto the bed and fell on the floor. Thoroughly wiped out, I stayed there and fell sound asleep.

I was awakened by the Captain calling, "Nita, Nita, please help us feed Butchy. We're short handed. Butchy needs to be fed. C'mon, gal, give us a hand."

The Captain begged. I raised my head. No, I wasn't going to feed anyone. I was not going to look at those horrible children anymore. I was going to call Dad right away.

"Please, Nita. Butch won't eat for anyone. Please help us out. He may eat for you."

Gradually I eased myself to a sitting position. God, you have forsaken me again. Sent me to this awful isolated place. I couldn't go back to the VA. What would they think of me, giving up so quickly? I couldn't go home. I'd die here. I gritted my teeth until I could not stand the pain. I would have to remain at least for the three months. I pleaded for God's help. I struggled to get up, but kept falling back. I eyed the night table praying it was strong enough to hold my grasp: With my right hand I reached for the top of the table, bearing all my weight on it while I pushed with my left hand on the wheelchair. Alleyoop, one, two, three—back on the floor—one, two, three—up, crashed into the chair puffing like a steam engine and perspiring like a longshoreman at the equator. My hands and feet were trembling. Perspiration dripped down my face. Matheny kept calling and whistling for me to come. I'd have to call my father to come back. Never! Tears fell like buckets.

"Okay, okay, I'm coming. I'm coming."

Chapter 26

As I ran a brush through my hair, I could envision every one of those kids who would be in the dining room. Lord, I never saw such horrible. . . As I raced through the halls I kept reminding myself just to focus on Butch.

The din of voices came to an abrupt stop when I entered. Spellbound eyes stared at me followed by a roar of grunts, weird sounds and guttural "Hi yas?" and "Who's she?" Butchy's high chair was the first one inside the dining room; the other faces faded out of my sight like old wash cloths.

"Gal, I appreciate this very much," Walt said. "We've had a heck of a time getting this little fella to eat. I think you're the one to help him."

I didn't answer, covering my left hand over the crossed fingers of my right. Walt maneuvered Butch, tied to a wooden highchair, to face me; I was stunned by the child's expressive eyes filled with fear and anger. Walt came around to move my chair alongside the child's. "You open his mouth with your left hand," he instructed, "put in a spoonful of food with your right, pushing gently toward the back of his mouth, careful that he doesn't choke." I was panic stricken. "Nita's going to feed you." The Captain said matter-of-factly. "You'll be fine. See you guys later."

The child's pitch black eyes dared me, his mouth and legs rigid as a barricade. It wasn't going to work. My hands felt clammy. Butch's lower lip began to quiver. . . I put my face down and could not look at Butch. Then I raised my eyes to face an exquisite little boy whose irate expression indicated that he was about to strike me.

"Hi. Remember me? I've never done this before and I'm just as scared as you." The dreaded expression on Butchy was still there. "Here's a nice piece of meat for you." Fresh springs were about to burst. He jammed his mouth shut. This two-year-old had

150

the strength of Atlas. I tried to force the spoon through his mouth. Was I crazy? A leg kicked me in the stomach. He began grinding his back teeth. Pulled my hair from the roots. This was involuntary? I broke the grip of his fingers.

"Haa," a small boy whose head was no bigger than a grapefruit, laughed hysterically. "Good for you, Butchy. That was a good kick. Give it to her again."

"Go home."

"Yer crippled. You can't feed him."

"Give it to her Butch."

Mean kids. I've got to control my emotions. I inhaled deeply. Aha, I recalled passing an empty physical therapy room right before the entrance to the dining room. Swiftly I turned Butchy's chair around. Set my pedals so I could push him, though his tray wiggled so hard I had to stop every few seconds. "We're going for a ride. Like a choo choo train." Struggling along we finally made it into the PT room. I faced the child's expression of sheer terror. How would I reach him? "Butch, I want to be your friend. I don't want you to get sick."

The child began to screech as though I was torturing him. An aide came to the door; I waved him away. Taking deep breaths, I slowly blew some air out of my mouth to stop my internal shaking.

Suddenly I had an idea."Hey, my new friend, I think you're like me. We start with the dessert first. How about some chocolate pudding?"

That did it. The child's jaw relaxed, his mouth stayed open, the pudding slid down his palate with the ease of a slippery eel. I mixed the potatoes with the green beans, with the ground beef, with the chocolate pudding. The child's eyes glistened like the reflections of a pure diamond. The involuntary kicking, and the various guttural sounds didn't bother me any more. The trick was to hold the tongue down with a small amount of food, tilt the spoon, remove it. Keep the soft palate relaxed by putting chocolate pudding in again.

"Hooray for Butch! That was wonderful. Let's try a few more green beans." Pow, a foot to my stomach. Look at that angel face, all innocence. I quickly gave him some pudding. This was not easy. Nothing in this place was going to be easy. Why was I doing it in the first place?

"Butchy," I exclaimed gleefully, "that was wonderful. You're happy and you've made me happy." I patted his cheek. "We'll do just fine. We're so much alike."

Matheny seemed to step out of a wall. "Holy cow, you fellas are okay. Can you come over here for a minute, gal? I'll take Butchy to Claire and be right back." He returned, pushing another child.

"Chucky, how good to see you." I wheeled around to the side of his chair to kiss his cheek. "Let me take a look at you. Goodness, how you've grown." Chucky was Matheny's son whom I had not seen since last summer at Cape Cod. Indeed, the child had grown considerably but Walt had written of his 'outstanding' progress, yet he was still drooling and grunting with his arms and legs jerking in involuntary spasms.

"Nita," Walt said. "I'd like you to join the staff for dinner at six. Pack it in early. Be ready for the works tomorrow."

"Sounds fine. I admit I'm a bit weary."

"My gosh, I almost forgot. There's a surprise waiting for you in the office." Turning to his son, "See you later, Chuck." The child bobbed his head back and forth. Walt ran me down to his office, handing me a florist's box that I took to my room and quickly opened.

The card read, "Welcome to your new home. Be a patient patient. Love Johnny." It was a magnificent orchid from my friend Dr. Weiss, the neurosurgeon at the VA. I wanted to rush to the phone to thank him but my new philosophy was to control my emotions. At a more convenient moment I would write him a thank you.

At dinner I picked at my food: mashed potatoes, watery green beans, dry canned beef, tapioca pudding. Ich. I could understand Butch better now. I excused myself and returned to my room.

The coming of evening had depleted all my enthusiasm. Was my father right? A run down school for outcasts! Three whole months before I could see anyone. That's right, feel sorry for yourself. The very first day. Jeepers, I lectured myself, give yourself a chance. Walt had been in charge of a large rehabilitation program up at Camp Edwards. He had to be good.

I started to undress when a frenzied piercing laugh from one of the rooms caused a tightness in my chest. It seemed to come from the room next to mine. It happened several times again. I heard more laughter then a soft voice followed with "goodnight" and a door closed. Silence. I got into bed but tossed and turned from one side to the other. I reached for the Bible my rabbi from Suffern had given me. The words blurred. I called out to God, "Please, please help me to adjust."

Wild screams reverberated through the wooden planks. I held my stomach, inhaling deeply. All was quiet. I pulled the covers over my head repeating to myself a hundred times: I need to relax. I need time to adjust. I must relax, I repeated over and over until I hypnotized myself into sleep.

The next day a small scrawny child was enrolled. For two days and nights, Sara would not touch a mouthful of food. The Captain was beside himself: the child was running a temperature. The staff was frustrated because Sara, unable to talk, cried constantly and only wanted to be carried. Matheny called her mother to ask if there was something more she could tell them about Sara. The mother was ready to leave from New York at once but Walt calmed her down and prevailed upon her to give him another couple of days.

"Hey, Nita," Walt called while I was feeding Butch. "Sara's grandmother takes care of her; she only speaks Jewish. Can you stop feeding Butch for a minute?"

So what did he want from me? My parents spoke Yiddish only when they didn't want me to understand. Let's see if I can remember anything. When Dad thought I was dressed to the hilt, he called me "chatchkele." Oh, that elicited a precious little smile from Sara. How about some ice cream, babele? How about a song "bai mir bist du shoen" . . . Unbelievable, my limited Yiddish worked miracles.

The following day my physical therapy began. The Captain had me contract and extend my quadricep muscles. Fifteen minutes in the morning, the same in the afternoon. "Don't overwork. Can't strain the muscles. You're doing great, gal." After two weeks I asked him when would I begin to walk. "Soon as those quads are stronger. Incidentally, some forms came from the VA. Stop in the office, hon, I need some info."

"Sure."

"Are you happy here?"

"Yes. Just a bit impatient to get going."

"Relax. Keep the faith." He patted my cheek. "You did well with Butch and Sara."

"It's hard. I've never fed anyone before."

"Give it more time, lady. Oh yes, from now on I'd like to

work in your room. Better for concentration." He looked pleased
with himself and left.

At the beginning of the third week when the Captain was in
my room, I was still contracting my quadricep muscles. "Mind if
I put on your radio? Like to get the afternoon racing results."

He was not even looking at my quads. What's to be nervous
about? So the whole VA pronounced him a quack. Give it time.

"That was good, gal." What was good? What did I do? "Can
you flex your right knee?" Pull, pull, gripped my fingers. Harder.
Beads of perspiration. "I can't."

"Oh, hon, don't be discouraged." Matheny was patronizing
me! "It takes time. Next time you'll bend your leg. Enough for
today." I transferred from my bed to my wheelchair. "Nita, you've
brought sunshine to this place." He moved closer, putting his hand
on my hair. I stiffened. He removed his hand. God, don't make
him a quack; he swore I could walk.

On Thursday the Captain announced he and his wife were
leaving for a few days, ". . . breathing time for innovative ideas
when we get back," giving me a knowing look. "Especially for
you, Nita, gal, got to get up on those gams of yours."

Maybe I was overreacting.

"Just great to have you here." He gave me a bear hug. "John
will be in charge."

John? Well, maybe I had more to learn about that man.

Chapter 27

It was hard to realize I had been at the school for almost a month. The day was March 12th, 1947. I flew into the dining room. "Morning, everyone." Ate all my meals with the staff. "I feel full of energy. John, please give me a thousand things to do." Indeed, it was John Muller who was hired as the new assistant director. In spite of his poor grammar, he was intelligent and very conscientious in his handling of the children. It was apparent that they liked him very much. Several nights I saw him in the office reading.

"Sure, there's plenty to do. After you feed Butch, read to Morris while he's in the standing bar. Do you think you can feed Pete?" I kept nodding. "Take an early lunch so you can handle the office from 12:30 to 1:30. Thanks a lot."

"And thank you." John lit a match for my cigarette. "Thanks." Keep busy, keep busy. Finished the chores. Sat in the office. Picked up last night's paper. The date jumped out at me. Began to get the shivers. My right thumb. I could still feel and remember the pain and the maddening throbbing. I cradled my thumb with the fingers of my left hand. The pain was becoming intolerable. God, I can't stand it! Emotions. Emotions. My hands covered my forehead and I closed my eyes. March 12, 1943, I could not shake that awful nightmare of four years ago.

My nails were bitten down to the skin. Suddenly I had been at Burnt Mills for two months. That awful habit I had kicked years ago reared its ugly head. My head ached from the realization that Matheny was not living up to his word.

Every night I prayed for patience, the will to resolve the problem, the frustration of where to go if I left? I knew it was hopeless to confront Walter. He was a man without shame. He had picked his patients well: adults and kids whose parents found it impossible to take care of them at home or those who were grate-

ful for the relief and the minimal exercises at Burnt Mills. On a
rare occasion he or another therapist did help someone, but usually it was a child who would have progressed naturally. Matheny
could state for the record there was "progress" and it would carry
him well with state assistance. I felt trapped, just like having those
bars on my windows in the VA. I knew without question that I
could never go home again. Certainly none of my relatives were
in a position to care for me: the cost factor was prohibitive. I
forced myself to eat and go through idiotic motions in therapy
with Matheny, knowing beyond a doubt, as far as I was concerned, the deal was over.

At dinner, Matheny announced that he and Marguerite would
be leaving for five days this time. "John will be in charge. Thank
you all for the double time. Hopefully we'll recruit some patients.
I'll say goodbye now because we'll be leaving early in the morning." He came over and kissed the top of my head.

The next morning I dragged myself to get dressed and
wheeled through the halls to feed Butchy. The child was cranky
that morning. I felt like putting my arms around him and moaning, "Hey, I feel the same way, only worse." Aides came for Butchy
and all the kids to be pottied and transported to their classes or
therapy rooms. I rolled over to the window where I sat staring at
the bleak dreary day.

"Nita, could you come into the office for a minute?"

I followed John Muller down the long hallway to Walt's office.

John sat in Walter's swivel chair. He held out a pack of cigarettes which I refused. Smoking in the morning made me nauseous. He took a long drag, his stare penetrated through me. "May
I ask why you came to this school?"

"Obviously to learn how to walk." I laughed snidely. "Certainly not for the luxurious surroundings," wondering what he
had in mind.

"Are you learning how to walk?"

The colossal nerve. My face felt hot.

"Hey, I'm sorry. I'm the last one to get personal. Plain and
simple I haven't seen you accomplish anything except to help the
kids, where you perform very nicely."

I was feeling very uncomfortable and I was becoming angry
over his inferences. "What business is it of yours what I do here?"

John took a deep breath. "I have a story, too. I'm going to be very frank with you. Before you came, all I heard from Walt was that a WAC named Nita was coming. Matheny was very excited. You were his entrance to the Veteran's Administration."

"What?" I was shocked!

"If he made any progress with you, it would open the door to hundreds of paralyzed veterans, and with them come their monthly checks."

I was stunned. My eyes smarted. I stared at this man. A light went on: I knew he was telling the truth. Matheny knew all along that I would never walk again. If he could get me out of the VA hospital and into his school it would afford him a grand opportunity. Walking in sixty days! What a joke. I must have been crazy. I sat like a stone. What could I do? Where would I go? How did the VA—?

John's voice was surprisingly warm and caring. "I know how upset you must be. I'm damn mad, too. I met Walter in a bar last summer shortly after he had moved here. I told him I was having difficulty with the union comin' into the chemical plant where I worked as a supervisor and I was becomin' very frustrated. The guy seen my misery and it wasn't long before he offered me a job. Not just any job, either. He said he needed an all-around person: someone to be his assistant director. Pardon me, bullshit. He needed someone who could do his dirty work and he was smart enough to hold out the promise that he would teach me how to work with them poor cerebral palsied children who needed help badly. He invited me and my wife to meet his wife and Chucky to see the old hotel. He was convertin' it into a school. All he needed from me was $10,000."

"You gave him all that money?" I was stupefied.

"It was the right time for me. A new lease on life. That kind a thing." Muller lit another cigarette. "I done a lot of maintenance work. All the paintin' and fixin' of this here place. If you think it's bad now you shoudda seen it in the beginnin'. I fell in love with the few kids who were there. I began reading every medical book Matheny had in his library plus books I found in the library on physical therapy. I begged him to teach me to work with the children. He taught me. Yeah, to carry them, change them, feed them. I'm nuthin but a handy man."

"I never dreamed you were a partner. What a pair of suckers.

John, I've been driving myself crazy. I don't know what to do. I'm so ashamed. I fought the VA to come here. God." I put my head down. I couldn't control the sobs.

"Nita," John said tenderly, "I think I can help you if you'll permit me. I'm not a qualified therapist but I got some theories about your spinal cord condition."

I looked at this man. Despite his speech there was a special quality about him. It was obvious that he was more intelligent than I had previously thought. Anyway, what did I have to lose? "What do you have in mind?"

"You have your braces here, don'tcha?"

"Yes but Matheny told me to put them away. Said I wouldn't need them any more."

"More of his half-baked promises. You'll have to wear them again and work until you become proficient. It will take a lot of hard work but I know it will be worth it. I'd like to help you reach that level at least."

"I expected to work hard when I came here."

Muller was really telling me there was no way I could walk independently in 60 days. Maybe never. But there was something I could do and do well. I smiled at him holding out my hand which he shook. "I'm ready any time you are."

"Well, let's go. I'll meet you in P.T."

After I put my braces on, I went to the therapy room. John locked my braces and strapped me in a standing table to get used to the upright position again. An hour later I bunny hopped through the halls with John at my side. When I became tired. I leaned against the wall, with John standing opposite me for safety. That night I slept soundly for the first time in ages. The next day John altered my routine somewhat. In the morning we did mat exercises without the braces; after lunch the steel went back on and I proceeded with the bunny hops.

"I don't think you need that pelvic band around your waist. Can we try walking without it?"

"Sure. As long as you don't move from my side."

All that day and the next I learned that I could bunny hop without the encumbrance of the band around my waist. The next day I began to swing through again.

"How do you get in and out of a chair?" John asked one afternoon while I was standing for a rest break. I had swung through my crutches all the way down the hall.

"Very shakily. It always scares me. My balance isn't that good."

"I would like to try a new technique." John proceeded to show me by using the law of gravity. If I could place my crutches in back of me, press down and raise my body from a chair, my braces would automatically lock and I would immediately place my crutches in front of me and stand erect.

"Oh, how wonderful. What a marvelous technique. John, you're incredible." The tall young man smiled modestly. I practiced over and over until I became frightened by the pounding of my heart and stopped.

After dinner John knocked at my door. He wore a pale blue wool sweater and navy tweed pants. "I have to go uptown for some medication. Would you care to come for a drive?"

"Oh, how lovely." I had not been out since my father brought me to Matheny's school.

We talked easily but I was always taken aback by the man's poor grammar. "John," I ventured carefully, "I'd like to do something for you."

"Really?"

I ignored the innuendo. "You know, for the bright man you are, your grammar and way of speaking leave a lot to be desired."

"I know. I've associated with too many factory workers for such a long time."

"I'd be happy to help you improve. I'm sure in no time at all you'll get out of the habit. You're too intelligent a man."

John's eyes were moist. "No one ever gave a damn before."

"You gave a damn about me, too, by sticking your neck out."

John pulled in front of a drug store. "Soon we're going to come down here to practice your walking. I'll be right back."

What an incentive: the chance to go shopping, select my own things. Life was becoming rosy again.

John came out with the medication. "How about stopping for a drink?"

"Oh, no, thanks."

"It would do you good. I bet you haven't had a real drink in a long time."

"You're very kind, and I appreciate the offer." I hesitated. "John, you're married. I don't want to start anything and you know how these things can get misinterpreted. If we're going to continue to work together, I think it's best that we keep our relationship confined to our goals." My stomach churned. I prayed that nothing would interfere with our therapy sessions.

"Sure, Nita. I had no intention of overstepping. Sorry." He extended his large hand. "Friends?" We smiled broadly at each other. "I'd like to show you the community but it's too dark. Save that for another time."

John talked all the way back about how he and his brother were raised on the grounds of the Douglas Dillon estate where his father was the superintendent and his parents still resided.

"I was raised in a small town too." I found it easy talking to John. For sure I was more relaxed than I had been in a long time. He was solid, no frills or false promises. He had broad shoulders and should be a good person to have for a friend. It was a lovely evening. Thank goodness there had been no complications.

Chapter 28

Walt and Marguerite returned in high spirits reporting that four new residents would be enrolled soon. Evidently John had clued Walt about doing therapy with me and I was relieved that there had been no recriminations. John and I continued to perfect my brace and crutch walking. Walter never commented about the obvious progress when he saw me swing through my braces with such ease.

In late April workmen began construction for the summer camp program that would start in early June. The men hammered away, making ramps and makeshift summer quarters to house the counselors and resident campers. Shiny bright green leaves filled the trees; tiny flowers were sprouting from bushes. I practiced ambulating on the long porch; my ability to swing through my crutches had improved considerably. John and I always had a lot to discuss. A few weeks later he said I was ready for my first trek into town.

"Oh my gosh, I can hardly wait. When, when?"

"How about this afternoon when the kids take their rest period?"

"You mean it? Today? Golly, gee."

I sat in John's car, my heart pounding from the excitement. It was like a miracle that John was taking me into town and that I would crutch-walk in a store. "Tell me about the local scenes. I'm so excited. Probably I'll fall on my face."

John laughed and then told me about his family. How his parents had come to this country from their respective countries, Ireland and Germany, and met while they were working on the Dillon estate. I was amazed how quickly his English had improved; he articulated as though he had never had a grammar problem. In a short while he drove into a small shopping section. "Would you like to stop at a card shop or a drug store?"

"A card shop would be fine. I need to get some cards and stationery."

John came around to the front door, opened it and reached in the back to get my crutches. His large face was all smiles. "Madam, are you ready for your first venture?"

"I think so. You've prepared me well." I lifted my feet and placed them on the ground in front of me, placing my crutches on either side, I pressed hard on the rims and brought myself to a standing position. I was perspiring profusely and started shuffling toward the store.

"Just a minute." John wiped my brow gently.

"Thanks," I murmured nervously and continued slowly up the slight incline toward the store. Oh, my god. I stopped on a dime. Looking down at my feet I hadn't noticed that the door opened suddenly and a patron was about to walk out—I stopped—she stopped. I took a long deep breath, waited until she left and then proceeded slowly.

John was quick to get to the door. "Allow me."

I crutch walked inside the store stealing a glance at John's proud expression, then quickly lowered my eyes to continue, looked up again briefly, and shuffled over to the birthday card rack, thrilled out of my mind that I was able to stand there long enough to take my time and read each card thoroughly. I ambulated over to the counter and happily paid the bill. I shuffled through the door, slowly making my way back to the car. John, proud as a peacock, opened the door. I was beside myself. Tears rolled down my cheeks and John tenderly wiped them away.

"This calls for a celebration. How about a hot fudge sundae?"

"Yummy. You know my passion for chocolate."

He drove to a nearby ice cream parlor. "I think you did enough for one day. How about if I bring them out to the car?"

"Fantastic."

John returned shortly.

"You know I would never have been able to accomplish any of what I did today if I had continued to work with Walt. You deserve a lot of credit for your patience and your confidence in me. Thanks, John, thanks a million."

"You don't have to thank me. You've done more for me, believe me." We concentrated on our fudge sundaes for a few moments. "Nita, I want to tell you about my personal life. I married when I was very young. Sixteen and a half." I gasped. "Rose was the first girl I dated. The marriage was rocky from the word go. I have left her several times but never obtained a legal separation, which I intend to do very soon."

"Why are you telling me all this?"

"You must know I'm nuts about you." He reached over to take my hand.

"John," I took a deep breath, withdrawing my hand, "I'm very fond of you but I cannot allow myself to fall in love with a non-Jewish man."

"What difference does religion make? I rejected Catholicism years ago. I believe in people, in their inherent goodness. Isn't that enough?"

"It would kill my parents, especially my father. It would break his heart. I can't allow myself to become involved."

John looked downcast then he picked up my hand and kissed it, looking directly at me. "Someday I'm going to marry you, Nita."

I tried to smile and act nonchalant, but the way John spoke, with such quiet determination, made me believe he would pursue this further. We finished our sundaes and went back to the school.

The following week Walt came down to my room. "Nita, you have a male visitor."

"Do you know his name?"

"He didn't say. You know, Nita, we always like to be informed if anyone is expecting visitors."

I detected the sarcasm. "Sorry, I have no idea who he might be." Slowly I wheeled into the waiting room. No one was waiting. The door to the verandah was open. I went out and saw the back of a tall dark haired man who was smoking.

"Hello," I greeted.

He turned around.

"Joeeeeeeeeeey!"

My childhood buddy swooped me into in his arms like a feather. We didn't stop hugging and kissing. My good pal. We were crying and laughing. It was the first time I had seen him in years, since he had married and was sent overseas. We'd been very close as youngsters; I always introduced him as my adopted brother. "Oh my golly, where did you come from?"

"I just got back from overseas. Went into your dad's store and he said you weren't allowed visitors but I wormed it out of him. What is this place, some kind of a prison?"

"No, silly, let me get a blanket and I'll tell you everything. First I'll pick up a couple of sandwiches and cokes. We'll have a picnic outside on the grass, away from all the tumult."

We spent the next three hours catching up on all the news: his marriage, my physical condition, army life, but I never revealed the details about how I became paralyzed.

"Aneet, did you get my last letter from England?"

"Yes, Joe . . ."

"I meant every word. I always loved you but I knew if I made any advances our relationship was over. Are you in love now? What happened to the Dutchman?"

"It didn't work. Different religion. Too many complications. I came here to work on my physical condition. When I leave, I'll get started on a career." I lowered my eyes for a second. "Joe, you're married now. You were the best thing that ever happened to me—having a brother—dear, kind—always there when I needed you."

"But, Aneet, I have to tell you something that pains me no end." His eyes filled with tears. I panicked. "Roz, my wife, can't tolerate the mention of your name. She said if I ever see you again she'll leave me. This will have to be our last meeting."

I was flabbergasted. We had been such good friends. He put his arms around me. We were both crying, holding on to each other for dear life. When Joey picked me up my blanket was soaking wet. I quickly grabbed it, placing the wet side on my lap, very thankful he never noticed.

Several days later John and I were working out in PT. I was just about to get out of a chair with the new technique he had taught me, when Matheny walked in the door.

"What the hell are you doing?" he yelled. "Sit down. Right now." The man was hysterical. He walked over to John. "Don't you ever do that again. Don't you ever let me see you allowing her to get out of a chair like that again. She could fall and hurt herself badly. Do you hear me?" Walt was yelling at the top of his lungs.

"Don't worry. I won't."

It happened at last. Sooner or later Walt would make it impossible for John to work with me. John and I looked at each other: we were truly bonded as of that moment.

Chapter 29

Someone was knocking on my door. "Coming for therapy?" John called.

"Sorry, John, not this morning. I have a bug of some kind. I'll try this afternoon."

"How about some tea and toast?"

"Mucho thanks." As soon as I heard him leave, I opened all the windows to spray the room with shots of cologne, then opened the door a crack as I had been plagued with diarrhea and hastened to freshen things up. About ten minutes later John returned carrying a tray decorated with four daisies plus tea, toast and jelly.

"You're very thoughtful."

"I'm going uptown this afternoon. There's a great delicatessen. Would you like a turkey sandwich on rye?"

"You're tempting me. I'm sure I'll be better by noon time. How about some money?"

"Forget it. We'll see about it later. Nita, you've been working too hard. A rest will do you good."

John was quite a guy. I was lucky to have found a friend in that place. After I finished my breakfast, I felt better and started writing a letter to Johnny Weiss, my neurologist friend at the VA, to thank him for the beautiful orchid and bring him up to date on my progress—but the words weren't making sense. Joey's prophecy kept haunting me, "I thought you were going to marry the Dutchman." Me, too. Me too. I have to put Herm out of my mind forever.

I felt drained of vim and vigor. Perhaps John was right: I was just plain exhausted. I couldn't wait to see Mar in a couple of weeks. My eyelids were getting heavy. I closed the door, got into bed and pulled the blanket over my head. Darn, oh, darn. I missed Herm awful again. Why did I ever let him go? I was so lonely. I had messed up my life. If only I could talk to him, but I would never—I promised. You miserable weakling. Stop dwelling on your rotten self. I'm tired. Tired of the struggle. I must have fallen asleep and was awakened to hear someone rapping on my door.

"Who is it?"

"The sandwich man."

Eeks, over four hours had passed. "Be right there." Grabbed my purse and opened the door.

John laughed, "Nita, put your pocketbook away. Hell, it's just a sandwich. If you're hungry, that's a good sign: it means you're feeling much better. You were very pale before."

How could this big hulk be such a lamb? "Well next time, it's on me. Smells yummy. Thanks."

"Okay, I'll take a rain check." He turned to go. "Sure there's nothing else? I'll be here all night if you need anything."

"What do you mean?" John usually went home after all the kids went to bed.

"I'll be moving to my parents' this weekend. My wife and I have separated."

That hit me like a bombshell. "I'm really sorry." Paused. "Are you sure? I don't mean to interfere. Would you like to talk?" How horrible for his wife.

"I don't mind talking. I'll come back after I tuck in Pete."

"May I come with you? I've never met your other patient."

"He's not a pretty sight."

"Please? It would be good for me. Get my mind off my miserable self." John looked at me quizzically but he didn't say anything and left. Usually I heard the door diagonally across from my room open—and—shut. Otherwise I never heard a sound except when someone was tending the patient.

The sandwich was delicious: turkey on fresh rye with Russian dressing, plus a coke. Poor John, perhaps I could convince him to stay with his wife and young daughter. The solid food and long nap had restored my energy. I finished the letter to my friend in the VA.

I began thinking about Mar. She was working in Paterson in the OR and last year had met a young man from Durham, North Carolina, a young engineer whom she brought to the VA a few months before I left. She and Harold Ornoff became engaged that December. In a few weeks, on June 22nd, my sister would be getting married and I would be going home for a week before the wedding to buy my outfit. I washed a few clothes. Did my nails. Wrote several more letters.

John returned about seven, carrying a tray. His change of attire caught me by surprise. He had changed into a light-blue sport shirt, gray slacks, gray suede casual shoes. He could easily have come from a wealthy family.

"I feel 100% better, thanks to you. Boy, was that sandwich good."

"Any time, but not for sickness." I followed him across the hall; he opened the door and flicked on the light. "Hi, Chris, ready for supper?"

A small bed with side rails was placed alongside the far wall. I could only see the stark white sheets. Rolled closer. Two glassy eyes flashed happily at John. God have mercy. . . the man appeared to be in his thirties, with straggly sandy brown hair; his flailing bony hands seemed to be waving; an attempt at smiling revealed two uneven buck teeth, saliva drooled down his chin.

"How do you like the pretty girl I brought to visit you tonight, Chris?" A loud guffaw. "This is Nita."

Darned if he didn't wink. "Nice to know you. How come you make so much noise?"

Another guffaw.

"Finally met Mr. Seclusion, the man of mystery." Chris obviously enjoyed bantering. He ate every morsel of his supper. He obviously adored John. I was spellbound observing the gentleness John displayed in taking care of this man. "Would you like me to read to you sometime?" A happy kind of a grunt.

"Chris gets letters from an aunt and uncle. You can read them over and over. He never tires of them. Got yourself another job, Nita." John paused, "I'll take care of big boy now, then see to Pete. Be back in about a half hour. By the way, Walt and Marguerite went to New York."

"Night. Chris, a pleasure to meet you," heading toward my room.

"Would you like a drink when I'm finished?"

"No thanks."

"Mind if I do?"

"Suit yourself."

When John returned, he had two glasses, a bottle and ice

cubes. He didn't ask but simply poured me a drink. "Ready for my confession?"

I took a sip. "Hey, what are you trying to do, kill me?"

"Sorry. I'll add some water." He went into my bathroom, returning with the glass, watered down. "This should be better. I'm a little heavy handed. Nostrovya."

"L'chaim."

"Salute."

"A votre sante."

John shook his head becoming more serious. "Where to begin this sad affair? My wife and I have been separated several times over the last ten years." I didn't realize he had been in such a troubled marriage. "We were both too young to be married. We've never been compatible. It was wrong from the beginning and it is bad for our ten year old daughter Ann. That's the story. This time I told my parents. My mother went into hysterics. She's Catholic and it was quite a shock to her." He took a long gulp of his drink. "Nita, I feel wonderful. Every day I learn more and more about the problems related to cerebral palsy, which is the affliction of most of the kids in this school, and feel even the lousy experience I've had with Matheny will come to some good. I have a gut feeling one day my future will be solely dedicated to the field of cerebral palsy." He sat back, very relaxed, as though ten pounds had been lifted from his soul.

"What can I say? I wish you the best of luck but feel badly for Ann." John nodded sadly. His separation wasn't a sudden decision after all. "Tell me about Chris. Why is he here? What can be done for him?"

"Another of Walt's manipulations to get bodies. Whether or not he can help them is immaterial. Chris gets fed, bathed, changed—period. He has no business in a rehab school. He should be in a custodial institution. He's a burden to everyone," John looked helpless. "I can't fight Walt on everything."

We talked and soon I excused myself to do more chores, wishing him the best of luck.

A few days later, John walked along while I ambulated on the veranda. I stopped at the far end, leaning my back against the shingled wooden frame. "John, I'm really pleased with my ambulation these days. What's next?"

"We're going to start curbs next week." He was always prepared.

"Great. When we practiced curbs back at the VA I was terrified. I never knew how to handle my crutches."

"Again it's a matter of balance and gravity. I don't think we'll have too much difficulty."

We stood there feeling good about each other. John took a step closer. Oh, no—John reached down, cupped my face up to his, gently touching his lips with mine.

"I love you Nita. I'm going to marry you."

Was I ever thankful I had those braces on to support me. "Please, John, don't ever do that again and don't say those things again—ever. Please."

"I know you don't love me. Never mind, I'll wait till hell freezes. You can't imagine what you've done for me." I was speechless. Surely it was the other way around. "I know I'm not free yet, but I'm going to marry you. I'll overcome any obstacle." He said this without doubt.

I shook my head slowly. "I'm sorry John. There can be nothing between us—ever. First of all, I'm never going to get married. Second, even if you weren't married, you're a Christian. John looked puzzled. "I told you I am Jewish. I don't date Gentile men. I had a serious relationship once that turned into a disaster. Never again. I took an oath. Your friendship means a lot to me and working with you has been the best thing that has happened." I stared directly into his eyes. "If you persist in talking like this, I'll have to leave this school."

John lit a cigarette, taking a deep drag. "All right. I guess I had no right . . . I'm a fool. I certainly don't want to cause you any trouble." He extended his hand. "I want to be your friend. Will you give me another chance?"

I shook hands with him. "I've forgotten the whole episode."

The following week Marilyn and her fiancé, Harold, came, bringing all kinds of surprises for my birthday. Every gift was wrapped with loving care. It was the first time my sister had acknowledged my birthday with so much ado. I was very touched by her caring.

"Mom and Dad are really anxious to see you, Neet."

"Another couple of weeks and they can come. I wanted to see you first."

Marilyn didn't know my father was picking me up the following week. A few of my aunts were making her a surprise shower in Paterson. Neither she nor Harold made any mention of my braces. "Come out and meet the kids. Can't wait for you to meet John Muller who has been working with me." Marilyn followed me.

Harold said timidly, "I'll wait on the porch." He was extremely shy or perhaps he just couldn't cope with the seriously deformed children. Harold was a good looking Jewish man. Although he was only twenty three, his brown curly hair had started receding at his forehead; he was about five feet ten, walked slowly and talked with a Southern drawl. He was not the type of man I would have expected her to choose. Marilyn was gregarious, laughed a lot, was quite opinionated and very certain of her actions. Harold seemed to go along with Sis but he rarely expressed his own thoughts, although he was very intelligent about anything to do with the field of engineering. I knew it would take a while before I really knew him. I was happy for Mar and felt in time I would get to know him better but as long as my sister and Harold loved each other, that was all that mattered to me.

My sister made a hit with everyone. I could tell that she adored Butchy but she was very friendly with all the kids. John came over and I introduced him. "Why don't we all go out to dinner? You can show your sister and her fiancé how well you've been doing."

"I've been dying to see your progress, Neet." John left to attend a child. "He's very nice."

"John has been my savior. I would have died here without his help. I can't tell you how much his friendship means to me." I whispered to Mar, "I'll tell you about Matheny another time." I showed her all around, introduced her to the staff, showed her the buildings that would house summer camp residents and introduced her to Walt and Marguerite. We met Harold on the veranda and chatted until John came to take us to dinner.

John drove further out in the country to the township of Far Hills, pulling up to a charming restaurant with a circular wooden porch. Many chaise lounges were positioned all around. He lowered his voice as I got out of the car, "I'll help you all the way. I'm going to leave your chair in the car but if you need it, I'll get it on the double." I gave him a brave smile. Harold opened the door but hurried off to wait inside the restaurant. Marilyn followed behind us. I bunny hopped to the steps and waited for John's help.

It was a struggle even with John's aid, but I made it into the dining room where I almost fell on the slippery floor, but somehow caught myself and eased into a comfortable chair. Mar ran over to kiss me repeatedly. "Oh, Neet, that was wonderful," and turned to John, "How can we ever thank you?"

I smiled proudly at him, too.

The restaurant had been a former mansion with a large first floor that had been converted into a series of small dining rooms. The maitre d' ushered us to a private alcove; John ordered a round of mint juleps and informed us that the house specialty was roast beef. Harold ordered fish because he kept Kosher. John ordered more drinks than any of us but never showed any signs of it. The food was excellent and the desserts were fabulous. We all indulged in the house specialty: German chocolate cake with a candle in my piece as the waiters and everyone sang "Happy Birthday." There were a few arguments over the bill, but John ended up paying.

I thanked everyone for the wonderful birthday.

After dinner we went out to the porch and sat in the lounge chairs. We had a nightcap while we talked about Marilyn and Harold's wedding and the summer camp soon to begin. My sister and John had a lot in common, talking about medical conditions. John easily related to people and I was also pleased at how easily he got along with Harold. A short time later John drove us back to Burnt Mills, where we bid each other good bye. John carried me up the steps and walked with me to my room. I thanked him again for the lovely evening while he waited for me to get back in my wheelchair and left. I sat quietly reflecting on the evening. I had to admit my feelings for John were growing stronger.

Within a few days, the workmen came: saws were buzzing, sawdust flying, hammers banging. Preparations were shaping up for summer camp where residents would soon be arriving for a couple of months. "Give the parents a respite, too," explained Matheny.

The fresh air was exhilarating and I crutch-walked outside to watch the daily progress. The days were getting warm. The children were lined up on the front porch or sitting under the trees or ambulating along the newly constructed ramps. To the left of the path adjacent to the property was a small stream. The land along the stream was like a beach and an ideal swimming hole for the camp. I had edged and bumped myself down to the stream on a hot day and found the water exhilarating and the terrain not too steep or rocky.

One afternoon after I swam and had been helped out of the water, I sat on a blanket, reading a novel. Next thing I knew, two big arms swooped me up. "John, what the deuce?" He quickly put me into the front seat of his car and took off like a demon.

I was in a stupor—in my wet suit—no towel—completely unprotected. "John, have you gone mad? Please, please take me back." John kept driving, ignoring my pleas. "Take me back," I screamed, "I'll—I'll open the door."

John remained calm. "What's the matter, Nita? Why are you so upset?"

"Please, take me back. Please."

He pulled off the main road, turning into a private driveway several hundred feet away from a house and turned off the engine. "Tell me why you insist on going back?"

"Are you crazy?" I yelled. "You must be completely insane." I lowered my voice to a whisper. "I am begging you to take me back. Please, John."

He did not move a muscle. "I want you to tell me why you're so upset. I haven't touched you. I merely took you for a little ride. Why are you . . . ?"

I swallowed hard. "It's my bladder." I raised my voice again. "Don't you understand? My bladder. I have no control." Tears ran down my face I wiped away as fast as I could.

"Nita," John said calmly, "I've known about your bladder since the first day I carried your bedpan. Even before that, I knew all about your condition. You act ashamed, like *you* caused your paralysis."

"It's awful. Horrible. I don't mind the loss of my legs. But this—my womanhood, my femininity. It's disgusting. I'm never sure how wet I am. I'm never sure my bowels won't act up." I turned away covering my eyes.

Two powerful arms held me. "Nita, let me love you. I have all this love for you. I don't want you to be miserable. Put your head on my shoulder." His strength eased my tension. . . "You're such a little thing. You shouldn't have to worry about anything. I know you don't love me, but one day you will. I promise. I'll never ever hurt you. Don't turn me away."

"John," I told him sadly, "it's not that I can't love you. I just know it would be a catastrophe. My parents—your parents. I can't begin to tell you how awful it would be. For your sake as well as mine."

"Have faith in me. I haven't let you down yet, have I? There's no obstacle in the world that can keep us apart. I promise. You are my heart's desire. All I want is to make you happy. I know we belong together."

I searched his face—finding only honesty and love. "Oh, John. How can you know? How can you be so sure?"

In a voice spoken with unusual determination, John said quietly, "There are some things you can't question." He kissed the top of my forehead. It felt warm. It felt right. It belonged.

Maybe my life could take on a more meaningful dimension with such a man. Perhaps we could work together to help handicapped children. If only my father would someday understand. John drove back, one hand on the wheel, one arm holding me close. He did not remove it until he made the turn into the driveway.

Chapter 30

The day before Marilyn and Harold were married, John offered to drive me home. "It would spare your father the trip."

I shook my head from side to side.

"Why do you do that, Nita?"

"You continue to amaze me. You're a dear, dear man"

"You're dearer." Placing his large hand over mine. "We'll leave after work."

We snuggled close all the way home. It felt good to be alone; it was a rare moment that we caught at Matheny's. "John, do you think everyone knows about us?"

"What if they do?"

I hesitated, "Suppose someone told your wife? She could make things very difficult for you."

"Don't worry about her. She'll have a boy friend soon," then added, "but, you're right, I guess we should be careful until all the papers are signed." John drove slowly. "Hon, don't you worry. Let me handle the situation. I want you to get stronger and stronger. After your sister's wedding, we're going to concentrate on mastering your braces and crutches to the point of complete independence."

"You really have faith in me, don't you, Johnny?"

"We're a team." In broad daylight, he pulled along the side of the road to kiss me passionately. "Will there ever come a time when I can show my love to you without sneaking a kiss here and there?"

"Now who's running out of patience? When our obstacles are solved, everything will fall into place. Right, my love?"

"Yes, sweetheart. Tell you what, pupsie, let's see if Marilyn is home. We'll take her out for a special dinner. What do you think?"

"You think of everything. She's not home but I have the

hospital number where she works. Please call her and make the arrangements."

We met Marilyn at the station in Suffern, then drove over to the Green Room in the Hotel Lafayette. John told me I wouldn't have to exert myself ambulating. It was a night to celebrate—and celebrate we did. He invited us to have a lobster dinner and champagne. Both John and Marilyn's laughter was infectious, causing many diners to laugh and join in with toasts to the bride. My sister was overjoyed. Only one thing made me uneasy: John always had a drink in his hand. When we ordered dessert, he had a cordial. I was not at all happy about his excessive drinking. We left about ten and I invited John to come in and to say 'hello' to my folks.

When one entered the small front porch of my parent's house there were only two steps instead of the five in the back. We had to pass through a dark narrow entry about eight feet long that opened into the small living room. It was always a shock not to see my piano across the room; my parents had given it away shortly after I became paralyzed—along with all my clothes. As though I'd died—as though I never was. Near the window on the far side were two old straight chairs with faded old rose velvet upholstery; along the back wall was the same second hand green and gold couch they had kept for years. A nine by twelve-piece of linoleum was placed in the middle of the floor exposing the dull hardwood floor around the perimeter. There wasn't anything I liked about the house. A light shone from the kitchen. "Mom. Dad. We're home," I called cheerfully.

My father walked in carrying a newspaper. "Dad, you remember John Muller. He brought me home."

John extended his hand. For a minute. . . then Dad shook his hand, "Thanks." Silence.

"You folks must need a good night's rest. Congratulations, I'll be heading back. Mr. Bloom, would you like me to come back for Nita?"

"I'll take Aneeda back next week." He coughed then sputtered, "Uh, thank you. Good night." John left. I was mortified. Neither Mar, nor I had said goodbye to him.

"Where's Mom? I wanted her to meet . . ."

"She's taking a bath."

"Dad," Marilyn's large brown eyes shone brightly, "John

showed us the best time. He has helped Nita . . ." She stopped. My father glared at her. She headed toward the bedroom. "I want to put some of my things away."

I was anxious to talk to my father about Marilyn's wedding gift. "Dad, have you got the check ready?" I had written to Mom asking her to withdraw $500 from my account as a gift to my sister and Harold. I was proud to be in a position to give them that substantial amount. My father banked my allotment checks; our understanding was that anytime I needed the money, either he or Mom could withdraw it.

My father's face was red. He had that horrible look again, but I stood my ground. He didn't frighten me anymore. I waited. "Aneeda, you don't have to give her such a big check," raising his voice, "she's just getting married. They don't need that much money."

I remained calm. "Hush, Dad. I don't want Marilyn to hear this conversation. It's something I want to do for her." I cleared my throat. "You know we have an understanding. I don't want any arguments, please."

My father's eyes began to bulge. "The money will go down the drain." Perspiration dripped on his forehead; his voice reached that crazy pitch. He didn't like being told what to do by a woman.

Marilyn raced into the room. I felt cold. My voice was strangely calm as I spoke, "Mar, please leave us alone. This is between Dad and me." Marilyn remained frozen. "Please."

"Tell her, Marilyn, you don't need much money right away. Right? You'll get a lot of presents. Won't you be satisfied if your sister gives you a hundred dollars? Won't you?" The pressure was on.

My sister looked from me to my father. "Yes, Nita, of course I'll be happy. Don't quarrel over me." Her eyes darkened; Her face looked painfully drawn. To think it was only an hour before that we were laughing and gay. Why did this ugly business have to happen? "Nita, Harold and I will appreciate whatever you give us, only let's not have an argument."

My mom came out of the bathroom kissing me and Mar warmly.

"Mom, didn't you. . . ?" My mother supposedly had withdrawn the money.

"Did you hear your sister?" Dad had me cornered. Mom looked shattered.

I took a long, deep breath. "Yes, Dad, give me the check for the hundred."

He opened his wallet, handing me a new one hundred dollar bill as though the ugly scene had never taken place.

"Don't spend it all in one place," I tried to be nonchalant. I turned my chair completely around, "Think I'll hit the hay. The bride should get a good night's sleep too." Sis and I slept in the same bed. "See you in the A.M." Keep cool, I kept repeating to myself. I kissed everybody goodnight as if nothing had happened. Mar and I didn't say a word. I was thankful the kid was going and I didn't have to live there.

The wedding took place in the Paramount Hotel in New York City. I was shocked. Only immediate family: aunts and uncles, the Ornoffs, their daughters and husbands and a few of their close friends were there. I had been looking forward to being with all my cousins. Hearing the familiar Yiddish music. There was no music. This wedding was not typical of the celebrations our family always enjoyed. I remembered Mar saying a few months ago, "Neet, will it bother you if I get married before you?" Then I ealized I wasn't the maid of honor. There were no bridesmaids. This was a fiasco. Marilyn did not wear a long white dress. The wedding list was incredibly small. Not even a flower girl. I was trembling. I felt I had ruined my sisters' wedding.

I felt that for the rest of my life people would try to spare my feelings because they didn't want to dance in front of me, knowing how much I had loved dancing. They didn't want to laugh too much or have a real simcha. I wanted to die. I wanted to leave— un away—kill myself. I shut my eyes. Pull yourself together girl. It's not your show. This is the way it's going to be forever. Always a freak. Soon John would be sick of the whole bloody mess. I made up my mind. I had to end that relationship.

The next day after the wedding Dad drove me back to school. The ride took forever. My father dragged Mr. Honig along. All they talked about was the ususal synagogue business while I sat in the back thinking about what was going to happen next.

John must have been on the lookout; he was always there at the right time. My father gave him a magnanimous "Thank you." Sure, John was a strong healthy goy who could take steps and carry suitcases. Dad didn't even bother going inside. He never questioned why it wasn't Matheny who had helped me when Mar had remarked how much John did. My father left shortly.

I was overjoyed to see John. As soon as we were alone in my room we embraced. I had forgotten everything I had planned to say to him but when I moved away I detected something was bothering him. He didn't say much and left saying he would get my suitcase. When he returned, I asked him if anything was wrong.

John grimaced, "We have a new PT. He has been assigned to work with you."

"I don't understand?"

"Walt is incensed about us. My wife met him uptown and accused him of breaking up our marriage. The captain thinks if you and I were separated in therapy we would stop seeing each other."

I felt lousy. "It's probably for the best," I said rather dejectedly, "I had a lot of second thoughts. I'm not comfortable about all your drinking. It's excessive. I think you needed female company and I was available. Maybe it's just as well this new PT has come on the scene."

John walked over to my chair. "Don't you want to be my girl?"

"Honestly, I don't know. Let's go along; take things as they come. You have a big job what with summer camp starting next week. I think we both need to think long and hard."

"For your information, I did a lot of serious thinking when I left you the other night. About my drinking—I'm on the wagon," grinning like he uncovered a treasure. "Like I said before, you are my angel. You bring out the best in me."

"Hey, that's great. I'm proud of you. I guess if there's going to be anything solid between us, a little time out won't hurt."

"If you insist. I have a lot to learn here. Everything will fall into shape. But don't ever forget, Nita, I love you." He kissed the top of my head and left.

A week after the wedding, Aunt Flo and Uncle Irv visited for the first time. After the hugs and kisses, my aunt spoke with a rare display of seriousness, "Neet, you didn't act your usual self at Marilyn's wedding."

I blurted out the details about my father withholding money from my sister as a wedding gift and we talked about my financial dependence. Uncle Irv was livid. "Why don't you have your checks sent here? Your father shouldn't have any more control over you. You're more than twenty-one and it's about time you stopped acting like a child."

John brought us several cokes and I introduced my aunt and uncle. Flo closed the door after John went out. "Neet, he seems like a charming young man. Is he the one who has helped you so much? You look sheepish. Tell us more?"

I filled in a few personal details, ". . . but I doubt anything will come of it. He's separated from his wife. Can you imagine how Dad would carry on?"

My aunt pursed her lips and shook her head. "Neet, take your happiness. You deserve every bit of it. If the two of you love each other, don't turn him away. Your parents have lived their lives. It's about time you had your chance." My uncle nodded in agreement.

"Well, if anything ever comes between John and me, it's comforting to know I can count on your support. Thanks for putting my head on straight."

Chapter 31

Compared to John, my therapy with the new PT fell short. John, who lacked formal training, was a master technician; compassionate, yet relentless when he observed a breadth of progress while my new therapist, though well qualified, lacked enthusiasm and motivation. He used old VA techniques and seemed indifferent to the possibility that any long-range progress of a chronic patient such as myself could be productive. Therapy sessions were boring.

I resented losing the independence I had achieved working with John. No longer were there any shopping trips or long walks around the veranda. My therapy was confined to the floor mat in the PT room and became dull and monotonous. I missed John more than ever and he was hurting for me. Whenever we met, he begged me to remain patient. "We'll find a way."

Soon campers and counselors began arriving for the summer camp program. I had to give the captain credit: he was a top notch promoter. He had enrolled campers from as far south as Florida and as far north as Maine.

John constructed the largest bonfire I had ever seen. Every weekend he took me and several of the counselors to a local pub where I was happy to see him continue his abstinence. He lost 25 pounds and was feeling more energetic than he had in ages. My heart was filled with pride for him. His enthusiasm touched each and every person. I never met anyone who didn't like and respect John. He was eager to share whatever he learned. John had a certain magic touch: not only could he get work out of a stone but he had the knack of bringing out the best qualities in that individual.

I continued to feed Butchy—taking him aside, making small jokes with him. I never gave him any gifts but I lavished a lot of tender loving care. One afternoon after lunch, while I was putting

Butchy's dishes on his tray, I found John looking at me rather strangely.

"Nita, when you're finished, I'd like to talk to you." I knew it wasn't going to be light.

"I would prefer that you did not feed Butch anymore. He eats . . . "

"Oh, please, John," my eyes filled, "don't. He's one of the few pleasures I have here."

In a firm voice that I never heard before, he said, "Nita, have you ever watched the other kids when you talk to Butchy and hold him or kiss him?" I didn't move a muscle. "When you take him away from the other kids? Did it ever occur to you that some of the others might need the same kind of attention?" John lit a cigarette, inhaling deeply, "I think Butchy is ready to come into the dining room. I'll find someone else for you."

For a second I wanted to slap his face. Then on second thought, I had to respect his integrity. "It will be hard for Butchy and me." I wheeled away from him for a second, then turned my chair around. "You're right—the time has come." John nodded and walked down the ramp. I was well aware of how difficult that task must have been for him.

Matheny hired a speech therapist to replace Marguerite who was assisting in the office. The young woman, Anna Mae, was twenty two years old, highly intelligent, and afflicted with cerebral palsy. Although her arms and legs were in constant spasms, somehow she had developed sufficient control over her involuntary jerks to walk, although with great difficulty. One had to concentrate to understand her strange somniferous speech. At first this was a strain for me, but I learned to pay close attention and found it was mostly a matter of developing the patience to listen carefully to the vowel sounds. In a few days I learned to interpret her speech.

Anna Mae had studied in a small college near Boston to become a speech therapist. At first I was skeptical, thinking that she, with her own poor speech could teach anyone else to talk. She never objected if I sat in with her. It was a revelation to watch the youngsters mimic her and the results were amazing. She would place her hands on their stomachs, their diaphragms, their chests, pucker their lips, spread their cheeks, make them smile, and the most difficult task of all, get them to blow for the 'th' sign. The kids made more progress in the short span of the summer than ever before. Anna Mae invited me to assist her on a daily basis; she was pleased with my efforts as well as my zeal.

She asked if I had ever considered becoming a speech therapist. "The field is sadly lacking in good technicians."

"I've thought about it, especially since I've been observing you, but even if I wanted to I don't have the money to go to college."

"There's always a way, Nita. Have you ever thought about applying for a scholarship? That's how I managed to attend school. It would be especially good for you — something you could handle easily from a wheelchair." The blind leading the blind.

I rolled over to give her a big hug. "Anna Mae, you're a genius. I'll put on my thinking cap."

The following week John knocked at my door, announcing sarcastically, "You have a visitor." I knew he wasn't talking about a woman.

Good old Ted Friedman waltzed in and came over to peck me on the cheek. The two men sized each other cooly. "Ted, I'd like you to meet John Muller." Two short grunts from the men. John left.

"Shaver," Ted said nastily, "what the hell are you doing here at the end of the world?"

Darn him. Still acting like he owned me. "Look here, Ted, if you came to give me a hard time, forget it. Do you want to enter like a human being or do you want to leave?"

"Come on, pack your things." His slanting eyes narrowed even more. Ted was prematurely bald. He reminded me of a detective on the prowl.

"You've got to be kidding."

"I'm not kidding. I just got out of the army, in case you haven't noticed. I found out where you were from your father."

I frowned. "Since when did you start talking to my father? Excuse me, I have to go to the bathroom." That guy always made me nervous. I started to get off my bed into my wheelchair. Ted rushed over but I motioned for him to stop. "Do you mind? I have to go—now."

I heard him rustling around my room. Opening and closing drawers. I couldn't void.

When I opened my door, sure enough, that monster was taking out my clothes and putting them on my bed. "What in the world do you think?"

"I own a hotel in upstate New York. I'm taking you there—the air will be good for you."

The man was unreal. "You've been drinking." He smiled awkwardly. "Darn you. I've had enough of your shenanigans. It's the first time I've begun to make real physical progress. That you have nothing whatsoever to do with my life? Do you have a need to hurt me?"

"Your father's not happy about your being here at all." He was getting cockier and his voice became louder. "I came to take you out, tonight."

John appeared in the doorway. "Anything wrong?"

"Nothing," I said haughtily, "this man was just leaving, weren't you?" I lowered my voice. "Thanks for coming. I'm very tired. You'll have to excuse me."

Ted's glassy eyes were clear now. He was conspicuously ashamed of himself. "Shaver, take good care of yourself."

I locked my door when he left. I didn't want any third degree. And I didn't care how far he had driven to see me.

The following day I received a letter from Johnny at the VA to say he was leaving the hospital and going back to Philadelphia to begin his practice in neurosurgery. The men in the military were picking up threads for their future. "Come see me when you're walking." I was relieved that neither he nor any of my friends at the VA ever came to visit. Perhaps they knew. Boy, would this place look like a dump to them.

When camp was over, the place was like a ghost town. The PT therapist was working with me on the mats. "Are you going home for the holidays?"

"Yep, I'll be leaving next week." It was the first time we shared something in common.

I hated the thought of going to my synagogue and facing all those steps again, recalling the last time when all the old men struggled with my chair. I would feign sickness as an excuse not to go. All those country yokels patronizing me: "Anita, it's sooo good to see you. You look sooo pretty. When will you get better?" Soon——some day—some year—when I'm dead and buried. One good thing about this year was that Mar and Harold would be with me. We could sit in the back and I could stay in my chair and not worry about my bladder spilling over. The ladies' room was down a flight of stairs. I wanted to go to synagogue on the High

Anita Bloomat 19, two years before enlisting in the Army

Leading Company B as left guide in Basic Training

Posing with buddies in Basic Training at Ft. Oglethorpe, GA

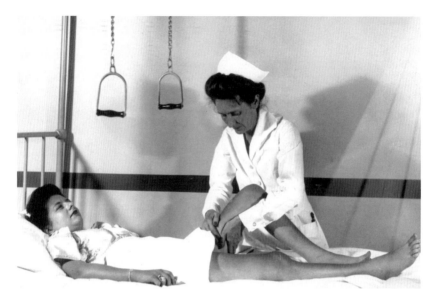

Physical therapy at the Bronx VA hospital

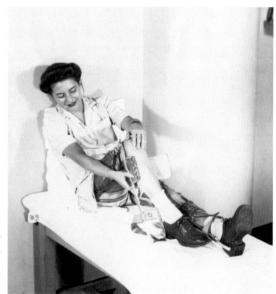

Installing leg braces following her paralysis, Bronx VA hospital

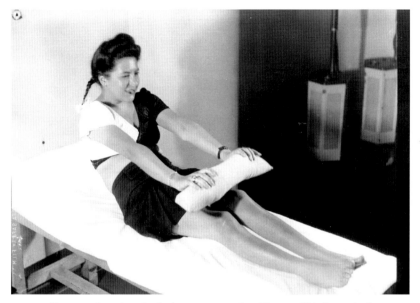

Sit-ups in physical therapy at the Bronx VA hospital

Receiving phonograph from National Jewish Council of America.

Relearning to swim with the help of Red Cross volunteers at the Bronx YMCA in July 1944

With Shawn, her physical therapist at the Bronx VA hospital

Receiving re-
freshments
from Red Cross
volunteers

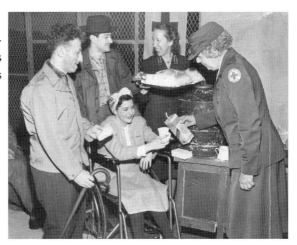

With Shirley Bernstein in
Chicago at Welcome Trav-
ellers Radio Show, where
Anita was a surprise guest

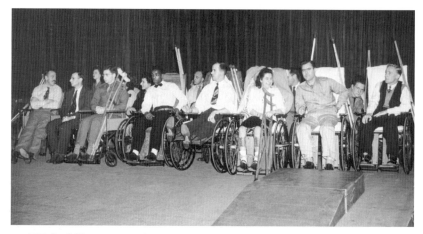

With fellow paraplegics in October 1944 at Madison Square Garden to demonstrate rehabilitation techniques

Brace walking practice on stage at the event sponsored by the Women's National Institute and American Occupational Therapy Association

With Bill Robinson (Mr. Bojangles) at Cafe Zanzibar in New York, November 1944; the photograph was signed by Ed Sullivan, Milton Berle, Danny Thomas and Ray Bolger, among many others.

A picnic at the exclusive Westchester Country Club for sixteen disabled veterans of the Bronx VA hospital in July 1944

Anita and Butchy, who became
friends at Matheny's makeshift
hospital

Anita and John Muller

Holy days, but the thought of that darn place made a nervous wreck out of me.

Early morning cast a shadow alongside my bed. A white piece of paper had been forced under the door.

"My dearest Nita, I know this place is getting you down. My sense is that your last visitor didn't make life any brighter. Let's have an Indian summer holiday to Delaware Water Gap this Saturday. I hope you've never been there before. I want to be with you when you experience that glorious view for the first time. Take your braces and crutches for the walking paths.

P. S. I love you."

Dear, thoughtful, understanding John. Why not? Why shouldn't I have a little happiness? With John things always looked bright and made me optimistic; with men like Ted the bleak side of life loomed. Yes, it was a stroke of luck that I came to this out of the way place. It wasn't my fault that John had problems with his wife. He was the first man who really cared who I was and who I would become. He never made me feel inadequate. He was a mentor, like my first love. Yikes, how could I ever explain to Dad? Drats, I wasn't ready for him, and I wasn't going to sever relations with John—not this time.

On Saturday I headed for the door carrying my crutches across my chair.

"Where are you going?" Marguerite called as she came down the steps to the waiting room.

"Today is John's day off. We're going on a holiday," I remarked casually.

"Oh, really?" She came over to me. "Do you think that's wise, Nita?"

"It's a lovely day. Please excuse me. See you later," wheeling my chair toward the door.

Her hands forced my wheelchair to a standstill. "Are you aware of the whole situation? The gossip? The anguish?"

"John is legally separated now." I responded quietly.

"We heard John is a runaround. A heavy drinker. You want him to ruin your life like he's done to his wife?"

"I appreciate your, uh, concern. John and I are good friends. Bye now." I edged forward. Marguerite released her grip.

Perhaps I had more to learn about John Muller. Well, that day would be a good beginning.

Chapter 32

One couldn't ask for anything more perfect than the day John chose for our Delaware Water Gap excursion. Huge white clouds edged the sky of soft shades of blue; the temperature in the high sixties was delightful; we were taking our first holiday, not for one or two hours, but a whole day.

"Oh, John, I'm breathless. The colors are spectacular. Such bright yellows, oranges, apricots and pure greens. Tell me about all these little towns." John knew the story of each little burg and its history.

Suddenly I felt a twinge. Oh, golly, not so soon.

John immediate sensed my discomfort. "You're unusually quiet, dear. Are you worried? Do you have to use the bathroom?" I shrugged my shoulders. "We'll find a gas station. Most of them have clean bathrooms. If you need me, I'll be right outside." That man was uncanny.

The bathroom was small but I managed — thankfully the sink was next to the commode where I could balance by holding on to it while I stood up to undress. I gave John a big kiss when I came out, snuggling close when we got back into the car. It had been years since I had spent a whole day with a man. John and I had a whole world to discover and we shared many common interests. Someone special had entered my life.

He stopped at a log cabin restaurant with the most charming indoor setting, especially the dark red stone fireplace and hearth that rose from floor to ceiling with a brightly lit fire aglow. I rolled over to embrace the warmth. Oops, I had to find the ladies' room — shucks the door was too narrow.

"I'm here."

I didn't deserve him. "Thanks, thanks."

We had ginger ales with our cigarettes in front of the fireplace and later moved to a table that overlooked an old barn abundant with vivid, colorful foliage in the distance. We talked about our plight at the school.

"John, I've been thinking a great deal about becoming a speech therapist ever since Anna Mae inspired me. She also told me how to go about getting a scholarship. I know an organization in New York that might possibly be in a position to sponsor me."

John took a bite of his BLT sandwich, laying the rest down. "You'll make a hell of a good therapist." He pursed his lips. "Then you're thinking about leaving?" Reaching for my hand to kiss it, John said reluctantly, "I knew all along you'd have to leave eventually. Don't think for a minute that will be the end of us." His light manner became serious. "I'm going to marry you, Nita, as sure as the sun rises. It might take longer than either of us anticipates. Will you have patience?"

"I'll wait." John leaned over to kiss me. We held hands for a long time. Patrons smiled.

"You know, John, something wonderful has happened to me. I couldn't have handled this school in my other life. Not for a second."

"Your other life?"

"My life before becoming paralyzed. I was quite selfish. Unconcerned about other people's illnesses. I couldn't visit people in a hospital. I was sure Aunt Flo would send me packing if I didn't visit her when she had her appendectomy. One time I forgot to feed her bird and it died while she was in the hospital giving birth to Bobby. That was stinking of me, considering I lived in her house." John started to interrupt. "No, don't make any excuses. I know what I was. An inconsiderate brat. Completely self-centered. If I had met Anna Mae before, I would have been repulsed. To think I might have missed this woman who might change my life."

"My future is changing for the better, too. I feel alive. There's meaning to my daily existence and it's all because of you, Pupsie. You're my everything." John's eyes warmed my whole body. "I'd die if I lost you but I know damned well you have to leave Burnt Mills. I've been doing a lot of thinking. There's nothing more for you at Matheny's. It killed me when Walt stopped me from working with you."

"John, *que sera sera*." I did my best to appear sophisticated and continued, "we still have a multitude of problems to resolve.

We have a lot to learn about each other," hesitating a moment. "By the way, have you been seeing other girls?"

"Not since I met you. What made you ask?"

"Someone insinuated . . . "

"You don't have to tell me. I know. That's called the pot calling . . . The captain knew all about my marital status. Several times he pestered me to get him a date. Frankly, I lost a lot of respect for him, always winking at me while he made remarks about his perfect marriage." He took a long drag on his cigarette. "Once I relented. He was disgusting. I don't like gossip but that bastard son of a—talking about me, when it's his own tail."

"From a selfish point, I feel relieved. Right now I feel like an investigator but I think if we're both honest with each other, in the long run it will be better for our relationship. Johnny, what about your work at the school? How long do you expect to stay?"

His eyes caressed my face. "I can't afford to go right now, but I love you for your insight. My plan is to stay another year until the debt is paid." He smiled broadly. "Now we're going back into the car so I can show you the Delaware Water Gap."

The drive to the reservoir took about an hour. Then John stopped at an overlook where we faced a scene that took my breath away. Before us was the largest reservoir I had ever seen. We remained enraptured until finally John started the car and drove to the other side of the road. He jumped out to clip a sprig of bright orange bittersweet for me. We took our time on the way back, stopping at a charming inn for a caesar salad and rare filet mignon. We didn't get back until eleven. Nothing in particular had delayed us. We were simply two young people very much in love.

Chapter 33

Dad insisted on taking me home for the Jewish holidays, bringing his usual crony, only this time when I asked to drive, he agreed and sat with Mr. Honig in the back. Sitting behind the wheel was always the perfect opportunity to collect my thoughts. I had written a letter to the National Council of Jewish Women, a women's philanthropic organization, informing them of my desire to attend New York University to become a speech therapist, and to inquire if there was any scholarship money available. I had also written to Dick Monfried to see if he had made any progress on my behalf since our last correspondence. Between the Jewish Holidays of Rosh Hashanah and Yom Kippur, I was going to meet with my Congresswoman, Katherine St. George, to push for the Veteran's benefits I had been denied.

"Dad, will you be able to go with me when I meet with Mrs. St. George?"

"Sure, Dollink, I know all about it. It vil be at Tony Cucolo's house." Mr. Cucolo's crew had built the Storm King Highway in the eastern part of New York State. He knew Congresswoman St. George and was almost certain that she could introduce the necessary legislation in Congress.

"Oh, that's wonderful. Thanks so much." My schoolmates and I used to ice skate at Bill Cucolo's pond. My memories reflected back to all the fun we had skating on my former classmate's pond and the marvelous Italian meals his mother prepared for us.

"If you ask me, I think it's a waste of time. The army is not going to pass a Bill for one person," Dad opined.

"Dad, I told you. I will keep on fighting for my rights forever. One day I know I'll be successful." Now I regretted not telling my parents all the sordid details.

I thought about how Matheny had practically ignored me

ever since John and I had our day in Delaware. My father would
have raised the roof if he ever heard about that escapade! Just as
I had detested keeping the secret of my relationship with Herm,
I knew it would take all my effort to keep John a secret. He meant
too much to me to sacrifice him because my father might have a
tirade. There was no way I was going to part with John.

If I received a positive response from the women's charity, I
would make plans to leave Burnt Mills. I thought about living in
New York City, where I speculated about getting to the theatre,
concerts, shopping. Wow. First and foremost I knew I had to appear before NYU's medical board before I could gain entrance to
NYU. I wondered if they had ever enrolled a paraplegic. I simply
had to convince them of my need for a college education. If it took
hell and high water, I was going to attend NYU.

Driving had always been a cinch for me; it didn't matter
whether I had to be in New York City or wherever. I took the
winding curves on route 202 like a pro. Good things were happening between John and me. I wondered if I would ever go all the
way with him. We loved each other passionately. He was so easy
to love. The kindest man I . . . well, but Herm was of the same
caliber. Not a mean streak in either of them: both averse to quar-
reling, always willing to compromise, generous with love for hu-
manity.

The only thing I prayed for was that John would continue his
abstinence. So far he was conscientious about his pledge. John
told me he had been drinking since he was a young teenager. His
father had encouraged both him and his brother to drink. His
mother used to feed him a swig of whiskey whenever he was sick.
How strange, I thought. Jewish people didn't drink much, only
wine on the Sabbath and on special occasions. I drank socially but
it was minimal compared to what John used to put away.

We were almost at Suffern and a few minutes later I pulled
into our driveway. The same unbearable struggle with Dad and
Mr. Honig dragging me up the back steps, but the minute I got
into the house, I went straight into the bathroom alone.

My father called, "I'll send Mama home but don't keep her
too long. I have to get a haircut."

I couldn't wait to call Midge, a friend I saw occasionally and
liked very much. She was a couple of years older than me, but
years ago, we both dated gentile boys and that created a strong

bond between us. We'd both parted from our sweethearts. Midge had been married a few years now and had a young son. Although we didn't see that much of each other, there was always a special closeness, probably made even stronger by the fact that the Suffern Jewish community had frowned on our behavior. When I phoned, she said she would come by after lunch.

Mom came home fairly soon. "Mom, you look gorgeous. I love your hair." Her black hair was neatly coiffed in a flattering style. I hadn't gone to a beauty parlor since I worked. My natural curly hair fell to my shoulders and I could wear it up or down depending on my mood. When I so desired, I could style it myself. We talked mostly about our clothes for the New Year. John and I had gone shopping and I had bought a stunning black two piece outfit, a new black felt hat and black suede sandals. We had lunch and she left shortly afterwards.

Within minutes Midge drove over. We embraced. It had been several years since we had seen each other, when I left for the service." Neet, you never looked more radiant."

"And you look terrific yourself." Midge was a short attractive woman. She characteristically wore the same hairstyle she had for years: straight with bangs. "I've been dying to tell you about John Muller. Yup, here I go again. It's quite a story," and proceeded to fill in the details.

"Neet, I'm happy for you. I know Marilyn feels the same way. But what about Poppa?" Her dark brown eyes probed mine. We had talked about our fathers' similar attitudes years ago.

"Dad will never change. I can't mention John's name. That's why I'm confiding in you. Please keep it on the QT. No sense causing grief to everyone. My folks only know that John was my therapist. He recently separated from his wife. There's a long way to go. Who knows, he could change his mind."

"You can count on me. You're wise to keep it on file in this community." She fiddled with her purse. "Take your happiness, sweetie. I have to go, hon. Hope to see you before you go back. Love to Mar."

We had to be in the synagogue about ten the next morning. Mar and Har came over, both looking terrific. Mar had put on most of the weight she had lost before the wedding but she looked marvelous with her long dark brown curly hair and expressive large dark brown eyes.

Mom outdid us all. She seldom wore black, but her dress with its pink satin collar and cuffs was stunning. My sister and I were shocked that she chose black because my dad was old fashioned about that color, and insisted, "It is only for mourning"; Dad's gray pinstripe suit with a gray and red abstract silk tie was most becoming. I was always proud of my parents when they dressed for a special occasion . I asked Harold to take pictures.

"Hurry," Dad called but I knew he was pleased to be photographed.

At one time we never drove to the synagogue on the High Holy days, but because of me, Dad parked on the lot adjacent to a Buick dealer across the street from the schul. No sooner did my father park the car than five men dashed across the street.

"She's in the car, Bill?"

"Don't worry. We'll help. Tell her not to move. Open the trunk. We'll get the—uh—the wheelchair."

Marilyn jumped out to open the front door. "Hi, good Yom Tov. Please put the chair here, facing the passenger side." One of the men blocked her way. "Please let me do this." Mar quickly opened my foot pedals. Much to their shock, I stood up and sat down.

"That's wonderful, Nita. Don't get overtired," one of the men remarked.

My father snatched my chair, bumping it across the road to the synagogue almost rattling my head off. I did my utmost to remain calm. Dozens of people were milling around, and every head turned my way, eyes glued to my legs. They don't move, ladies and gentlemen. Smile pretty. "Hi's" to familiar faces. Marilyn politely shooed them away. "Okay men, let's try the stone steps," giving instructions while I kept my eyes shut tight. They approached the steps head on. I could envision a broken nose. Vel, I could use a nose job.

Someone tilted my chair. I thought my head would fall off. "We'll tip her back, Bill. Hey, Anita, you're looking sensational."

"We'll tip her back further, Bill." I shut my eyes.

"Tilt her back further, stupid . . ." someone else yelled.

Step one. Fourteen to go. We could have had the service on the lawn. More steps. Slammed into the sanctuary door. "Open the door. Turn her around." Mar looked horrified. Where is Harold? Mom and Dad? A plastered smile remained on my face. Could there be a talent scout in the crowd? Open them portals. Get your tickets. The show is starting.

Father took over, pushing me to the family pew all the way in the front where the most prominent members sat.

Then came the opening curtain. I braked my chair, stood up and crashed hard on the wooden pew. What did it matter? Minimal sensation, well padded. Swung my legs to the right as far as I could, permitting the rest of the family to get to their seats. My legs jumped from spasms. Good old Dad stepped on my toes. I was grabbed from behind.

"Anita, darling," Mom's friend gasped, "you're as beautiful as ever." Just let me live a little longer. Whup! Getting strangled from all sides. Did they put money in the pushke for the chance to strangle me? Mar and I started having hysterics. Tears rolling down our faces. We both knew—I was peeing in my pants. Oy, the Rabbi's sermon. Forty five minutes on the High Holy Days. Why didn't the Rabbi talk about the needs of cerebral palsied children? Thought about John. I couldn't concentrate on the Siddur. Who understood what they were mumbling? Dad's voice rang out the loudest.

"Neet, you'll stay at our house next time you come to Suffern," consoled Mar. She and Har had moved to a one room apartment in a converted garage.

Next time? The blessings. Amen.

The following week my father and I met with Congresswoman Katherine St. George. Mrs. St. George was a tall imposing woman, obviously cultured and articulate. After the usual amenities, she asked me to relate the details leading up to my paralysis. "Miss Bloom, I want you to tell me in your own words why you feel you should be entitled to veterans' benefits."

In as few words as possible and careful not to include anything about Five-by-Five, I complied with her request. I knew I had to convince this woman that it was only because of a technicality that I was denied veterans' benefits. We talked for several more minutes, then I asked Mrs. St. George, "Do you think you can help me?"

Mrs. St. George never took her eyes from my face and responded, "Anita, if I may call you Anita, it's such a pretty name."

"Thank you."

"You can be assured that I will do everything in my power

to see to it that justice is done." Neither I nor Katherine St. George knew that on January 3, 1947, (ten months prior) Congresswoman Edith Nourse Rogers of Massachusetts had introduced a Bill into the eightieth Congress, first session, H. R. 143. This Bill was referred to the Committee on Veterans' Affairs and was to provide benefits based upon active military service as a member of the WAAC. If this Bill were passed, it would be the answer to my prayers, providing me with financial and educational benefits that I desperately needed to enable me to function as a contributing member of society.

The ten days between Rosh Hashana and Yom Kippur went well. I stayed with my sister and brother-in-law. Harold was working as an engineer for Wright Aeronautical in New Jersey on the late shift; I was company for Mar in their apartment over a garage and would stand up to wash the dishes every night. John phoned several times.

I particularly loved the Kol Nidre service. Mar and Har took the steps by themselves. I wore white, a linen suit I had bought on sale at the end of the summer. The cantor was exceptional that year and I was thankful for the peace and tranquility.

Mom had the customary Break-the-fast for many friends. She made her gefilte fish and Dad contributed his super homemade pickled herring and chopped herring salad. Before I left for Burnt Mills, Dad handed me a large wrapped package. "There's a nice suit for Chucky and a dress for the little blond girl."

"Oh, Dad, you're wonderful." I left my parent's home on a happy note.

Mar and Har drove to a midpoint where we met John for a short rendezvous and I transferred to John's car. After waving our goodbyes he handed me a New Year's gift. It was his first real gift: a silver marquisette star of David on a sterling chain. "I can't breathe when you're not here."

"Thanks. It's magnificent." We embraced for several minutes. "What a beautiful necklace." I have sinned. I have transgressed. I repeated to myself as it is stated in the service.

"How were your holidays?"

"John, I'd rather not talk about it. I'm not big on organized religion. It's difficult to explain. I love being Jewish. I adhere to many of the tenets, love many of the customs and I adore Jewish music. I have my own unique way of praying. I know there's something bigger than man." I shook my head, "John, I think you might enjoy attending a service one day."

"Can I go with you sometime?"

"My father would have a fit."

"One day. Do you want to do anything special? Dinner?"

"Oh, dear, we ate so much. I brought back a care package for you. I'm rather tired and need to hit the hay early tonight." What a pleasure it was when John took me up the front steps. He returned with my suitcase, kissed me, and left.

I was in the middle of unpacking when someone knocked at my door. "Mind if I come in?" Walt questioned.

"Sure. Hi, is it anything important? I'm very tired."

"Had a heavy night? Too much for you?" He moved my suitcase and sat on my bed, his lips puckered. I continued to unpack. "Nita," with his inimitable soft drawl, "what's going on between you and John?"

"I beg your pardon?"

"You told us you and John were just good friends. Next thing I hear is that you've spent a whole day . . . "

Okay. Let's get it over with, mister. I spoke harshly, letting my anger boil out at him at last. "You were the one who encouraged me to come here—for the express purpose of working with me. More specifically, to get me on my feet—out of my wheelchair. Without braces. Without crutches. *In sixty days*. It's now September. Do you see me walking?" Bless Anna Mae's speech lessons in emphasis. "The government allowed me to come because of you," deliberate slower speech, "quote: guaranteed progress."

He started to interrupt but I ignored him. "I was making phenomenal improvement when I worked with John. Evidently too much to suit you. I have practically stagnated with the new PT. My commitment here was to improve my physical condition . . . "

"We'll get to your physical condition. The scandal you've both caused. We can't have that kind of behavior." Walt squared his shoulders, keeping a stiff upper lip.

"What scandal?"

"John was a happily married man," Walt pontificated, "with a lovely wife. Unless you promise to stop seeing John, I will have to ask you to leave."

Somehow I had not moved a muscle—nor did my eyes leave

his face. "Now you listen carefully. Do not interrupt me until I am finished. I plan to leave this school on December 30th 1947. I am going to college. The final arrangements are being made. I will continue to work out in PT doing the best I can with the least amount of support I receive here. I am more than twenty-one years old. I will not discuss my private life with you. I expect your complete cooperation or I will report you to the United States Employees Compensation Commission for failing to provide the required therapy. If necessary I have a few choice bits I will inform your wife. I will apprize my parents of your false promises, which I'm sure they've already suspected." I took a long sigh. "I'll give you one second to get out of my room or I'll yell for help. And, yes, I expect you to treat me cordially at all times."

He stood at the end of my bed grabbing the two posters, his fists were shaking; his face had turned purple with rage.

I sat quietly with folded hands; my eyes penetrated his. "I hope we can continue to be cooperative as long as I'm here. My father sent Chucky and Barbara a present," handing him the package. "Daddy is grateful for all you have done for me." I swung my chair away from him, turning my back toward my suitcase.

God, I beseeched, don't let him choke me.

The bed creaked. His feet thumped out. He did not close the door. Yes, John, you said there would be obstacles? We were totally committed to each other but we were well aware of all the obstacles ahead. John was certain we would overcome each and every one of them. But—my father? He would be the last hurdle, the hardest one of all.

Chapter 34

What pleased me the most about my introduction to Congresswoman Katherine St. George was that I was certain it would lead to other contacts in the Congress. Dick Monfried told me he would write to her as soon as I informed him that she was going to champion my cause.

When I was a patient at the VA in the Bronx, a group of ladies from the New York Chapter of the National Council of Jewish Women of America used to visit me from time to time. On Chanukah 1945, the year before I left the VA, they presented me with a record player and several albums of classical music. I had written to ask if they could consider granting me a scholarship so that I might attend New York University. I wanted to apply to NYU for the semester beginning in February 1948. I told them that my contribution to this venture had to be limited to the $90 per month I received from the U.S. Compensation Commission.

Marguerite called me to the phone one morning to take a call from the secretary of the National Council.

"Miss Bloom, it's almost unheard of . . . er, ah, doesn't your father want to contribute something toward your education? Your father has his own business. Ninety dollars would hardly take care of . . ."

I was humiliated, particularly in front of Marguerite, but I hated to sound like a beggar. "I can't ask my father for any money. I promise to get a job to supplement . . ."

"Look, my dear, we don't expect you to work if you're brave enough to tackle NYU. It's just, well, we're not set up to give full scholarships. We've never done it before."

"I'll manage on whatever you send. I appreciate anything you can do for me."

"We'll discuss your problem at our next board meeting." She

cleared her throat. "Miss Bloom, we always try to assist whenever we can. By the way, who is paying for your stay at this school for rehabilitation?"

"The VA, but they won't pay for my education. Unfortunately, none of this would be necessary under the GI Bill of Rights, which you know I don't have, but believe me, I'm working on it. I can't tell you how much I appreciate your efforts." I hung up without saying another word.

Two weeks later I was more than grateful to receive an affirmative note that said the Council would pay me one hundred and twenty-five dollars a month. I had never discussed my plans for college with my father; I couldn't bear his refusal. Somehow I was going to NYU and I prayed that one day in the not too distant future I would become a bona fide veteran. I would continue to press for that day until I became successful.

The following Sunday, John asked me to take a ride. "Nita, don't wear your braces today." Within a short while we came to a large estate, I clasped my hands tightly. "Not today?"

John didn't answer and after a short distance he turned down onto a long, private macadam driveway that bordered the most tremendous lawn I had ever seen. In the distance I could see a magnificent brick mansion surrounded by many elegant formal gardens. John's father was a superintendent of the Douglas Dillon grounds.

"One of these days, Dad will give you the cook's tour. He doesn't like to show the place to visitors, which means no one dares to step into those gardens unless he takes them," John said, with a touch of irony that surprised me. He stopped in front of a brown shingled building that looked like an oversized garage.

A door opened and it was then I realized that a small house was attached to this building. A stocky red faced man headed toward us shouting, "Hi." Mr. Muller's clear blue eyes were twinkling.

John got out and went around to the other side of the car to get my chair. "Excuse me, Dad."

"That's okay. I'll open the door for this attractive lady." Mr. Muller's thick German accent caught me off guard.

John pushed his father aside, saying curtly, "I want to bring my friend into the house," John sounded annoyed. "Nita, this is my father."

I had never heard that abrupt tone in John's voice before.

Perhaps this was a sign of friction between John and his father.

"How do you do, Mr. Muller?"

The man stepped aside, apparently confused as John reached in and swiftly picked me up to carry me into a small living room where he sat me on the couch. My dress was way over my knees and I wiggled to get it down. A slightly stooped, dark-haired elderly woman stood in the middle of the room, her eyes almost popping out of her head.

"Mom, this is Nita Bloom."

"How are ye?" Her voice croaked in a high-pitched Irish brogue. "Ye'll take a bit of tea, won't ye?"

For me, tea was only for colds. "Thank you. Tea would be lovely."

John had urged me to eat. "That's all my mother lives for. Her biggest pleasure in life." His mother quickly left the room. A small kitchen table was visible from where I sat.

"Okay, hon?" John nodded. "I'll get your chair."

"Oh, no, not now." John and his father came in together. "John, is there a powder room?"

"Sure. Right here in the garage." He started to bring my chair over.

"What the hell do you mean—garage?" bellowed his father. "The toilet's upstairs."

Without a word John carried me up a full flight of steep stairs that curved sharply midway, breathing so hard I thought his heart would burst.

"Stop a minute," I pleaded. He continued until he almost fell into the bathroom, landing me hard on the toilet seat.

"Can you take care?" perspiration dripping down his forehead. I shook my head resignedly. Somehow I managed.

Things went better after I was settled back on the couch. His mother wanted to know where I came from; how long I had been at the school where Johnny worked with "them certified palsied" children? Questions that enabled me to tell them what a fine therapist John was and how much he had helped me.

"Oh, I couldn't go there," his mother said emphatically. "I can't bear them crippled children. I don't see how John . . ."

"Mom, these tarts are the best." His mother's face lightened with a huge smile. "The next time Nita visits, she's going to walk in."

"Ye are?" she screamed.

"John doesn't mean walk in the sense . . ."

"How 'bout a drink? " Mr. Muller offered.

"Dad, I told you . . ."

"I don't know what the hell's the matter with you these days." His father turned to me. "How about you, Nita, Conchita. I sure like that name. What'll you have? Rye? Scotch, Nita, Juanita. Are you Spanish?"

"No, Herr Muller, I'm Jewish." And crippled. And I wet my pants. And I'm unworthy of your son. Damnation. "Tea is fine for me now, thanks."

Grudgingly, his father poured himself half a glass of whiskey, took a big slug, let out a belch, then smiled innocently at me and turned to John, "When the hell are we going hunting, Son? It's been a long time."

"I don't know, Dad. We're very busy at school now. Soon as I have some free time I'll call you." My stomach churned. Jewish people didn't go hunting. Well, I thought, there were going to be a lot of compromises if we continued to go with each other.

"Yer Jewish, are ya?" piped his mother, "I knew a Jewish man. Wonderful. Remember Sol, Daddy? Ye knew him too, didn't you Sonny? He used to come out here with lots of nice things."

"Charged a helluva lot, too." His father said wryly.

"But Daddy, he never pestered me for the money. He's a very nice man." Her voice was much softer now. "He'd come in me kitchen and I'd make him a lovely cuppa tea. He took it with a teaspoon of sugar and a piece of lemon. "With folded hands and smiling pleasantly she continued, "I take mine with a little milk. Do ye Jewish people always take sugar and lemon?"

"I'm not sure. My father does and always drinks his tea from a glass. My grandfather did it the same way." John looked as if he was going to have a convulsion.

"Well, ye don't say. You hear that, Daddy? Then she turned around to John, speaking petulantly, "Ye'll stay for supper, won't ye, Sonny?"

"Not this time, Mom, I have to be on duty."

His mother's teary eyes reminded me of a Basset hound. "Ye just got here, Sonny. Can't ye stay for another few minutes? Since he's working those certified palsied. . ."

"Now, Mom," pacified John, "I'll bring Nita back another

time. We have to go now." They both walked outside with us to the car. I stood up straight, turned around and got in.

"Thanks very much for a lovely afternoon. It was a pleasure meeting you both."

"Well, isn't that nice?" complimented his mother. "And pretty soon ye'll be walking, just like Johnny told me." John pulled out of the driveway, his parents waving until we passed the curve. "You made a hit with my folks, you gorgeous creature."

"What?"

"I know my parents. One day I'll tell you. . .oh, what's the difference?" John raced out of the driveway, swung the car off the road, pulled me to him and kissed me passionately.

"Hon, that's enough. We'll get a ticket."

He roared with his inimitable laughter. "We're going to my brother's house for dinner. I think you'll find this visit quite different."

"I think I've had enough . . ."

John's gentle tone calmed me, "Please be patient. I know my family will love you."

"I would like to stop for a box of candy." John looked puzzled. "If we're going to dinner, I would like to bring a little something."

He grinned from ear to ear. "What a thoughtful gesture. That's what I love about you, Pupsie, you're always thinking of the other fella."

After we stopped at a local pharmacy for the sweets, John drove a few miles then stopped in front of a white two story wooden frame house. A tall slim man, who resembled John approached the car. "Hi. You're Nita. I'm Charley," he greeted as he opened the door, extending his hand to me. "Tell me what to do."

"Hi, Charley."

"It's okay." John's voice was amazingly formal. "I'll take care of getting Nita out of the car."

"Tell me what I can do, for Christ sake." Not a word.

I took my time standing up, slowly pivoting to get into my chair without being klutzy. A darling pug-nosed child of about seven came running to the car.

"Here's Lucia. Honey, meet Nita." Charley introduced us.

I pivoted my chair around, "Hello. My, you're wearing a pretty dress." John pushed me toward the steps. Six steps. His brother tried to assist John going up the steps but he tilted the wheelchair too far back almost knocking John on his back.

"Goddamn it. I told you I would handle Nita. I do this work every day, you know."

"Please John, " I said, "your brother was only trying to help. Simply give him instructions." I raised my hand to let John know that he should calm down.

"He won't listen." John said childishly, looking directly at his older brother. "We'll be okay if you simply let me handle this part alone. When I need your help, I'll ask." His brother released the chair.

I gave Charley a big smile. "I'll give the instructions next time myself. Thanks for the offer." I was surprised to see John so sensitive.

"Oh, Nita, it's good to meet you at last." A lovely young woman greeted me like a long lost friend and extended her hand. "I've heard nothing from John but Nita this and Nita that."

"Eleanor, it's a pleasure to meet you. John speaks very highly of you, too."

A small child was crawling around the living room. Eleanor quickly swooped the baby up in her arms, bringing her close to my face. "You have a kiss for Nita." The baby put her lips to my face. "Oh, Maureenie, that's wonderful. Come, Nita, let me show you all the things we've done to this place. We've only been here a few months but Lord we've worked hard. Charley did most of the construction himself. I'm amazed at how much he's done in the short time we've been here. We haven't stopped fixing since we came, but it's great to have the extra room. Our home in Newark was much smaller. How do you like the kitchen, love?" addressing John who had done the painting.

"I'm very impressed," I said, smiling proudly at John. The kitchen was most attractive with bold yellow and white stripes and multi-flowered curtains. John looked over at me, I had a feeling that one day? Good old bladder again. "May I use your facilities?"

"Good thing you have this big lug," Eleanor laughed kindly. "In fact you have two of them at your service."

I might have known: the bathroom was a flight up very steep steps, and thankfully John allowed his brother to assist him.

The Mullers' were warm and welcoming. I was relieved to see that John had relaxed; he and his brother's hearty laughs were identical and it was hard to distinguish one from the other. Eleanor was the conversationalist. She knew all about Burnt Mills, the kids, my progress, our relationship. She was interested, concerned, witty. It was evident that Eleanor had a lot of respect and love for John. The two brothers laughed a lot without ever getting serious in their discussions. Eleanor smiled at me and said,

"We're expecting you for Thanksgiving, Nita. I'd love you to meet my parents." I looked at John a little puzzled. I was not aware of this invitation.

"We'll be here." He leaned over to kiss his sister-in-law.

I sat quietly in the car on the way back. Sure, we'll be here. What if I have to go to the john, come downstairs, only to go right back up again? Or if I'm nervous with all those people damning me for ruining your marriage? Why the heck didn't you settle your personal affairs before trapping me into something sordid?

John parked the car in an isolated spot. His fingers lightly touched my hair, my face, my lips. "I've done a terrible thing to you, Nita." His eyes were misty. "I love you so much. I want the whole world to meet you, but if it's too much, I won't accept any more invitations for us until I'm divorced."

This man was unbelievable. What was the matter with me? Always thinking of myself. I reached up to put my arms around his substantial frame. "The suffering will fade once everything is solved. Perhaps it's because I've just met your family and I'm petrified they wouldn't like me. The bathroom. . . "

"I know. I thought about that, too. But honey, that's the real world. You're not going to have everything convenient." He kissed me gently. "We'll make it, won't we?" Our kisses were becoming more and more passionate and we were finding it more difficult to part.

In the beginning of December, the kids at school were practicing for the Christmas show. Marguerite was coaching and used a record player for accompaniment. Carols were heard throughout the day and night. There was a positive side in that it motivated the children. They produced whatever sounds their lungs could project; those who weren't capable of singing contributed in whatever way they could.

"Nita, you play the piano," Marguerite spoke in the kindest tone I'd heard in some time. "Would you play the carols for us?"

I was on the spot. It would have been easy to refuse. Because of my Jewish faith I had never played or sung Christmas carols in my life. "You know I only play to amuse myself. You're better off with the record player."

"Please, it would be more personal."

Oh, well. "Okay."

The piano had always been fun. When I started lessons at the age of eight, my mother used to sneak a dollar for the teacher out of the register. It was during the depression and Dad wasn't at all interested. I would practice on the piano in the synagogue. I loved it and somehow Mom persuaded my father to allow me to take lessons. A few years later Aunt Jen found an old piano and had it sent to me. I was invited to play at several local concerts and soon I was taking lessons from a New York teacher who would slap my hands with a ruler if I made a mistake. Dad would ask me to play whenever we had company. I played jazz extemporaneously and Mom and I would sing when she was home.

During the holidays I played while everyone sang. There was a lot more spontaneity. John was proud. Soon I found myself humming, then singing. My favorite was "Jesu Babino", a charming carol the captain and his wife taught everyone. The best fun was when Marguerite, in a fairly full mezzo soprano, belted out "Down on your knees" while I crashed the crescendo with all the power I could muster without ever needing the pedals. The play was a huge success. All the kids who were without speech were dressed like angels. I would never forget those faces.

John gave me a beautiful gold watch for an engagement present. "One day I'll give you a ring, but I hope you'll accept this with the same commitment."

Tears sprang to my eyes. "Thank you. I'm very proud. It's truly lovely and I'll cherish it forever." Yes, it was true. John Muller was the love of my life.

Chapter 35

The days were endless, boring and wasteful. John found me outside reading. "Have you told your parents what day you'll be coming home?"

"I plan to call home tonight."

John cupped one side of his face, whispering intimately, "Tell them you'll be home on New Year's Day."

"Really," I said coyly. "And where will I be on the eve, pray tell?"

"With me."

Just like that. With me. I knew I was blushing.

"Tell your folks you've been invited to a New Year's celebration."

"I can't, John . . ."

"Gotta go now," he coldly responded.

"No," I insisted. "I don't want to lie."

"Please, darling. Trust me." We looked at each other in silence.

Aunt Flo's prescription of "Take all the happiness you deserve," kept nudging me. Faces came before me: Ralph and other paraplegics who were already buried. How long would my kidneys . . .? There had been so much I'd had to overcome, I felt I was enititled to some happiness.

Early in December I began to prepare the kids for my departure. On December 23rd, Walt, Marguerite and Chucky left for an extended winter holiday until New Years' Eve. John invited me to his home for Christmas dinner.

At first I refused. "No, I can't. Thanks, but I'd rather not intrude. All those religious symbols. You enjoy your holiday . . ."

"It will be exactly like Thanksgiving. My folks don't even have a tree anymore. It would mean a lot to them."

It was always easy to compromise with John who was such

an angel. He asked very little of me. "I'd be delighted to go. It was kind of your mom and dad to include me."

His grateful smile was sufficient thanks.

I turned and wheeled down to my room. Yes, I reminisced, Thanksgiving at Charley and Eleanor's had been lovely. The dinner was super: I had never seen so many courses in my life: hors d'oeuvres, cranberry sauce, mashed potatoes, candied sweet potatoes, a squash casserole, turkey and four different pies. John's mother brought the best apple pie I had ever tasted. Eleanor's table was elegantly set with beautiful china, crystal glassware and sterling silver that graced her damask off-white tablecloth with matching napkins. I was horrified by the excessive drinking, though thankful that John drank ginger ale, which annoyed not only his brother and his father but Eleanor's father, who kept urging him to have a drink with them. I wasn't happy about that aspect of the festivities but John kept his promise.

When John first brought me to his brother's house, I did not remember that he had told me he had lived there with his wife and daughter. As I was carried up the steps to the bedroom this realization hit me hard, causing me to be very tense. I wanted to leave. I only stayed to please John. I became nauseous and almost threw up the whole meal.

Despite that episode, I felt grateful to Charley and Eleanor for their warmth and acceptance in a difficult situation. They were dear, loving people, but I wondered if my father in reverse circumstances would have been so tolerant. These people accepted me without question. I wasn't going to torture myself thinking it was all a false front. I knew I had to please John and share Christmas with him.

At Epstein's, a local department store, I bought a good-looking yellow silk dress. John surprised me with a gorgeous yellow hand corsage of tiny roses. But I couldn't get my father's warnings out of my mind:

"Aneeda, you're not to go out with him anymore. Do you hear me? I'll kill you and him together." When Christmas came the Cossacks marched into the Polish ghetto. They raped Jewish women; they stole; they killed.

Aneeda. I'm warning you. When he gets drunk, he'll call you 'a dirty Jew.'"

"Dad, you're in America. Forget those ugly . . ."

"Aneeda, believe me, it's not different. They drink all the time.

"Soon you'll hear 'you lousy Jew.' Everyone of them are the same. I'll kill you. Do you hear?"

Dad, oh, Dad, I said to myself, you came from another era. I trust John. With my life. I couldn't hurt him.

We drove to his parents and parked, just as his brother pulled alongside our car. The elder Mullers came out to greet us.

"Merry Christmas everyone," Eleanor greeted. "Nita you look simply divine."

"So do you. All of you. Lucia, your velvet dress is beautiful. Maureenie looks precious. And you, Charley, handsome. Everyone looks wonderful."

"Merry Christmas."

"Merry Christmas."

"Well, what are ye standing here for? It's me dinner ye'll be wantin'. And isn't it nice ye could come out for Christmas, Nita?" As John brought me in, I noticed his mother hurriedly set another place setting for me. It was obvious that I was unexpected, and I could hardly restrain from sobbing.

Mrs. Muller's dinner was splendid. I never tasted a chestnut stuffing before and found it a delectable side dish. When everyone exchanged gifts, his mother handed me a box that had been addressed to someone else whose name was crossed out, with my first name scribbled incorrectly.

On the day I left Burnt Mills, the children were eating dinner. I could not bring myself to say goodbye. John carried my belongings and we got in the car; I slumped way down into the seat and promptly dozed off to awaken shortly before we stopped. I remained silent. We had reached a log cabin about seventy-five miles away from Pluckemin. We were going to spend the night and the next day we would go back to celebrate his father's annual New Year's Day birthday dinner before heading for Suffern. I sat rigidly while John registered at the main lodge giving a phoney name, no doubt. If his wife ever found out . . . Room #24 had a double bed with matching red corduroy drapes and spread. A charming maple dresser was placed against the wall, with two small night tables, lamps and two comfortable upholstered chairs. The room was too narrow for me to turn around. John rearranged the furniture, placing one of the chairs in the bathtub. I hadn't stirred. I was just plain miserable.

"I think we did the wrong thing. Please, please, John, let's get out of here." He swooped me out of my chair, lifting me on the bed. "John, I don't like anything about this. You promised . . . "

The man looked beat. "You don't trust me, do you?"

His remark annoyed me. "What do you mean trust? This place . . . ?"

John turned his back putting his face in his hands."I will never . . ." He didn't say anything for a few minutes. "I told you I would never have intercourse with you until we're married."

"I'm sorry I hurt you."

"Pupsie, I'm human. I want to be close to you." He picked up my chin. "Don't you feel the same way? All these months of stolen time. A few minutes here and there."

I knew it was easier for me to have self control: I was half out of my mind about my sexual inadequacy. How could I please a normal man? My tight spastic leg muscles? I swallowed hard. "Up until now you haven't made any demands."

"Nita," John fumbled for words, "I love you. I want to be close to you. We have a lot to learn about each other, even without going all the way." He looked like a sad sheep dog. "Don't you feel the same way?" He was struggling to appease me. God, he was exhausted.

Suddenly the room took on a special warmth. I pulled him close. "Yes, dear, I do love you." He resisted only a second before his irresistible smile emerged. "I truly want us to be happy. You're my teacher. I'm your willing student. You're right. We haven't had much time for each other."

"Just to have you all to myself. To ring in a New Year." He hugged me tightly. "I'm the luckiest guy." We edged down on the bed slowly turning toward each other.

"Oops, excuse . . . " I dashed to the bathroom, thankful the door was wide enough for my chair. I was frightened, yet eager, full of anticipation. I stayed in the bathroom for a long time, washing and primping, before finally taking a deep breath and coming out. John was lying on the bed, stretched to his full six feet— sound asleep. I had to admit I was disappointed. I transferred into bed trying my best to make an easy transition.

"Boo! Thought I was asleep? Like hell." He reached for me.

"John, why do you use that language?"

"My father didn't allow my brother and me to use any profanity at home, even though he swore constantly. No doubt my work in the chemical plant with all the men was another factor. Hey, it's fun. A release. Why don't you try? Like, why in the hell did that sonofabitch have to go off without a decent 'goodbye?'"

"Cause he's a yellow bellied . . . "

"Yellow bellied what?" egged John

"Yellow bellied sonofabitch." We roared.

John's long kisses were delicious—becoming more intimate, gradually leading to passionate soul kisses. I was breathless and pushed him away.

"What's wrong?"

"I'm nervous."

He kissed my face, my ears, drawing me closer, unbuttoned my blouse, undid my bra.

"John, please," I pleaded. "That's all. That's enough." I had not moved an inch.

He unzipped my skirt, pulled down my panty girdle, plastic bloomers, pads, tossing everything on the floor. I was terrified. He began kissing my lips, soul kissing, then he slowly massaged my breasts. "God, you're gorgeous." He murmured breathlessly and began to suck them until I cried in passion. When he began stroking the side of my leg, I pushed his hand away.

"Please stop," I whispered, "I can't stand to be touched on the lower part of my legs. They're very sensitive."

"How's this?" caressing my thighs very gently.

"Better." What was he trying to do? Experiment on me? Feel this—feel that? Mark it down for the record?

"What's the—you're angry?" John was perplexed.

"You think I'm a mechanical toy, don't you? I think you're using me to further your own gains." Lord what was wrong with me? The man turned white. He was crushed. "Oh, John forgive me. I can't bear myself. Those horrible bloomers. How can you say I'm a woman?"

"You make me feel like a king," he said, kissing my lips lovingly. "I have to ask questions because I don't ever want to hurt you. No other woman has ever had such an effect on me. You're exciting. You must have had a lot of boyfriends."

"I've had a lot of dates. I was truly in love only once." I

wasn't ready to discuss my first love. "John, this holiday costs a pretty penny. How did you manage?"

He grinned. "No problem. I saved for my Pupsie doll. You know, staying at Mom's. There's a restaurant on the premises. We'll choose from the menu and have all our meals right here in Paradise." What a darling.

We toasted the end of 1947 with love and ginger ale. And stayed in bed until it was time to leave for Pluckemin.

John's gentleness had made it natural for me to overcome my embarrassment. We matched each other's satisfactions, met each other's strengths, without going all the way. What a revelation. My paralysis didn't stop me from being really sexy and I could please my love to peak levels. But intercourse? I didn't have to worry about that, yet.

"Darling you're glowing."

"You become me."

Hail to 1948.

Chapter 36

My plan was to go home until I left for NYU, providing I was accepted by their medical board. Each day I spent in my parent's house was a nightmare. They had recently moved into the first floor of a white wooden two story house with steps in front and back. I felt like a captive. Occasionally I saw Midge or a few old friends. Mar visited several times a week in the evenings, after her long day at the hospital, but I didn't want her to stay long because she worked very hard as an operating room nurse and I knew she was exhausted. The mere mention of John's name caused my father's voice to escalate. I couldn't wait to receive a letter from the NYU medical board.

Almost a year before, Edith Nourse Rogers had written assuring me of her continued dedication to women veterans' rights. She was sympathetic to my plight as well as to the thousands of other WAACs who were not entitled to veterans' status. She had written a new Bill that would offer veterans' status to any WAAC who served in the military before it became part of the regular army. Oh, that was music to my ears. I wrote letters to Congressmen and Senators to support the Bill until I was blue in the face.

Dad drove me into New York the second week in January 1948 for my hearing for acceptance to NYU. "I hope I won't be long, Dad," aware of his impatient nature.

"It's all right Dolling. I'll get a cup of coffee."

I waited nervously until my name was called, then wheeled into an office to face a panel of three men, one being Dr. George Deaver, whom I'd met four years ago when he introduced the technique of brace and crutch ambulation to the paraplegics at the VA. I took comfort in his broad smile compared to the deadpan expressions of the other two physicians.

Dr. Deaver spoke first. "How nice to see you, Miss Bloom," and proceeded to introduce the two other doctors.

A stern pair of eyes faced me. "Miss Bloom, in the face of your extreme difficulty, why would you consider attending NYU, which is not accessible to anyone in a wheelchair? Why would you want to bring such hardship upon yourself?"

My stomach churned. I felt my legs becoming tense. "I want to become a speech therapist. I feel I can make a contribution to society if I become a viable, hardworking citizen."

The slimmest man nodded rather condescendingly, "That's all well and good, but how will you manage in the crowded halls, the narrow bathrooms, the overcrowded cafeteria?"

My right hand pinched my left tight as I struggled to answer. "Sir, everything you mention will be an obstacle, only one of many that I'll have to face every day of my life. Somehow I will find a way to cope. I plan to take fewer courses than the average freshman. I know it will take me longer to graduate but I have faith that if I persevere I will succeed."

The other doctor asked, "How will you manage to live in New York?"

Dr. Deaver queried, "Where will you live?"

God only knew where I could afford to live, but I assured the board that I would find suitable quarters.

"How often do you have to have a doctor in attendance?" And on and on. They continued to interrogate me with mundane questions for over an hour. There were no smiles of approval or any indication as to whether I had persuaded them. Dr. Deaver thanked me for coming and said I would be notified within ten days.

I raced to one of the bathrooms as soon as the interview ended, thankful the place was empty. I couldn't help but wish the members of the board could have seen me using the "inaccessible facilities." School would not commence until early February. I chose to take a positive attitude, blocking out any negative fears.

On the way home I tried to explain to my father what a mammoth job John had accomplished to bring me to the point in my life where I could even consider living in New York and attending NYU.

"Aneeda, I am happy you are going to go to college. It will give you something to do, but I don't want to hear anymore about the shaygets. You are away from that terrible place. Finished. Do you understand?"

I understood. I understood that by hook or by crook I was going to get out of my parents' home—and live my own life—which would definitely include John Muller.

I managed to keep busy writing letters to Dick Monfried, the lawyer, Mrs. St. George, Mrs. Rogers, and anyone else I thought could help. Shopping for clothes was always a chore but with Marilyn's help I purchased a few necessities.

A letter arrived from Dick Monfried that included copies of two letters he had received from Katherine St. George in regard to HR 143. She stated in one of her letters, " . . . this Bill has strong opposition in the committee" and she is "preparing to introduce a private Bill to grant relief to Miss Bloom in the hope that this move will focus attention on her neglect by our government."

In Dick's response to Mrs. St. George he offered to help in connection with the approval of HR 143 to provide veterans' benefits to all the women in the WAAC, such as myself. He volunteered to contact certain of his friends and clients to obtain publicity, showing the plight of the WAACs and their unfortunate situation. He added, "if you feel that it will be helpful to have Miss Bloom come to Washington at the time you appear before Mrs. Roger's committee to act as a sort of Exhibit A, I will be glad to make the necessary arrangements to have her in Washington and will be glad to come down with her."

The next day I called one of my mom's sisters, Aunt Min, Aunt Jen's twin sister, to ask, if I was accepted to NYU, could I spend my last week with her in Paterson. She was more than pleased to have me. Ten days later I was overjoyed to receive my acceptance to NYU.

Dad, who hardly spoke to me while I was living at home, was kind enough to drive me into the city for my interview with the Dean of Women and to inquire about housing.

A statuesque gray-haired woman recommended the Number One Fifth Avenue Hotel for the female students. Dad and I went over to see it, but the rates were prohibitive for my meager funds and we returned to the dean.

"Miss Bloom, as I understand your situation, you are more than twenty-one, served in the WAAC and I would think, are perfectly capable of taking care of yourself." I nodded and waited curiously to hear the rest. "I would like you to go over to the Broadway Central Hotel, which is fairly close to NYU and where I'm sure the cost per week is considerably less. If you're comfortable there, you will open the door to other students who also find Number One Fifth Avenue too high priced."

Dad drove over to the hotel. Sure enough, there were a few unsavory characters sitting in the hotel lobby, but the manager was very kind, assuring me and my father that if I minded my own business no one would bother me. The price was right; the large room was more than adequate. Taxi fare would be relatively inexpensive for the short distance to college. The mere thought of living in the Big Apple was more than I could bear. I could hardly wait. I told Dad repeatedly how much I appreciated his efforts that day.

A few days later my father drove me to Paterson. The sojourn at my aunt's house was wonderful. She knew about John and was eager to meet him. I called to ask when he would visit and was flabbergasted when he said, "Pupsie, I just got over the mumps, but don't worry, the doctor assured me I was okay, if you know what I mean."

"Oh, gosh, John . . ."

"Hon, before you say another word, the doctor also assured me that once you break out, you're not contagious anymore. The swelling will go away in a few days. So help me. No one will come down with the mumps."

On Friday night my aunt answered the doorbell. "Oh, no," I heard. "You can't come in here. I have two children." The door slammed. I raced in.

"Aunt Min, please let me talk to John." I opened the door to see a dejected swollen-cheeked John.

After hearing what the doctor said to John, that the mumps were no longer contagious, Aunt Min let him in. I introduced them and was very proud my John had the forethought to bring her a huge box of candy. The two of them hit it off like old friends. Aunt Min had a delicious sense of humor, relating to people as easily as John. Soon we were having a merry time. John was wonderful with Larry and Debbie, playing games with them and regaling them with delightful stories. Uncle Jules came home about six o'clock from his work as manager of a large drug store. We lit the Sabbath candles; I said the prayers. My aunt had made a delicious brisket, mashed potatoes, fresh green beans, cole slaw, cake and coffee. It was the first night since I left John that I felt contentment. No one ever contracted mumps.

The following Sunday my parents accompanied me to the Broadway Central Hotel. They were reluctant to leave me but I reassured them I would be safe and sound. John arrived early Monday morning to do a dry run with me the first couple of days. He registered at the hotel for his own room. We ate a quick breakfast, then waited more than twenty minutes before a taxi would stop. I began to get anxious, realizing this was going to be a big problem for me each day.

When we arrived at the school I almost had a stroke. I couldn't say the medical board hadn't warned me: sheer unadulterated bedlam, crowded elevators, doors almost slamming in my face, difficulty in locating classes, and getting shoved from all sides in the bookstore. John was a blessing. Without him it would have been disaster. There was no way I could have coped.

After school, we discovered inexpensive restaurants, talked forever about the problems at Burnt Mills, how difficult it was becoming for him to work there and caught up on family news, and how difficult it was going to be for me living alone in New York.

"Pupsie," John comforted me, "the cue is to take one day at a time. I have faith in you."

"I'll give it my best shot." I most assuredly didn't have any confidence and I knew that when the time came for us to part, it was going to be murder. The most delicious part of his stay was our intimate time together. We were never bored.

School was slightly easier the next day but again I was thankful for John's presence. He had to leave after dinner and it took every bit of self control I could muster to say goodbye. I felt badly for John, knowing how difficult it was for him to go back to Burnt Mills.

The next morning I awoke early, dressed, grabbed my books, raced down to the restaurant, and waited endlessly for a cab to stop. Tears blinded my eyes when taxi after taxi passed until finally, one kind soul stopped. The driver, after putting my wheelchair in the trunk, complained of a terrible backache all during the short ride to NYU. He struggled to get the chair out and it was very difficult for me to get back into my wheelchair, pay the tab and give the man a small tip.

Slowly, I wheeled over to the imposing heavy metal doors and was grateful to the young man who opened one of them for me. I almost fainted as I was being crushed amidst the throngs of students. If John hadn't done a first walk through, I don't know how I would have survived. I was nervous and barely concentrated on my first course, English 101. The dining room was impossible but I managed to squeeze in between the students to buy an apple. I faced the same difficulty hailing a taxi returning to the hotel. As soon as I got to my room, I fell on the bed exhausted. In the evening I went into the hotel for a light supper, convinced John on the phone later that I was fine, listened to WQXR and fell asleep with the light on. For the next few days, I wanted to give up the whole idea of college but somehow I got through the week and before I realized it my John was back for the weekend. The following week passed without incident: I arose an hour earlier, ate a small breakfast on the run and just waited for a cab to stop.

The following weekend John and I went to Central Park on a brisk day and

I practiced brace walking. It had been weeks since I had crutch walked but in no time I was swinging through again. John was pleased. After we had dinner Sunday night, we returned to the Broadway Central. I was still wearing my braces and had to use the bathroom. When I came out, I went into a state of shock. John was gone. My wheelchair was no longer in the room.

"That no good. . . " Oh, my God, what would I do? I hobbled over to my bed, sat down and simply stared. I was completely shaken. About fifteen minutes later the phone rang.

"Hi, pupsie . . ."

"Don't you pupsie me, you no-good sonofabitch," I shrieked, "What have you done? You bring my chair back instantly or I'll never see you again. Do you hear me?"

"I hear you, hon."

"Stop calling me 'hon.' You're a complete bastard. You bring my chair right back. Now."

"I can't. I'm just going on to the George Washington Bridge. If you calm down, we can talk about how you'll manage."

"No," I screamed, "I can't manage. It's too awful. Taxis whizzing by, elevator doors slamming in my face. Are you crazy? If you don't bring back my chair, I'll—I'll have you arrested. It's too much to ask of me. Please, please, John," I began to cry, "on bended knees, bring my chair back."

"Nita, darling, listen to me. You can swing through the lobby. Taxi cabs will be easier to hail. Soon you will find a steady taxi driver who will come for you three times a week. Just take it slow and easy in school. I left a strap for your books on your night table. I have the utmost confidence in you. It will take a little time but I know you. Sooner than you ever dreamed possible, you'll be doing fine. Trust me."

I choked back my tears. "It's too hard. I'm not ready."

"Pupsie," John consoled, "I'm right here in the lobby. Your wheelchair is here. I'll bring it up."

Oh, God, that man had so much confidence in me. In my heart of hearts I knew I couldn't disappoint him. "Leave it there, you crazy idiot. I'll try. But first I need you to hold me close before I go to bed, you wonderful man."

Chapter 37

After John left, I devoted myself to my homework, fiddled aimlessly with toiletries, shuffled and crashed on the bed. Although I was totally wiped out, all I did was toss and turn and question my stupidity. What a fool I was to allow John to take my wheelchair away. How in God's name would I manage? I knew I could always persuade the manager to get the chair for me, but I simply had to make the effort—even if only to please John.

My first class began at 9:00 A.M., which meant I had to get up at 6:00 A.M. in order to start drinking the first one of the prescribed 10 glasses of water I needed daily to keep my kidneys flushed. The screeching alarm clock shocked me into reality. Still half asleep, I struggled to get my braces on, then shuffled to the bathroom. Thankfully the commode was next to the sink where I could wash, and by stretching my neck, brush my teeth. I bunny hopped back, then struggled to carry my clothes that I clumsily dragged over to the bed. It was a pain in the neck to strap my books onto my crutches and then face the problem of how was I going to hold my damned pocketbook which I ended up clutching to the wooden bar of one of my crutches. I opened the door—goddamnit, forgot my keys. I went back to the dresser, picked up the keys, and swung through my crutches down the long hall to the elevator, praying the damned elevator door wouldn't slam in my face! I was sweating profusely. Was that man insane?

How I managed to get out of the elevator, all the time keeping my eyes glued to the floor as I shuffled, was a mystery. No way would I swing through the shiny marble floor even if it wasn't wet. Perspiration dripped down my cheeks. My sweater was soaking wet. Slowly I meandered across the hall, keeping my eyes down and headed for the restaurant where I crashed into a chair. I said,"Good morning" to a waiter who was rooted to the spot, gaping as though he had seen an apparition. Finally he asked for my order.

After breakfast I blanked out the thought of going all the way back to my room to the bathroom. I bunny hopped across that damned floor, coming to a halt in front of the glass revolving doors, taking long breaths to steady myself. Thankfully a man who obviously knew how to keep the doors separated came to my assistance. I nodded my appreciation, ignoring his stunned expression and bunny hopped outside. The whiz of the cars roaring down Broadway scared me half to death. My legs were trembling. I felt weak. I edged closer to the curb, trying to hail a cab but they all sped by. Finally one pulled over to the curb and I forced myself to ignore the shocked stare on the driver's face when I asked to go to NYU.

In the cab, the driver cross examined me: "What on earth is a young lady like yourself doing on the streets of Broadway?"

"I'm going to NYU. Today is my first day of school without my wheelchair."

"Isn't anyone going with you?"

I choked back my tears. "No, I'm alone."

"Who the hell would allow you to go out in your condition all by yourself?"

"It's my decision." Yeah, sure. It's that damn John who wants to kill me. I couldn't wait to get to school. I didn't need that man's badgering.

"Where are your parents?

"They're working." He drove up to the black iron gate, stopping a distance from the curb.

The acrid taste in my mouth was sickening. "Would you kindly pull close to the curb? Thanks," trying to ignore the puzzled look on his face. I paid the fare and tip. He went around the front to open the door. I struggled to get out and just stood rooted to that spot.

Hundreds of young people raced around, in front, in back and alongside of me. Like a snail, I shuffled toward the metal doors, praying some kind soul would open one for me. I was petrified that one of the doors would swing out and knock me down, but the door remained solid as a statue. Slowly I pulled on one of the knobs. No luck. I tried again, pulling with all my might.

"Allow me," a young man offered.

"Oh, thank you," I said, giving him a grateful nod of appreciation without looking up. I navigated toward the elevator. The door opened to a tumultuous din. I froze. Where was John when I needed him? His goddamned instructions. What the hell was the matter with him subjecting me to this kind of torture? I shuffled into the elevator like a frozen potato. Somehow I got out and headed for my first class: math. I didn't hear a word the professor said. Besides, I hated math and resented the requirement. The next class, English 101, was on the second floor. I edged over to the elevator certain I'd have a stroke when the door opened. In agony, I entered the elevator facing the rear. Second floor. I hadn't turned around. Up to the fifth before I could manage to turn around. Down to the second. Door crashed open to admit tons of bodies pushing against me as I weaseled out in a panic. I found my class and ever so slowly slid down into a seat, smiling broadly—to no one. No one paid the slightest attention to me. The professor entered and English 101 began. My mind was a blank.

How I got into the cafeteria at lunchtime was a mystery. I picked up a tray—and just stood there. How would I carry everything? "Please," I asked the cashier meekly, "can someone help me carry my tray?"

"You'll have to wait, miss. We're busy now."

Sure I'll wait—till hell freezes over. Then I'll miss my afternoon class and go back to my hotel. Boy, will that John get a" you-know-what-for" call from me. We're finished. Done. Forever. Someone brought me a tray, and to save time, I gave the woman my order and devoured every morsel within a few minutes. No one approached me. No hellos. No nothing. Well, I didn't go to NYU for socialization. Thankfully I found a ladies room not too far from the cafeteria and, praise be to the Lord, by some miracle I was safe and successful. After lunch, I found my way to social studies.

At 3:00 P.M. I went outside and was overjoyed to see the same driver who had picked me up earlier, parked close to the curb. I thanked him profusely, and he said he would be there in the morning.

Feeling much relieved, I headed towards the door of my hotel, when a drunk rushed in front of me. "C'n I do sumthin' for yuh?"

"Thank you. If you'll be so kind as to open the door."

"What door, lady?"

"The door to the hotel. Right there."

"I don't see any door." Oh, God. I hopped over to the door. The drunk followed me. "Where yuh goin'?"

"Can you please open the door?"

"No, I want you to come with me."

Good Lord. No one was in sight. I started to pull on the door but the man blocked the entrance. "Wanna swig?" he said, pulling out a bottle from his filthy pants.

"No. Please let me go inside."

"No," he began to raise his voice. "I want you to come with me. Yer pretty. C'mon, I'm a good screwer."

My eyes filled. I was afraid to antagonize him. I stared into his besotted eyes for a few minutes.

"Aw, screw you, you lousy cripple, screw you," he mumbled, as he wobbled down the street. Shaking like a leaf I waited several minutes until another man showed up to open the door. I thanked him profusely, and by the look on his face I knew he thought I was off my rocker.

Suddenly a tall good-looking man approached me. "You're Miss Bloom, if I recall? The student from NYU?" I nodded without looking up at him. "I'm Ross Baker, the manager of this hotel. I want to welcome you. If there's anything I can do for you, please don't hesitate to call me."

Looking up for a second into Mr. Baker's smiling countenance I saw the first cheerful sign I had seen all day. "I'm pleased to make your acquaintance. Today was my first day at college without my wheelchair, and I have to admit I'm exhausted. I appreciate your kind offer. Good day." I took the elevator, opened the door to my room, going directly to my bed where I crashed, completely stunned that John's prophecy had come true—at least for one day.

The next morning after breakfast I went out to hail a cab and found my same driver parked along the curb. He jumped out as soon as he saw me and with a big smile on his face, he bowed saying "Ernie, at your service. Would you like me to pick you up every day at this time?"

"Oh, bless your heart, I'd be eternally grateful." Ernie picked me up on the mornings I had classes. We became good pals. I was thankful that he never probed about my personal life the way he had when he first met me.

All of a sudden it was Friday night and John was back. Was I ever happy to see him. He was jubilant when I told him about my successful week. "Time for celebration, my wonder woman. But first this man needs a lot of tender loving care. I was some lonely guy."

"Me, too."

His strong arms, the touch of his lips and his tender caresses were all sheer ecstasy. Soon we confessed our ravenous hunger, and were content in the knowledge there would be plenty of time when we returned. The manager had given John a room for a mere $10 a night, adding that it would remain the same whenever he visited. Proudly I accompanied him to the elevator, but when we got off, he asked me to swing through the lobby instead of bunny hopping. I was amazed how easily I managed.

"Just be careful when the floors are wet. That's when you do bunny hops, but otherwise you swing through. You'll see, it will be a hell of a lot easier."

"Yes, confidence man."

We drove to Greenwich Village and dined in a small mom and pop Chinese restaurant. Their Wonton soup and Moo Shu Pork were outstanding. I was pleased when the waiter folded the little pancakes for me. They never looked as neat when I did it. We talked for about three hours. The adoring expression on John's face was worth a million dollars when I told him how I used the straps he had brought to fasten my books.

"I knew you could do it. You're going to become even more proficient as time goes by." He leaned across the table to kiss me. "I'm very proud of you, Pupsie. Very proud. I love you so much. Now I have something very important to tell you. Ben Pakula, a resident of Suffern whose seven-year-old cerebral palsied daughter, Sandy, was a resident at Burnt Mills, asked if I would consider being the director of a clinic in Suffern."

"Wow."

"At present there are seven families who started the Rockland County Society and are now operating minimally with a physical and speech therapist in the basement of the Suffern High School. They're hoping to expand the facilities to include more services."

"What?" I shrieked and to my embarrassment the waiter dashed over to our table. "Sorry," I apologized. "Oh, John, I can't believe it."

"Of course I can't accept anything until the year is up, but Ben said by that time the board would be notified of the whole idea and ready to go. In the meantime I'm not going to approach Rose for the divorce. I'll wait until I leave. Right now she's still mad as a hornet. I feel it's wise to wait." I nodded, trying to understand.

After dinner I ambulated a short distance to a night club where we had a couple of cokes and listened to a raucous dame belt out the blues. Later we drove around the area looking for other amusements for the future. We returned to the hotel tired, but not so totally exhausted that we couldn't take time out for more love making.

Saturday was a bitter cold day. We went uptown, and I ventured into Orbachs' department store. The crowds were overwhelming but with John's guidance I bunny hopped slowly through. I bought a sweater, some hosiery, a small pocketbook; John purchased a shirt—all at fantastically low prices. We took in a movie, and found an Indian restaurant where no one looked at me as a creature from outer space. I was enchanted with the food except for the rose petal tea that was not particularly pleasing to either of us.

"I have to go to the bathroom before we leave." I got up to shuffle around to the back where I was given the directions. When I came out I had to pass the kitchen. I became nauseous when I saw all the raw meats lying around the counter top, vegetables thrown around, lots of rotten fruit. Ugh. I hopped away as fast as I could. John waited at the end with a puzzled look on his face. "Tell you later," I mumbled. Such a disappointing end to the super inexpensive meal.

Sunday came all too soon. Parting was always difficult but we resolved to act mature. In truth, there was no other option.

After John left, I went over my checkbook and then panicked. I was running short of money. Despite all the pleading from the waiter to eat more, I kept lunches down to half a sandwich; the other half to be kept in the hotel's refrigerator for the next day. Dinner consisted of the least expensive entree. No dessert or coffee. It was only because John was living at his mother's that he could afford the few extra dollars when he came to New York. If only I had the GI Bill of Rights to pay for my education. I prayed for a more hopeful letter from Congresswoman St. George.

One day on my return from school, I saw Ross Baker in the lobby. A light went on: Approaching him, I took the plunge. "Mr. Baker, would you by chance have a small job for me? I really need the extra money."

"Let me think about it Miss Bloom. I'll call you later."

"Please call me, Nita. Miss Bloom makes me feel old."

"I'm Ross."

It was early March when I received an update from Dick Monfried. He had written Congresswoman Katharine St. George stating that he had watched for an article in the newspapers concerning H. R. 143 but had not seen anything. He asked her if the Committee had taken any further action. Dick updated her on the fact that I was attending classes at NYU, living at the Broadway Central Hotel and had arranged to get to college by taxi. He emphasized the fact that it had been a financial strain on me, living away from home and outside the Veterans' Hospital where it was necessary to pay for room and meals. ". . . It is becoming quite severe and she is barely able to make ends meet on the small allowance she is receiving from the Compensation Bureau," further stating, "that if she did not feel there was a possibility of H R 143 being enacted into law at this session, did she think that it would be worthwhile to introduce a private Bill under which Miss Bloom would receive the equivalent of the benefits of HR 143. If you wish Miss Bloom and me to discuss this matter we would be only too happy to come to Washington."

Congresswoman St George replied ". . . recognizing Miss Bloom's situation and happy to hear that she is attending school and assisting herself. She stated that she had spoken to Mrs. Roger's office relative to HR 143 and it had been indicated to her that it would shortly be put down for hearings. Mrs. Rogers, who is the author of the Bill, is most anxious that it pass, and I shall gladly do any act possible to work with her on it. In the event no action has been taken on this Bill by the middle of April, remind me, and I will introduce a private Bill although I think that HR 143 can better serve relief for Miss Bloom than a private Bill."

There was little leisure time for me, what with studying, washing my undies and writing to the various representatives in Congress. Whenever I ate in the restaurant and a patron left the *Times*, I always read the weekly articles that Dr. Howard Rusk, a noted rehabilitation specialist, wrote about the disabled community. One morning I had a brainstorm and decided to phone him. His secretary took my name as well as a brief summary of why I wanted to talk to the doctor. She called back several days later with the good news that Dr. Rusk would give me an interview the following week.

I took a cab uptown to the *Times* building, swung through the lobby and took the elevator up to Dr. Rusk's office. Soon I was face to face with the renowned physician.

Dr. Rusk was quite handsome. His dark brown hair sprinkled with silver streaks and his friendly dark brown eyes quickly relieved my tension. "Please, make yourself comfortable." I maneuvered into the straight leather chair somewhat gracefully. "Miss Bloom, tell me how a beautiful woman like yourself came to join the Women's Army?"

"Thank you for the compliment. It's very simple sir. When my country called for women to serve, I felt it my privilege and duty to join the WAAC."

"You must have been very young."

"I was twenty one years old when I enlisted, full of vim and vigor, and most eager to serve until this unfortunate happening took place.

"Won't you please tell me what occurred?" Dr. Rusk paused, "I hope it won't be too stressful for you."

"Yes, many incidents are painful, but I need to explain them and the reasons why I feel I should be recognized as a veteran. I'll try to be brief and I do appreciate the valuable time you have taken to hear me out." Dr. Rusk's eyes never left my face. He was visibly shocked when I told him the gory details of the thumb infection. I related the pertinent incidents as quickly as possible, then sat with folded hands waiting for him to respond.

"Miss Bloom," Dr. Rusk said emphatically, "I promise you that I will do anything I can on your behalf. I do have many friends in both the House and the Senate. Suppose you write me a letter stating how you became paralyzed and all the circumstances leading up to the injustice of your not being recognized as a veteran. I shall write to each and every one of the representatives on the House Veteran's Committee. I hope something positive will be effected."

"How can I thank you?" I shook my head in awe. "No wonder. Your articles are always filled with innovative, encouraging ideas to the handicapped community. I pray that most of your theories will come to pass one day."

Dr. Rusk rose from his chair as he came around the table. "I would like to watch you crutch walk. You must have worked very hard. Was George Deaver responsible for any of your progress?"

"Yes, Dr. Deaver came to the Bronx VA where I was fitted for my braces several years ago. My fiancé John Muller became my therapist, and he has done more for me than anyone else."

"He must be very special."

"He is. Thank you." I arose from my chair to get up to swing through my crutches around his office.

"You are an example of what it takes to survive in this world. I admire your indomitable spirit, and I sincerely hope I can help you in your struggle to be recognized as a veteran."

"It has been a privilege to meet you, sir. If anyone can help, I know it will be you. I'll get that letter out immediately." We shook hands. "Goodbye. God bless you to continue your worthy endeavors." I left on cloud nine.

The following Sunday Mom and Dad were coming to visit for the first time. I asked John to leave early, as much as it pained me to do so. He was compassionate as usual, adding that it was no problem at all. My parents came in the early afternoon and I was genuinely happy to see them. I missed them and prayed their visit would not bring any problems.

"Noo, vat are you doing?"

"Dad, I love school. At first it was difficult to resume my study habits but now I'm in the swing of things."

"Nita, you look great," Mom exuded. "How do you get to school?"

I sat quietly. "Just fine."

"I don't like this hotel. I don't like the characters I saw sitting in the lobby. One of them looked like he was a drunkard."

"Dad, I mind my own business just like the dean advised. You remember? Would you like to go out for a bite? You know Katz's Deli on the East Side. It's not far from here."

My father's expression turned to shock. "How are you going? I don't see your wheelchair?"

I took a deep breath, counting to three. "Dad, if it weren't for John. . . "

"That shaygets has been to New York?" His voice became

louder. "Aneeda, you know I don't approve. I vant you to stop. Do you hear me? I vant you to stop seeing him."

"Dad, please listen to me," I pleaded, "John has helped me more than any other person on earth. He spent a whole day going with me to NYU, and when he was sure I would be able to manage on my braces and crutches alone, he took my wheelchair away. Do you know I call a cab, attend classes and return to the hotel almost every day? Please try to understand how much he is helping me."

Dad looked at me angrily.

"Now, Bill," Mom placated, "don't get yourself excited."

"Why don't we go to Katz's? Remember you took me there when I was a teenager? I hear it's still great. The best corned beef sandwiches in the world."

"No, I'm not hungry. You take care of yourself. Come, Til, I vant to go."

I was terrified at my Mom's sad expression, well aware that I could cause her to have a nervous breakdown. My father would never understand. I shouldn't have mentioned John's name. In the future I would keep my personal life private.

About an hour and a half later the phone rang. It was John. "Pupsie, how did it go?"

I couldn't control my sobs. "Sweetheart, I suspected something like that. Don't you worry. They'll come around." We made small talk. Ten minutes later there was a short rap on my door.

"John, you're wonderful."

"You don't think I'd allow my pupsie to go to bed sad." We had a light dinner in the hotel. He stayed for a while and left me on a happy note. I enjoyed doing my homework and fell asleep quick as a wink.

As he had promised, Dick wrote to Katharine St. George on April 19 to remind her about the status of HR 143 stating that: "Newspaper articles have been printing a number of stories recently about paraplegics and as a result I believe the country has become conscious of the situation affecting those people. It is therefore my humble opinion that the time is now most advantageous for the introduction of a Bill to help Miss Bloom and for pressure to be exerted on the Committee to take the action to help her and the others similarly affected."

Katharine St. George quickly responded, stating HR 143 has

been referred to the Sub-Committee on Compensation and Pensions of the Committee on Veterans Affairs of the House and ". . .it is generally felt that a report will shortly be made." She said that she would hold up introducing a private Bill pending the results of that report.

One day later when I returned from school, to my amazement, I received copies of some of the responses from the letters that Dr. Rusk had received from his June request on my behalf. All of them were sympathetic, but some were most informative.

From Congressman Frank Karsten, of the 13th District, Missouri: ". . .this is a most deserving case, and to my mind it is one that certainly should be recognized under the Training Program provided for veterans. As you know, members of the Women's Army Corps are entitled to veterans benefits and it is certainly discriminatory to deny the same benefits to those who served in the Women's Auxiliary Army Corps. The failure to include members of the Women's Auxiliary Army Corps is simply based on a technicality. While it is true they were not actually members of the Army, to all intents and purposes they were subject to similar rules and regulations that applied to the Women's Army Corps later on, when the women were taken into the Army. Nevertheless, the Subcommittee received an adverse report from the Veterans Administration. Mrs. Rogers seems to think the adverse report was based on the fact that such a program would increase the budget of the Veterans Bureau. It is expected Congress will adjourn within the next two weeks. A great deal of veterans legislation is pending and I doubt whether HR 143 will be advanced."

Other letters were from Senator John Sparkman of Alabama, Senator James E. Murray of Montana, Senator J. W. Fulbright of Arkansas, Senator Lister Hill of Alabama, Senator Kenneth S. Wherry of Nebraska, Senator Joseph H. Ball of Michigan, and Senator Irving M. Ives of New York, all expressing sympathy and pledging to support the Bill on my behalf.

One letter in particular clarified the so called "technicality" and made my blood boil. It was a response from Senator Elbert D. Thomas of Utah: . . . "As you know, I was the author of the WAAC Bill and I was the first to advocate putting the WAAC in the Army. The sentiment against women in the Army was great. If at some time you are interested in reading the debate you will find it in the Congressional Record of April 27, 1942. I was literally driven off the floor. Miss Bloom is wrong in saying she is not recognized as a Veteran simply because of a technicality. No, it was quite deliberate that only those WAACs who did enter the WAC would receive Veteran's considerations. I pleaded with my colleagues in the Conference Committee not to make this distinction, but the zeal of the branches of the Service and the zeal of the Veterans Organizations prevailed and the distinction was made."

More letters arrived from Congressmen Hugh D. Scott, Jr. of Pennsylvania, Carl Hinshaw of California, Oren Harris of Arkansas, Harris Ellsworth of Oregon, George Smathers of Florida, Eugene J. Keogh of New York, Augustine B. Kelly of Pennsylvania, Claude I. Bakewell of Missouri and Speaker Joseph W. Martin of Massachusetts, all pledging support of the Bill on my behalf.

My most bitter battle was about to begin.

Chapter 38

The early summer of 1948 was a time of great fun. I went home on several weekends and could enjoy being with Mom, Dad, Marilyn and Harold, who loved to picnic. I especially liked Lake Sebago, a recreational area about fifteen miles from Suffern. During our childhood years, Joey and I used to ride our bikes there. I never owned a bicycle, but Joey made a makeshift model for me by removing parts from his old bikes. Lake Sebago was a popular area where NYU and other institutions sponsored summer camps. Our picturesque picnic surroundings included a shoreline surrounded by hiking paths, tables and barbeque grills.

While Dad and Harold fished, Mar would wheel me down to the lake where I would ease myself out of my chair, slide into the water and swim a far distance out to the ladder alongside the raft where I could hold on to the steps and rest. Years ago I used to climb on the raft and sunbathe before returning. Now when I tried to hike myself back into the wheelchair, more often than not, some kind stranger would rush over to assist, but if he or she refused my instructions I'd thank the person and keep struggling until I got up myself. Mar was in the seventh month of pregnancy and there was no way I would allow her to do any lifting.

When the men returned, Dad immediately went to the grill to cook the "best" hamburgers and hot dogs; Mom contributed by bringing her inimitable potato salad and cole slaw. On many occasions our younger cousins came to visit my parents and couldn't wait to go to Lake Sebago with them.

One Sunday afternoon Dad and Harold wanted to remain and fish, saying they would come home with one of Dad's friends. I drove Mom and Mar home, sitting on a towel because of my wet suit. The windows were wide open, and my hair was blowing in the soft breeze. As we pulled into the driveway, the mirror reflected a large black car pulling in front of our house.

Marilyn was beside herself "Neet," she said excitedly, "It's Herm!"

"What?" I hadn't seen my first love since the day we parted shortly after my eighteenth birthday. He had married a woman I knew from our old neighborhood.

Within a minute Herm was leaning in the window staring at me. Mom and Marilyn greeted him, then disappeared quickly into the house. The two of us stared teary eyed without uttering a word. Herm spoke first. "Nita, I was sick over what happened to you. You look wonderful. You're apparently coping?"

"I'm doing fine. Excuse my appearance. . ."

"I want you to know how badly I felt when Mom told me you were injured. I wanted to fly to you at once but . . . "

"I understand. I wanted to see you in the worst way, too. Your final words were that our parting was irrevocable." I forced myself to smile, "How is your wife?"

"Joan's fine. More relaxed since I got out of the army. She's in the car. I had just turned the corner when I saw you pull in. I had to see you. I'm very thankful you're in good health. Nita, were you swimming?" I nodded. "That's terrific. I have every confidence that whatever path you take, you'll be successful. Darl— er, uh, Nita, you must have had a really bad time."

"Things were rough in the beginning." The pain that I was feeling in seeing him again was almost too much to bear. My heart pounded until I was afraid that I would have an attack. I thought I would faint, but somehow I summoned my courage enough to say, "You best go back to your wife now. Thanks for stopping by. Peace be with you."

"You too." We drank in every look, every feature, every memory.

Goodbye. Goodbye forever. I remained in a stupor. . . As soon as Herm's car left, Mom and Mar flew out to take my wheelchair from the trunk. John had taught me how to pull up on its wheels to lessen the burden on someone who was assisting me up steps and the three of us took the two steps easily, making it very easy for Mom and Mar. No one said a word. As soon as we entered the living room, I couldn't control the flood of tears. Marilyn held me. She, too, had adored Herm. No one said a word. I was relieved to return to New York the next day.

The following Friday I happily reported my academic accomplishments to John when we were having dinner. "I got A's, B's and only one C in biology this past semester." He shook his head smiling proudly. I put down my fork, and continued, "Johnny, in a couple of weeks you'll be starting your last camp season at Matheny's."

John nodded in agreement. "You know it will be good to work outdoors, away from Matheny's nasty looks. I'm counting the days until December." We clinked our water glasses to December.

My first course in summer school at NYU was thoroughly enjoyable: I breezed through conversational Hebrew. As a youngster attending Hebrew school, I never enjoyed the language because it was all biblical and never held my interest compared to this course, which was alive and fun. We learned to speak Hebrew, as well as to sing at least twenty modern Israeli songs that we belted out like true Israelis.

I went home for a few days to stay with Marilyn and Harold. When Dad drove me back to New York it was the first time we were in the car alone. I tried to make light conversation, but it wasn't easy. I knew what he was thinking; I wasn't in the mood for his machinations.

Upon my return, I received a short letter from Mrs. Rogers acknowledging receipt of my letter of June 1948, enclosing two newspaper articles and pictures of the wheelchair demonstrations by veterans in New York City. I recall that it took every bit of my strength to get to the congested street where the demonstrations took place. I struggled to flag a taxi to take me from the Broadway Central Hotel to the place of action. These demonstrations were very important to emphasize the need for service connected spinal cord injured veterans to receive monetary benefits for specially constructed housing. Mrs. Rogers stated that the Senate acted favorably on the House Bill, HR 4244. I felt my presence was another voice in favor of the Bill. Her letter also referred to HR 143 stating that no action had been taken. She ended, "I sincerely hope that legislation proving beneficial to your case may be enacted." Patience, I kept reminding myself.

My mother's unmarried sister, Aunt Mary, with whom I had

a close relationship, was an attractive petite brunette. She lived in the city and enjoyed a good position with a well-known lingerie firm. She was in her late forties, but very naive and unsophisticated in the ways of the world—especially when it came to men. Therefore we were pleased when she began seeing Martin, a gentle and creative man, who was always tinkering with some kind of weird invention. Much to our amazement, the couple announced they would be married in mid-August. Aunt Mary made me doubly happy by inviting John to the wedding.

John drove me to the hotel in Suffern where the festivities were to take place. My relatives were friendly to John, with the exception of my father who ignored him completely. Our rabbi, Moses Rosenthal, performed the ceremony, and we all thought it would never end. When champagne toasts were offered, Marilyn goaded John into taking a glass.

"You have to toast Aunt Mary," she insisted. I didn't say a word. I had never forewarned Mar that alcohol was a problem for John. He took the drink whispering that it was of no consequence. I nodded, but I wasn't consoled.

Before the reception, Mar, Harold and John ran upstairs to where Aunt Mary and Martin were spending the night and tied their bed sheets tight as a drum. We had dinner in the hotel's "Green Room" ending with toasts to Aunt Mary and Martin for a long and happy life.

The semester progressed a lot more smoothly. John allowed me to use my wheelchair when I went home or if I visited anyone where steps were involved, but he insisted that as soon as I returned to the Broadway Central and school, I only use my braces and crutches.

One gal at NYU befriended me in the ladies' room and occasionally the two of us had lunch. It was still a hassle getting into the cafeteria, but it was much easier since my new acquaintance, Hazel, carried my tray. I appreciated her kindness immensely. Several students and I had a "Hi, how you doing?" relationship. My study habits improved considerably and, always to my amazement, the studying went quickly.

Ross Baker offered me a part time job at the switchboard on the mornings or afternoons when I didn't have classes. The extra money was helpful. In the beginning I would invariably disconnect the person or interrupt one party connecting him to the wrong

line. Eventually I caught on and was ever thankful, but far be it
for me to say I was in any way, manner, shape, or form, a telephone operator.

In May of 1948 Mar and Harold were expecting their first
baby. I could hardly wait to become an aunt, but I was determined
about one thing: the child would never call me "aunt." Aunt Flo
had given me permission to call her Flo right from the beginning.
"Don't make me feel old." She demanded. I remembered how
pleased I was to be on a first name relationship with an aunt and
made up my mind about this as a young girl.

Once in a while Aunt Mary came downtown, although not as
much since she was married. Usually she brought me one of her
hand-me-downs, stayed for an hour and on occasion remained for
an early dinner. Mom and Dad visited once in a while. Their visits
were disturbing; I always had to be on guard not to mention John.
Occasionally we went over to Katz's for deli. John would remain
in his room, but, when they left, would magically appear within
five minutes of their departure.

When I visited Mar she gave me a blow by blow description
of Dad coming over every morning to bring her freshly baked
buns, but it didn't take long until he started on his usual tirade
about my relationship with John, and she would have to ask him
to leave. Dad wasn't at all perturbed and would return the next
morning with the sweet rolls and the same conversation. It hurt
that Mar had to defend me against Dad.

Friday night was always a highlight. It was when John returned. We found many places to enjoy, mostly museums that
were free. On an occasion we took in a movie; but we rarely
purchased tickets for the theatre because John could only afford
the balcony, and I didn't appreciate it because it meant he had to
carry me up many steps. Music, the theatre, ballets were my biggest pleasure, and I vowed to have more of a cultural life when he
became director of the proposed clinic.

John lamented, "I never had time or friends who were interested in music or art. I love being with you Pupsie, for I'm certain
many new horizons will open for me." He lit a cigarette, "Butchy
always looks at me with those incredible eyes. I know he's asking
about you, Nita. I always give him some tidbit to elicit his inimitable smile. His parents live in Rockland County. I'm almost certain he'll be coming to the new clinic."

"Oh, darling, I can hardly wait. What a marvelous future we'll be facing. You, the director and me; your faithful employee." We giggled like two happy kids licking ice cream cones.

From time to time John was also meeting with the leaders of the Rockland County Society group, preparing for his job as the new director. John knew at least five children who were coming and one of his first projects would be to recruit new clients as soon as he was free of Burnt Mills.

I signed up for two more courses, and in the beginning of September, I went home for a couple of weeks before school began, hoping I would be there when my sister gave birth. Harold worked as an engineer during the night shift at Wright Aeronautical. On September 9th, my sister, Midge, and I were having dinner at a local restaurant. Marilyn went to the ladies room and raced back to the table all flushed.

"Please, Midge, my water just broke. I have to go to the hospital right now!"

"Oh my golly. Let's go." Midge drove her to Good Samaritan and we sped back to their apartment to await my brother-in-law. We rehearsed the scenario. Harold was very innocent, shy and reserved: we didn't want to frighten him. He returned about midnight. As soon as he saw Midge's car in the driveway, he raced down the steep hill, yelling into our window, "I'm off to the hospital," then ran back up the hill and all the way to the hospital. He didn't need our assistance at all.

At eight o'clock the next morning my brother-in-law called. "You have a redheaded niece."

I was flabbergasted. Redheads were my passion. "Oh, golly. That's great. How is Marilyn?'

"She's fine. But, Neet, I have to confess, the baby doesn't have a single hair on her head. I was only kidding."

"Oh, that's okay. I'm thrilled. Just thrilled. Are you sure Mar's okay?" My baby sister having a baby—wow. I couldn't wait to see her, touch her, hold her. I couldn't wait to call John.

"What's her name?"

"Ellen."

"Sounds like music. Ellen. I can't wait to see her. All my love to Mar."

Several days later two men from the Ramapo Valley Democratic club paid me a visit while I was at my parents' house.

"Miss Bloom, we have a wonderful opportunity for you. Would you be willing to run for Rockland County Comptroller?"

"Oh my goodness. I'd love to, but I don't have any experience in accounting, and besides, I attend school at NYU and I couldn't sacrifice my education."

"Oh, no, we know all about that," one of the men said as a matter of fact. "We have no intentions of asking you to stop anything that interferes with your education in New York. You'll have plenty of assistance, besides this position pays very well. You only have to appear once in a while and believe me, you'll have more help than you need. We need to get the Republican incumbent out. As a disabled veteran, we feel you'll succeed."

I wasn't at all happy about being chosen because I was a disabled veteran, but I was pleased that I was being considered a "veteran" by my fellow Democrats. I was struggling so hard with finances that I knew if things didn't improve I would have to stop school. The extra money was very enticing: I would have no problem handling my expenses. "Thank you very much. I need a little time to think it over. How about if I let you know in a few days?"

When Dad drove me to New York the next morning for my fall semester, I didn't discuss the subject. I called John that night, and he thought it might work out if what they promised "wasn't baloney." Then I called Dad, who was excited about the whole idea—obviously he had prior knowledge.

The fall semester included a class on traffic control, which necessitated my going to and from night court one night a week, and the course presented difficulties. I had to wait on the corner to hail a taxi and I was scared out of my wits. Sometimes there was no one around and it took ages until one stopped. Although the classes were fascinating I was relieved when they were over.

One day I came back to the hotel to find a surprise waiting for me in the lobby. "Mom, how delightful. Is Dad parking the car?"

"No, I came by myself. Took the bus downtown after I did a little shopping for the store."

Her voice sounded exhausted, her face was pale. Something was wrong. To come all the way downtown by herself? "How about we go in for a cup of coffee?"

"No, honey, let's go up to your room?"

Oh, I thought, this was really going to be serious. I proudly swung through the lobby, onto the elevator, down to my room. My mother was impressed because I'd had little opportunity to show off in my parent's small home.

"You're doing beautifully, Neet."

I sat on the bed. Mom pulled up a chair. "Mom, I owe it all to John. He has been an angel in my life."

Mom didn't smile. She lowered her sad eyes. When she looked up, they were filled with tears. "Daddy said to tell you that if you persist in seeing John, we can't see you anymore. We are very much against your going with a gentile, and in addition, one who is married."

Tears rolled down my cheeks. I couldn't look at my mom. I weighed my response carefully not to agitate her further. "Mom, I took an oath once: never to date a gentile man again. Certainly I never planned to meet a man like John. Not only has he helped me therapeutically but he has befriended me in more instances than I can relate. I couldn't help falling in love with him." I had to restrain myself from telling her that when the time came, we planned to be married. My mother's face was white. "Mom, John doesn't belong to any religious institution. Can't you persuade Daddy? You don't have to tell him every single thing. It's going to be a long struggle. John is still married although eventually he plans to get a divorce. Besides I have to get my degree. Did you hear that John is going to be the director of the Rockland County Center for the Physically Handicapped in Suffern after the first of the year?"

"Ben told Dad, but that doesn't change his mind. Neet, he is very upset about this relationship. Perhaps it's for the best that we have a separation for the time being." The poor woman looked desperate. I fought back my desire to fight for my own happiness. Sadly, I said goodbye to my mother.

A letter dated November 4th came from the Veterans Administration, Board of Veterans Appeals concerning my appeal for a new car as a veteran. The evidence fails to show that Anita Bloom, by reason of her service in the Woman's Army Auxiliary Corps, served in the "active military service" or acquired a military status that would establish basic eligibility for benefits under Public Law 663, 79th Congress, as amended. She, therefore, is not a veteran of World War II within the requirements of the law. The appeal is denied.

Reading those words I became very weak, but quickly gritted my teeth and became more determined than ever to fight for what I knew was right for me; my veterans' rights. I agonized for weeks that I had to fight harder to convince the U.S. Government to correct my status. I decided to take positive action and wrote a letter to General Eisenhower, the U.S. Military Chief of Staff. I thought this was the best way to plead my case.

On December 13 I received a response from Mr. George E. Brown, Director, Veterans Claims Service. He stated "your communication has been referred for consideration and reply to the office having jurisdiction, the Veterans Administration. Regional Office . . ."

On December 24th John made his last payment to Matheny. He came into New York and we celebrated into the wee hours of the night. The following week we rang in 1949 with Mar, Har and a couple of close friends.

On January 5th, 1949, John was welcomed as the new director of the Rockland County Center for the Physically Handicapped. I had no idea how he would cope with all the hard work. Within a short time he found available space in the basement of the Suffern High School and he hired workmen to partition walls to include classrooms for speech therapy, occupational rooms, and a physical therapy area. He began scouting the county and located several more cerebral palsied children, some who had been hidden for years. He hired a secretary, a speech therapist and occupational therapist. It was the most exciting time of his life. The downside was in not being able to share the wonderful news with my parents; but even worse, was not being allowed to see them. Mar, Har, and Midge celebrated with us.

Over my winter holiday I spent a few days with my sister. Mar taught me how to diaper, change, and feed Ellen her bottle. I was beside myself with joy.

Was it possible, I kept thinking, that such a miracle could happen to me?

Chapter 39

If it weren't for the courses that kept me busy day and night, I would have suffered a nervous collapse. Dad and Mom continued their boycott; the only news I had from home was when I spoke to Marilyn or my mom's sisters. John pleaded with me to keep faith, certain that my dad would relent before we were married.

Equally disturbing was the cost factor: I lived from hand to mouth. The Broadway Central charged $50 per month for my room; I had to pay $20 a week for taxi service to and from NYU and $6 for a bellboy to transport me to and from the Old Cooper Union annex of NYU for a night course. I tried skimping on lunches by merely eating a piece of fruit. At least I drank the required amount of water. The only source of compensation I had was $141.00 from the U. S. Employee's Compensation Commission in addition to the monthly stipend from the National Council of Jewish Women. I was at my wit's end as to how in the world I could continue—certainly not from the ten dollars I received when I occasionally manned the switchboard. Since I lost the election by less than 300 votes, the job offered to me by the Democratic Party of Suffern did not materialize. In early 1949 I felt that I was on a see-saw. One minute my spirits were soaring and the next they were dashed.

I received a letter from Robert Moss, executive secretary of the Eastern Paralyzed Veterans' Association at the end of January 1949 stating, ". . .enclosed you will find your 1949 membership card. You are now eligible for all the benefits (in theory, but not actually), which members of that organization are entitled to."

At long last I was at least considered to be a veteran by a national veterans' organization. A few weeks later, Congressman Sol Bloom sent an uplifting letter stating that he had introduced, on my behalf, HR 1453. He enclosed a copy of the Bill. My hopes were dashed within days when I received a letter from Congressman Emanuel Cellers, chairman of the Committee on the Judiciary, stating, "HR1453 cannot receive favorable consideration for the reason that it comes within the jurisdiction of the Employees Compensation Commission and under the rules of our committee no consideration shall be given private legislation which is covered by this act."

My spirits hit rock bottom. Several days later another letter came from Katherine St. George enclosing Bill HR291 which provides veterans benefits based upon service as a WAAC. She wrote that she would support either her Bill or the one that Sol Bloom had introduced. I prayed that either one would be effective.

Other actions supported my cause despite the lack of government action. Richard Schneiderman, adjutant of Post 859 American Legion in Suffern, forwarded me a letter he had received in response to his letter supporting HR1453 to Congressman Emanuel Cellers. Again came the response stating that this Bill would be rejected.

It looked as if nothing good was going to come from all my hard work. I received sympathy from Senators and Congressmen but no action. I was getting depressed over the whole situation. In desperation, I wrote to Dr. Rusk again, asking for his assistance.

I informed Dr. Rusk at the *Times* of HR1453, giving him the unpleasant picture and asking if he would be so kind as to send letters to the various members of the House Judiciary sub-committee on my behalf. Fourteen letters were forwarded to me all pledging the Congressmen's cooperation.

In February I began my spring semester. I had been a leading lady in most of my High School plays, and I was certain that when I enrolled in a public speaking course for the spring semester it would be a breeze. I was wrong. I had never projected my voice from a wheelchair—a totally different experience. I couldn't open my mouth for several minutes for fear I would shout. Finally I sputtered a few garbled words.

"Miss Bloom, your voice must be heard by everyone in the room. Anyone who doesn't hear Miss Bloom, raise your hand," the professor instructed.

I tried again and again, embarrassed by all the hands that flew up. Taking a few deep breaths to clear my throat, I started again and persisted until I began to articulate properly. A few times I noticed a hand or two but I didn't get nervous and proceeded to concentrate on projecting and looking at the students until I was finished with my little talk about the joy of living in the Greenwich Village area. At the end of the course, I was pleased to receive an A. On the other hand, math was a tough sweat—I was thankful to get a C- and even more surprised to receive a B in history because I had been totally bored in high school, merely getting by with an average C plus.

In early March of 1949, Justice Benjamin Shalleck, a noted judge of the municipal court of New York City, responded to a letter I had written him vis a vis one of his close friends, stating that ". . .with the unfortunate death of our very great friend Congressman Sol Bloom we will just have to bide our time and see what steps are necessary to help you out of your dilemma." How sad it was that I could never meet the man who was so sensitive to my plight. I had to force myself to eat and to go to school.

One Monday evening, I was reading the N.Y. *Post*. Oh, my golly, I said to myself, and gulped down the scrambled eggs. I grabbed my crutches and swung through the lobby as quickly as possible to return to my room to call John. I almost fell on the floor before reaching the phone. "Johnny, please, oh please, say you can come into New York Friday night."

"Pupsie, I have an important meeting with the Board. What's up?"

"Congressman Emanuel Celler is speaking at one of the synagogues on the lower east side this Friday night. He's chairman of the House Judiciary committee. Can you believe? Oh, my God, I have to go."

"Neet, I don't want you going down to that section alone. I'll postpone the meeting. Sweetheart, don't you worry, I'll be there."

"You're wonderful."

"No, you are. Love you, hon." The tone of his voice never failed to arouse me. "Shall we have dinner before or after?"

"After. I'll be too excited to eat."

"On second thought, I'll come in early and we'll have a light bite. If we're still hungry after, we'll stop in the Village. Who knows, we might be celebrating. Stay sweet."

John was so kind. If only my dad would allow himself to see beyond his personal prejudice.

Friday evening John and I had a sandwich in the hotel and

afterwards he drove downtown for the lecture. There was no way I would have managed that feat alone. Ten imposing steps faced John, who took them like a breeze. We arrived about fifteen minutes before the service started. I found the Conservative Service familiar to me. Soon John sat proudly, taking pleasure in hearing me sing the Hebrew songs I had known since childhood. Several congregants nodded approvingly.

After the service, Congressman Celler was introduced. He was a man with an imposing demeanor. Tall and aristocratic in appearance, he spoke compassionately about the latest information regarding his recent trip to Israel, urging the audience to contribute as much as possible to the needy country. The lecture lasted about forty five minutes and afterwards many people encircled the bimah to question him. I waited until everyone left. He noticed me and came down the steps.

Sitting straight as a ramrod, I stretched my neck as high as I could in order to speak to him directly. "Sir, I was very impressed with your description of Israel. I hope one day to visit. I have to confess that I came here for only one reason—a personal matter. May I have a few minutes of your precious time?"

The man sighed for a moment. "Yes, if you make it brief. It's been a long day."

I introduced myself and proceeded to give a bird's eye view of my problem about being denied my veteran's status. "For anything you can do to help, I would be eternally grateful."

He was silent for what seemed like forever. "Miss Bloom, I think I can arrange for you to appear before the Judiciary House sub-committee for a hearing on your Bill. May I have your address?"

Wonder of wonders, I thought, as I opened my purse to find a notebook for the necessary information, and thanked him profusely for his consideration.

I didn't say a word to John until we were safely back in the car. For a moment I sat motionless and although John was totally unaware of the verdict, he respected my silence. "Hon,"I shouted at the top of my lungs.

"Yes, yes," he said, "yes."

"He's going to send a letter inviting me to testify before the sub-committee." We went to our favorite little spot in the village to celebrate and talked for a couple of hours, planning my presentation before the Judiciary committee.

I could not resist the urge to call my parents on Sunday.

"Dad, it's me."

"I know. How are you?" I could sense his agony.

"I'm fine. I'm finishing my freshman year now. Dad, I called to tell you and Mom I'm going to be invited to the House Judiciary sub-committee for a hearing on my Bill."

"Dat's good. I'll tell Momma. Don't get your hopes up. Thanks for calling. Good luck."

Tears flowed unceasingly. John crushed his cigarette racing over to cradle me in his arms. "Someday he'll forgive you. Believe me. You are my life, and I promise I'll do whatever it takes to make you happy."

During the next few weeks I was on pins and needles waiting to hear from the sub-committee. Several weeks later I received a letter inviting me to appear before the committee on April 20th; then I was devastated a week later when another letter from them arrived. My hands shook as I read the contents. The hearing was changed to May 4th. At long last I was invited to appear for a hearing on my claim before the House Judiciary sub-committee and to bring witnesses, if any, to testify on my behalf. The meeting would take place in Room 327 of the Old House Office Building. I was truly elated. I felt my dream would be realized once the subcommittee heard the facts from me.

My former WAAC buddy, Helen, and I always kept in close touch. She had married and was living in Virginia. When I brought her up to date about the upcoming hearing, she insisted that I stay with them, anxious for me to meet her husband, John. In addition, I wrote to my former social worker Rhoda Golub at the Washington VA to ask if she could join me, as well as the Eastern Paralyzed Association, Congresswoman Katherine St. George, Edith Nourse Rogers, and Congressman Jacob Javits.

John, God bless his heart, offered to pay for my plane trip. Helen wrote back to say that she and her husband felt it would be more convenient for the two of us to stay at the Hay Adams Hotel in Washington which would be closer to the Old House Building.

This would be my golden opportunity. I had to win. If I succeeded, it would open the doors to all the other deserving members of the WAAC.

I closed my eyes. Are *you* listening?

Chapter 40

The trip to Washington was causing me all kinds of anxieties. I felt certain the plane would crash. My stomach was tight and I was perspiring profusely when John drove me to the airport, knowing he would have to carry me up many steps onto the plane. As always, the passengers gawked like I came from Mars. At one point John stumbled—I thought I would have a stroke. He finally plopped me on my seat, but it hurt me to see what it must have taken out of him to get me on the plane. I was a wreck. The shocked expression of an elderly gentleman across the aisle frightened me; I thought for sure he was going to have a heart attack.

John opened his wallet. "Hon, here's $50 to buy champagne for everyone."

"But you've already paid for this trip," I protested and he shrugged off. "Do you really think I stand a chance?"

"Once the Congressmen hear your story first hand, I know you'll convince them to do the right thing."

I reached up to kiss him. "You're always on my side, sweetheart."

"Will you be okay?"

I gave him the thumbs up sign. "I'm fine, Johnny, just fine."

Dr. Rusk had cautioned about getting my hopes up too high. "The subcommittee has already rejected the Bill. Chances are the full committee won't consider it favorably either. There's one chance in a million that your personal appearance could change their minds."

Yes sir, that's what I'm counting on. One chance.

As soon as the doors closed, I began to panic. Who would take me off the plane? Would my wheelchair be in one piece? What if—what if? The motors revved up and, after what seemed an inordinate amount of time, the plane took to the air. I should have been frightened from the way my heart was pounding, but I was really thrilled because I finally had a chance to plead my case. In a few minutes we soared above the clouds. If ever there was a place called heaven, I felt I was there, floating on a blanket of cotton candy. Forty five minutes passed quickly, and in a short time I could see the majesty of our nation's Capitol with its magnificent tall, white buildings surrounding the city. All at once I became petrified. How would we land? What if . . .but there wasn't time for "if's." The wheels screeched down and the plane hit the ground hard as I lurched forward to grab the sides of my seat, holding on for dear life. Good Lord, was I thankful that I had plenty of time to collect myself because all the other passengers departed first.

Half an hour later two men came for me. "Miss. We're going to carry you down the steps."

How nice, I'm going to get off the plane at last. "I would appreciate that very much." They carried me off the plane like a sack of potatoes. Someday, I promised myself, I would give lessons on how to carry a wheelchair-bound individual from a plane.

Helen, looking more beautiful than ever, met me at the airport and drove to her attractive apartment in Virginia, where I met her husband John for the first time. We enjoyed a glass of wine with caviar and crackers, a gourmet dinner that she had evidently prepared earlier, and a lavish French pastry dessert served hot with cinnamon apples and ice cream. I caught up with a blow by blow description of their wedding that was held in a castle in France that I wasn't able to attend. Her husband told me about his future position with the American Embassy in Washington.

Later, he bid me good luck and Helen drove me to the historic Hay Adams Hotel where she had reserved a suite for the two of us. The hotel in the lobby was decorated with many fascinating pieces of Victorian furnishings. Our sitting room was indeed splendid, although much too plush and overcrowded with furniture, making it difficult for me to get around. Helen and I spent most of the night reminiscing and laughing about the good old days in the WAAC, talked about Connie, her parents and her marriage until Helen saw I was exhausted and suggested a leisurely hot bath.

The large tub was a blessing, but I was nervous until I figured out how to get into the huge thing: I put my legs over the side and slowly edged myself down without the assistance of any bars. I enjoyed the luxurious bath but almost killed myself getting out. I was totally exhausted and fell asleep as soon as my head hit the pillow—but not for long. Suddenly I woke and the rest of the night I tossed and turned: suppose I lost my voice—suppose I become tongue tied? Suppose, suppose, suppose—until finally sleep took a firm hold.

On May 4 I awoke and promised Helen to take an optimistic attitude. I was confident that my presentation of the whole truth would convince any jury to do the right thing. The day of reckoning was granted to me so I could demonstrate to the powers that be that my patriotism was genuine, that I had had every intention of returning to the WAAC and most certainly would have reenlisted in the WAC.

Helen had ordered room service, including juice, bacon and eggs and delicious fresh-brewed coffee, which came elegantly served with a fresh rose in a silver vase. I almost refused, but the delicious aromas lured me and I ate every drop on my plate.

After breakfast I put on the navy gabardine suit John and I had selected from Orbachs' with a navy and white striped silk blouse, navy leather pumps, pocketbook and kid gloves to match.

"Nita, you look very attractive," Helen said approvingly.

"Thanks. I tried. By the way, you do, too. Helen, I don't want you to pay for all of this luxury. You and John just got back from Europe. I know you have many expenses . . . I can contribute my share. . ."

"Nita, I want to do this for you. If ever there was a deserving woman entitled to become a veteran, it's you." John took no issue at all. "He wants to do this for you as much as I do. No thanks ever. Promise?"

"I don't know what to say. You're too generous."

"Are you ready?"

"As ready as I'll ever be."

"Then we're off for Nita's day in Congress."

The bellboy hailed a taxi to take us to the Old House Office Building and the driver dropped us off at the mouth of a pedestrian tunnel near the Capital. Helen pushed my wheelchair as fast as her feet would go through the darkness, to the elevator and finally to the third floor. Butterflies swirled in my stomach. Try as

I might, I could not relax. Finally we arrived at the House hearing room #327.

No one had arrived. Helen and I took seats near the front. The room was very impressive with a huge cathedral ceiling encircled by a dome with small windows shooting rays of sunlight down inside. Deep wine mahogany leather chairs were placed around a huge desk that rested on a long raised platform. Helen said that she would take a seat among the spectators' chairs to allow me a few minutes of privacy.

I sat quietly at the side of one of the front rows. That awesome environment was just beginning to have its effect. In a few minutes, I was going to appear before the Congress of the United States of America. Somehow, some way, I had to reverse the verdict in order to be acknowledged as a veteran and be eligible for all the benefits and never, never become a burden to anyone for as long as I lived. I had to have money, not only for a college education, which the GI Bill of Rights guaranteed, but also for the high cost of living my disability created. I never wanted John to go into debt on my account. I had to win.

Mrs. Golub arrived, greeting me warmly, as did Congresspersons Jacob Javits and Katherine St. George, and two representatives from the Eastern Paralyzed Veteran's Association. At the stroke of 10:05AM six Congressmen came in and took their places.

The Honorable William Byrne of N.Y. state presided, giving the opening statement, then called upon Katherine St. George to introduce the nature of my presence which she did eloquently: "She is young and she is brave; she does not want to be a charge; she does not want to beg. But she feels that had this same thing happened to her in September instead of March 1943, when the WAAC was taken into the regular Army, she would have her veteran's status, which was all she wanted or desired." Mrs. St. George went on to say that ". . . passage of this Bill would not start a precedent because there were very few cases of this kind that would ever come up."

"My dear friends," continued Mr. Byrne, "we have for consideration before us, I believe, a Bill that the late Mr. Bloom introduced back in January 13, 1949, known as HR 1453 for the relief of Anita Bloom. . . We are now ready to hear her and her witnesses."

The following statements are taken from the actual hearing, a copy of which was provided to me by Mrs. St. George.

Addressing me, Mr. Byrne said, "Speak right up and tell us the things that you have in your good mind."

I thanked the committee for the privilege of appearing before them and proceeded to state the facts, beginning with my induction on January 28, 1943 when I was sent to Fort Oglethorpe, Georgia, for six weeks of basic training.

"On completion of the training I was sent to the Steven F. Austin College, Nacogdoches, Texas. On the morning of March 12, I awoke with a stinging pain in my thumb. I immediately reported to sick call. There was no doctor; there was no nurse on duty that morning.

"A WAAC Sargent assumed that I had an infection, and she picked up a razor blade and incised my thumb. She gave me some Epsom salts and told me to soak my finger in boiling water. Even the military doctor on the base was uninterested until the infection got worse and the pain unbearable. Then they sent me to a civilian physician in town."

Mr. Byrne interrupted, "Who was the doctor they sent you to?"

I simply replied, "Dr. Nelson in Nacogdoches."

I continued to explain that for five and a half weeks I suffered and although the regular army general hospital (Harmon General Hospital) was only seventy miles away in Longview, Texas, they did not send me there. I was kept at the WAAC post, which was at the college.

I told them that on April 6, the morning that my class was to have its picture taken for graduation, I began to feel very weak, and I sat down while the photographer was getting ready.

"That evening I began to run a temperature, and my buddies called the infirmary and reported that I had a temperature, but I was ordered to get up and walk over to the infirmary instead of remaining in my barracks.

"I was kept there for a couple of days, and the pain was getting worse all the time.

"On April 8, the WAAC attendant told me that I was finally going to a civilian hospital. She tossed my clothes at me and told me to get up and get dressed, and as I did, I reached over to pick up my shoes. I fell off the bed and I did not have any feeling from my waist down. I was put in a truck and taken to a civilian hospital."

Mr. Byrne interrupted again, "Sent where?"

"To the civilian hospital, Memorial Hospital in Nacogdoches, Texas. I remained there overnight, and the next day I was sent by ambulance to Harmon."

"Three hours later, after I arrived at Harmon, they operated on my spine, and when I became conscious, I realized that I was paralyzed from the waist down with complete loss of bladder and bowel control.

"My mother came from Suffern, New York to see me and she learned when she arrived that I would be sent nearer home. Of course that made her very happy. I was very miserable because I wanted to remain in the Army. And of course, I did not realize I was so seriously ill, and the one thing I wanted was to hurry up and get well and go back on duty.

"However as soon as my mother left I was transferred to the Bronx Veteran's Hospital against my will. I never did sign my discharge, not out of stubbornness, but I just wanted to remain in the Army."

I was about to tell something about my arrival in the Veteran's Hospital when I was interrupted again by Mr. Byrne.

"You came up all the way by train?"

"Yes I did."

Mr. Byrne: "From down there?"

"That was on May 29."

"May 29?"

"Yes. After I arrived there, I learned that my jurisdiction came under the Employees' Compensation Commission, which is known today as the Federal Security Agency. They settled my case as a service-connected one and allocated me $91 per month."

At that time, "military benefits meant little to me. I was primarily interested in my physical condition, to get well, and I did not realize that because my jurisdiction came under the Federal Security Agency that I was not considered a veteran. Well, I was there altogether 3 ½ years, but in 1946. . ."

Mr. Byrne questioned. "In the Bronx Hospital for 3 ½ years?"

"Yes."

Mr. Byrne asked. "You are now at home, are you?"

"No, sir; now I am going to New York University."

Mr. Byrne again interrupted. "You are attending New York University?"

"Yes, I am.

"In 1946 the government gave an allotment toward a hand controlled automobile to service-connected paraplegics. I thought that was the most wonderful thing in the world—to be able to get into a car and drive around myself; to get out of this chariot and become independent enough to take my place with other able bodied people. I immediately passed the test for my license. I sent for my car, and I was told that I was not a veteran and, therefore, I am not entitled to any benefits whatsoever."

Mr. Byrne stated, "That is the situation."

"When the WAAC turned over in September 1943, I was lying in bed paralyzed and this is the technicality that makes my case different from all the others.

"I was never asked whether or not I wanted to go into the service; you see, it was a voluntary re-enlistment, and the girls could go in or go out, but I was never even asked whether I wanted to, and, sir, the people around me were more than aware of my intentions. I was proud to be a WAAC and I certainly wanted to reenlist in the regular army. I fought to do it, actually."

Mr. Byrne interrupted, "How old were you at the time that you went into the service?"

"Twenty-one."

"I beg your pardon?"

"Twenty-one years old."

Mr. Bryne asked, "And today you are what?"

"I will be twenty-eight this month."

Mr. Denton asked, "Are you drawing veterans' benefits to go to school?"

"When I moved to attend school, I received $141.00. I am supposed to live on that amount of money. That is all."

Mr. Denton questioned again, "How much do you draw a month now?"

"$141.00 per month."

Mr. Byrne asked, "That is what you get now?"

"That is right."

Mr. Denton asked again, "And if you get Veteran's Benefits?"

I answered, "$360.00 per month; an allotment for a hand-controlled automobile; up to $10,000 for a specially constructed home, which I need desperately; and my school benefits."

I answered his question and many more germane to my status.

Mr. Jennings, "What was the purpose of the Bill?"

Mr. Denton explained the differences between the WAAC and the WAC.

Mr. Jennings, "In other words, the WAAC was a government service, and later she would have been in the WAC if she had not suffered this disability?"

Within a matter of seconds Mr. Jennings proclaimed, "And she is to be given the status of a veteran? I am ready to vote on it."

I broke out into a sweat.

Mr. Frazier: "I am too."

Mr. Jennings: "She has already won her case. I have seen people lose lawsuits talking after somebody has won his lawsuit."

I could hardly believe my ears! I was beaming. Everyone was smiling.

Jennings asked all the people who came on my behalf to speak briefly. As soon as the meeting was adjourned, I ecstatically invited all my supporters to join me for champagne cocktails. Congressman Jacob Javits and Katherine St. George congratulated me, saying they would be happy to come.

I flew into Congressman Celler's office to relate the news and to invite him to join us.

His angry expression stopped me cold. "Did you see anyone pick up a pen?"

"But, sir—?" His face looked like a mean bulldog.

"There are no buts, Miss Bloom. The Bill has to go before the full committee. Chances are the Bill will be thrown out."

"Sir, I don't understand. They said I won my case."

"Your Bill will open the door to thousands of WAACs who did not join the regular army when it became the WAC. No one had the courage to tell you." I stared incredulously at him. Then I bowed my head, straining to control my tears. He suggested I contact members of the Senate to put pressure on the full committee to put a similar Bill in the hopper.

"Thank you for trying," I managed.

It was a sad me when I had to return to inform everyone of the facts. My mouth was dry and my energy was depleted. The people seemed to disappear into the woodworks. I felt like a fool. Helen remained. She was savvy about Washington politics and pleaded with me to go to Senator Ives's office immediately to get a Bill rolling in the Senate.

Katherine St. George invited the two of us to lunch along with Edith Nourse Rogers, who had championed several unsuccessful Bills. Mrs. St. George informed me in the early afternoon that Senator Ives put a companion Bill to HR 1453 (Bill S 1761) and I went to his office to thank him. The Senator tried to buoy my spirits.

"Don't give up, young lady. Keep those bright eyes shining."

It was hard. It was hard.

Later that evening, John met my plane. My phony grin in no way deceived him. "Gosh, Pupsie, what happened?"

I blurted out the details and felt the worse for it. John had made reservations at the Tavern-on-the-Green restaurant insisting we go there. He probably had been saving well before I went in order to afford such extravagance. He looked at me downheartedly, then reached for my hand. "Nita, dearest, you have to stop fretting. You'll make yourself sick over this goddamned Bill."

"John, I'll try not to dwell on the morbid side, but I'm the one who went through the nightmare. I know right from wrong and I have every confidence that my government does, too. I don't intend to stop until the wrong is righted." I took a bite of steak, swallowed and put my fork down. "I promise I won't burden you anymore. I'll take care of my business until it's finished." I forced myself to smile at him. "We have each other. That's the most important thing in the world, isn't it?"

Chapter 41

Shortly after I returned to the Broadway Central Hotel, I received a letter from Dwyer W. Shageue, Council to Senator Ives, who sent several copies of S 1761, which was introduced by Senator Ives on the day of my visit to Washington. As soon as I notified Dr. Rusk about the Bill, he immediately wrote letters to many Senators requesting their support on my behalf. I was gratified to see their responses. All through the month of May, I was heartened by copies from the various correspondents on my behalf: Anthony Cucolo, Rabbi Moses Rosenthal, Suffern Mayor Maurice Lonergan, Bernard Shufelt, president of PVA, Lester Duberstein, Executive Director of N. Y. Jewish War Veterans, and Bernard Weitzer, National Legislation Representative of Jewish War Veterans of the USA.

In early June, Wright Aeronautical, the company for which Harold worked, laid off approximately eight hundred engineers, and he was forced to seek employment elsewhere. My heart broke not only for my brother-in-law, who had what appeared to be a brilliant engineering career with that company, but especially for Mar and the baby. Harold was unsuccessful in locating another engineering job in the area and, within a few weeks, Marilyn called to say they would be leaving for Durham, North Carolina, the city where Harold was raised and attended Duke University and where he would be working for his father in the textile business. The move was to take place in the next couple of weeks. I was crushed. For years I had practically ignored my younger sister. It was only after I joined the WAAC that I began to realize I had a gem of a sister. For the last few years we had been bosom pals. The thought that she and baby Ellen, whom I adored, were going to leave at the end of June was most distressing.

Buckets of sad events filled my calendar. One evening John

came to New York looking very downcast. "My wife promised to give me a legal separation, but every single time she promises to sign the papers and I drive all the way to Jersey, she backs out. I think she's just being spiteful."

"I'm truly sorry, John." It hurt to see John's usually happy countenance display such misery.

"I just don't know. She's playing games with me," drumming his fingers on my night table. Suddenly he squared his shoulders and smiled, "Pupsie, I know that one of these days everything will come up daisies. We can't lose faith, can we?"

I tried to share his upbeat attitude. "It's merely another obstacle." It wasn't easy for me, although I tried my best not to harangue him on the subject. I detested the fact that the man I loved was a married man. I was also uncomfortable to observe that John had started drinking several glasses of beer. He swore that two or three glasses were his limit and pleaded with me not to worry, but I was concerned that he was retreating into his old habits.

The following week, Johnny Weiss from the VA called to invite me out to dinner. He was pleased to see how easily I swung though my crutches. Over dinner he was very tactful not to mention Walt's promise that I would be walking unaided within six months. The young neurologist said I was lucky I wasn't in the VA hospital any more because most of the good physicians had left to return to private practice. His intention was to return to Philadelphia to resume his practice as a neurologist.

My thoughts were constantly centered on whom I should contact to assist me in the Congress. I thought a letter to Eleanor Roosevelt might be helpful concerning the various Bills that were pending. Her response was short and to the point: "I have your letter and I have forwarded it to my son, Franklin, Junior, but I never make any requests of my children on anything." I was surprised when within the week I received a letter from Congressman Franklin D. Roosevelt, Jr. in which he stated: ". . .Be assured that I want to do everything I can to help in your matter, but I have been told that nothing further can be done until additional reports are received from the agencies involved."

I continued to receive updates from both Congresswoman Katharine St. George and Congressman Celler indicating that reports from the Department of the Army and the U.S. Employees

Compensation Commission had not been issued. Mrs. St. George stated: ". . . In an effort to speed the matter, I have requested that reports from both agencies be expedited so that we may get action on this Bill during the present Congress . . ."

In early August, I took the bold step of writing to President Truman. The reply came from the Executive Office of the President, Bureau of the Budget. It stated that my letter to the president was referred to them and went on to say: ". . . the President's schedules do not permit your being granted an interview. Your attention is invited to the fact that further action with respect to HR 1453 is in the hands of Congress."

I was really downhearted when I received the letter from the Executive Office of the President. My disapppointment was compounded by a letter from Congresswoman Katharine St. George on August 15, 1949 stating, "I cannot tell you how disappointed I was when I learned that the Committee on the Judiciary had unfavorably reported HR 1453. I do not believe we should consider this matter closed."

In early September I forgot about my Bill temporarily and took my second plane trip to visit my sister, arriving in Durham by September the tenth, Ellen's first birthday. The thought of flying again held no fear. But when I saw the flight of over a dozen steps facing John, I was downright miserable. In addition, he had to carry me all the way to the rear, almost passing out until he plopped me down into a seat next to the very last row. I mopped his brow hugging him for dear life until he had to get off the plane. As soon as the doors locked, the pilot announced there was a possible hurricane and he might not be able to land at the Raleigh-Durham airport. "Oh, no," I moaned—to no one.

A man sitting in the row behind me shoved an opened bottle of scotch in front of me saying. "Take a swig. Do you good." I did. "I'm from Canada. Where you from? Was that your husband?"

We talked and kept passing the bottle back and forth. I was scarcely aware that an hour and a half had passed or even that we had taken off when the pilot's announcement came to fasten our seatbelts for the landing in fifteen minutes. I thought the end of my life had come when the plane nosed down. I shut my eyes and was totally shocked to find we had landed in Durham, NC, safe and sound.

To my dismay, out in front, alongside my sister, Harold and

Ellen, stood an elderly couple I presumed were my brother-in-law's parents. I wasn't too steady on my crutches. I was ever thankful to the pilot who carried me down the steps where I stood and began ambulating toward everyone very shakily.

"Hi, 'cuse, please, just a lil' drunk," I muttered, explaining the possible dangers that we had faced and how the friendly man in back of me diverted my attention to calm my nerves. Mar laughed uproariously; Harold's family simply gawked.

Ellen was precious. She had saucer brown sparkling eyes and a head full of dark brown curls. She captivated me talking a mile a minute. When she said, "Naayda" in a southern drawl I became her everlasting slave. For Ellen's first birthday Mar baked a cake in the shape of a lamb that she unmolded, spread vanilla icing over and sprinkled with coconut flakes. Everyone raved about her culinary talents, but there was no doubt about who the real star was. Ellen was full of herself, and I predicted right then and there she was destined to become an actress. I had a delightful time and returned to New York sober as a judge. Someday, my dream was, I would fly a hand controlled plane.

After a few courses in summer school at NYU, I registered as a full-fledged sophomore. John was busy combing the county searching for new clients for the Center. One afternoon about five-thirty John called from Suffern to tell me not to eat until he got there."

"Is everything okay?"

"I'll tell you when I get there."

I managed to get most of my homework finished before he arrived, but the suspense as to why he was coming during the middle of the week kept interfering with my concentration.

John arrived carrying a lovely bouquet of flowers. "Pupsie, you'll never believe what's going on. Let's have supper and I'll tell you everything." We went down to the hotel's restaurant, which was certain to be quiet on a weekday.

"Darling, this is a night to celebrate. What will you have?"

"Scotch and water on the rocks."

John had a beer, then proceeded to relate the unbelievable happening. A woman recently visited the Center who had been a former physical therapist in New York, now living in Rockland County. Miss Hawkins became fascinated when she heard about the new clinic in the county, paid John a visit and was very impressed. He invited her to lunch and she related that she had been a therapist to the cerebral palsied son of the Graces of the Grace Lines shipping company. Miss Hawkins then informed him about a thirty-eight-acre piece of property in New City, not far from the clinic, that belonged to the Edwin Gould Foundation, adding that the Graces and Goulds were friends. She further revealed that at one time the property had been a girl scout camp and had not been used for many years.

"She drove me out to see the area Nita, and when we drove onto the property and got out of the car, I stopped dead in my tracks: before me was a well-kept large lawn surrounded by several large log cabin type wooden buildings, which housed sleeping quarters, a long ramp leading to another large building, which I later discovered had a fully equipped kitchen. To my left was the director's cottage, which could be our quarters soon, Pupsie, and it has a huge fireplace in the living room. There's a spacious room for the infirmary and quarters for a nurse. We walked down a long hill to find a good size swimming pool surrounded by trees and several large bushes. Can you picture our children getting their first opportunity to swim? Neet, I was speechless. In my wildest dreams I never imagined anything like it. Oh, yes, I met Herb, the maintenance man who lives with his family in a home on one side of the property. He was friendly and eager to do whatever we needed to get the place in shape for the summer." We were speechless for a few minutes, simply staring at each other unbelievingly.

"Oh, darling, I'm delighted for you and for the Center, but mostly for all the children who desperately need the camp experience, as well as for their parents who need a rest from their responsibilities."

"We will start as a day camp of course and hope to expand into a resident camp in the foreseeable future, to include seriously handicapped children who have never enjoyed a camping experience."

"Are you certain all this will come to pass?"

"Just keep saying your good Jewish prayers."

A few months later, John and I had another opportunity to celebrate: the signed papers of his legal separation. "All we can pray for now is that Rose will find a boyfriend. Pupsie, I'm half out of my mind with hope."

As much as I tried, nothing but nothing could prevent me from worrying. I tried my best to obliterate the dismal thoughts of how long we would have to wait or if, God forbid, because his wife was Catholic, she would ever grant him a divorce. I was more than thankful that studying and writing letters to members of Congress and other influential persons dominated my time.

Eleanor Roosevelt read about my case in the newspapers and wrote that, "she was sympathetic but had no influence in Congress," I was pleased to know she cared.

Congresswoman Katharine St. George introduced another Bill on my behalf, HR 6085. I had received a letter from Franklin Roosevelt, Jr. stating that he was greatly disappointed to receive the Committee's adverse report on HR 1453 and that he had appealed to the Committee for a reconsideration. He also sent me a copy of a very strong letter he had written to Emanuel Celler pleading with him to look more favorably on that Bill.

A letter from Mrs. St. George included copies of the new Bill, HR 6085 which was introduced to the Committee on Veterans Affairs and asked that I start writing to John Rankin, Chairman of that Committee. She further stated that this Bill was applicable to a very limited group to remove as many objections as possible.

I wrote to John Rankin, but his response was not encouraging. He stated that, at the present time, no hearings had been held on this measure and none were scheduled. As a result of all this bad news I started having headaches more frequently, which affected my study habits.

John was busier than ever making plans for the opening of the summer day camp. He called one night enthusiastically, "Herb came up with the perfect name for the camp. How do you like Camp Jawonio? It means independence—an old Indian name. Neet, eventually we will have one of the few camps in the state that take severely disabled children. I'll have to hire an above average staff and I'll be interviewing several counselors soon."

"The name is perfect. Just perfect. Tell Herb I'm proud of him. Have you thought of having an orientation program for the counselors? Working with severely disabled youngsters will be quite different from working at an ordinary camp, don't you agree?"

"Pupsie, you always come up with just the right suggestions."

In October, Franklin Roosevelt Jr. wrote that he had asked Chairman John Rankin to do everything he could to schedule an early hearing on HR 6085. He felt the political climate wasn't encouraging for hearings before January 1950. However, you can be assured "that I'll keep after the committee members and do everything I can to secure an early hearing."

A friend introduced me to Thomas J. Wiley, the Executive Vice President of the Commerce and Industry Association of New York, Inc. Mr. Wiley became interested in my case and told me he would write to his friend Tracy S. Voorhees, Under Secretary of the Army. He sent me a copy of his response in December. Mr. Voorhees's response stated "he would not be of any help in this particular case. If you desire, I will have the case looked into further." However Mr. Wiley said that he could not help through his organization—"but in your case, in which I am tremendously interested, I'd be glad to do so as an individual."

I began to get support from women veterans and on January 21, 1950, I was delighted to hear from Isabelle Biafini, president of Womens' Army Corps-Veterans' Association of Greater New York, chapter #11 in which she informed me: "her chapter had adopted a resolution in support of HR 6085 and she is forwarding a copy to all New York State representatives in Congress and also to the national and local chapters of the WAC-VETs'." She indicated that the legislative committee of her chapter would start a "lobbying" campaign. The resolution from her chapter that was going to the Senators and Congressmen started with, "We, in New York, feel if this Bill is passed by Congress, it will help the cause, not only for the disabled WAACs to whom it applies, but of all former members of the auxiliary corps . . ." She further stated that she was trying to get a mention, along with my name and address, in the organization's newspaper, The *Channel*. This would allow other WAACs who were discharged for a disability to get in touch with me. For me, and all the other WAACs, this action was necessary and right.

I wrote to Congresswoman Rogers concerning the status of my Bill. She recalled the "pleasant" lunch we had together last May and mentioned that she was very "interested in seeing that former WAACs receive veterans' status ". . . the greatest difficulty we face is in getting the Chairman of the Veterans' Affairs Committee to bring up the legislation." Was there no end to this battle?

Support came from strange places—reporters, political friends of Franklin Roosevelt, Jr, all putting pressure on John Rankin to take some kind of action for my plight. People I had met casually who had influence responded positively. Questions that were posed from these acquaintances were sent to Franklin Jr, included the following: "What action can be taken to force the Bill out of Rankin's committee? Is there any particular publicity procedure to follow that will put pressure on the Congress as a whole or the committee members?" On May tenth Roosevelt wrote, "I have again talked with the committee chairman about this Bill and it appears that prospects are not too bright for its early consideration."

Roosevelt had not given up. A week later he pleaded with the committee for early consideration but it did not look good for that session. What else was new?

I met with Mrs. St. George in Goshen, New York in June and we discussed every option possible. I was a sad sack when I left.

I completed another summer program and looked forward to continuing my sophomore year. Letter by letter, we prepared my cause in 1950. There seemed to be a dead-end to my struggle. I was beginning to doubt if anything would ever materialize.

In mid-June camp counselors arrived in New City for their orientation before the campers arrived, and John brought several of the youngsters from the clinic for observation. A few of the counselors could not cope with the serious condition of the children and their malformations. When they first saw the sadly afflicted children they wanted to leave immediately, but John prevailed upon them to stay until orientation was over. After the five-day period, only one young woman left. Camp Jawonio opened the summer of 1950.

I had a week between classes; John was busy around the clock. I scrimped a few dollars so that my friend Midge and I were able to plan a few days in the Berkshires to attend concerts, theater and ballet. John loaned me his car that had hand controls installed. We went swimming, boating, antique shopping, attended the ballet at Jacob's Pillow, the Williamstown theatre, but mostly we went to concerts at Tanglewood. We had the pleasure of watching Serge Koussevitsky present Leonard Bernstein to conduct his first formal concert there.

I was pleased that my energy was high, enabling me to ambulate most of the time. I only used my wheelchair when absolutely necessary. I knew Midge would have enjoyed more physical activities but I was content to enjoy both the comradery and our holiday. The night before we left, I called Mar to find out how she was feeling, because she was due to expect her second baby any day. She sounded in high spirits but cut our conversation short, explaining they were going out for the evening and they were late. I was going home penniless, thankful my money had lasted and more thankful I still had the job as a telephone operator.

Midge and I returned the afternoon of July 31st. Mom came running out to greet us. "Neet, we have another granddaughter, Naomi." I burst into tears. I learned afterward that the moment I had called, Harold was practically dragging Marilyn away from the phone to take her to the hospital. Must have been ESP! Six weeks later John paid for me to fly to Durham to see Marilyn, Ellen and to hold my new fair-haired niece, Naomi.

The desire to have a baby did not cross my mind. John and I had made a pact when we got married: no dogs and no babies.

Chapter 42

One miracle in my life as a paraplegic was my ability to stand on my own two feet. As long as I held on to a stable surface, I could remain in an upright position for a couple of minutes. However, when I stood, my feet were not flat on the floor: I stood on tip toes and I had to be certain there was something solid I could grab before I released the other hand in order to perform whatever duty was necessary. John asked the Center's orthopedist, Dr. Robert Martin, to examine me and he felt I should be fitted with knee high night braces that should bring my feet to a ninety-degree angle—flat on the floor. If that procedure didn't work within a year's time, he would consider remedial surgery. I was fitted for the braces and every night I slept with them. The prosthesis was a drag, but if it worked I wouldn't be a ballerina on point anymore.

On Saturdays when it was sunny, John and I went up to Central Park where I swung through with my crutches further than ever before. We enjoyed the park outdoors, stopping to feed the ducks, or sitting on a bench drinking a coke or simply people watching. Somehow the air seemed purer, and the grass looked greener, all very reminiscent of our country roots.

One afternoon when we went to the park, John parked near one of the walking paths. I got out as I always did and began ambulating for a short distance when all of a sudden, John swooped me up in his arms, planting kiss after kiss on my lips shouting, "You did it, you wonderful angel!"

"Did what?"

"I unlocked your braces before you put them on this morning. I was convinced you didn't need the upper part. Do you know what that means?" John queried. I simply stared unbelievingly, and he repeated himself. "While you were in the bathroom this morning, I unlocked your braces. Your braces were unlocked and you walked." His rich laughter rippled through the bare trees. "I'm going to remove the top of that clumsy waist band so everyone can see your gorgeous figure "

I held onto him for dear life. "I can't believe it. Oh, darling let me down or I'll have to pick you up."

"We are going to have a special dinner tonight." We embraced for the longest time. People giggled when they passed. I ambulated three more times before we left. We had a luscious Italian meal, and when John left my room that night the sun had begun to rise. I never used the waist band or the upper part of my braces again.

In early June of 1951, by some miracle, I eked out enough money to pay for a trip to visit my friend Shirley Rosenbloom, who had married and was then living in Chicago. In the early forties, Shirley, a former WAAC, was brought into the VA in critical condition late one night. Her father had not arrived from Pennsylvania to meet her. Because we were of the same faith, I was asked to keep vigil at her bedside until he arrived. One of the nurses informed me the young woman had a bleeding ulcer and might not live through the night.

Shirley survived, and when her father left in the late afternoons I took his place every evening until I was told she was well on her way to recovery. One night I felt someone crawl into my bed whispering to me, "Are you sleeping?"

"No," I replied softly.

"I'm Shirley Rosenbloom, the WAAC you sat with all those nights. One of the nurses gave me your room number. I wanted to meet you and say thanks from the bottom of my heart."

We yakked until 2:00 A.M., making plans to eat lunch together the next day. Shirley told me that because she had always eaten kosher food before entering the service, she had developed an ulcer because of the trauma of eating non-kosher meat. She was of medium height, I think, (from my wheelchair I wasn't always the best judge of height) with long, thick curly dark-brown hair that fell to her shoulders, a most pleasing voice and a terrific personality. What struck me most about Shirley was her openness and sincerity.

Shirl's mother died when she was very young and she was the caretaker to her elderly father and her two younger brothers, whom she practically raised and adored. We shared the ability to take life as it came and not become maudlin about tragedies over which we had no control. We had a lot in common and talked about everything under the earth, including a young lieutenant she had met in England whom she very much desired to hear from again.

Aunt Flo called one Sunday to say she'd purchased theatre tickets for the three of us for "The Song of Norway." I was thrilled that Flo included Shirl and was out of my mind with the thought of going back to Broadway. It was Shirley's very first exposure to a New York theatre. We donned our best bibs and waited for my aunt to pick us up at the hospital. The first time my aunt handled my wheelchair, I was amazed at her ability to pick it up and lay it in the trunk of the car. The hustle and bustle of Broadway was as thrilling as it had ever been before. However, when we came into the theatre the manager went into shock.

"We cannot allow you into the theatre with her," he said, not looking directly at me, "it's against our policy. We don't carry insurance for—uh—uh her," the man sputtered.

Aunt Flo's lips grew taut. "Sir," drawing herself up to her full five-foot six-inch height to glare at him, "I beg your pardon, we paid for these tickets and you will see to it we are taken to our seats—right now."

The manager sputtered and spewed, finally uttering something about removing one of the seats to accommodate me. I said nothing about my ability to transfer to a seat because I wanted to be sure the next disabled person would not be treated in the same horrendous manner. The show was outstanding. What a fantastic gift Aunt Flo had given us.

In 1949 Shirley married her army sweetheart Joe Bernstein, the same person we had spoken about in the hospital, and the couple moved to the north side of Chicago. Two years later their daughter, Merle, was born, and I was anxious to see all of them. John took me to the airport for my trip to visit Shirley. I arrived tired and starved, but seeing her again was like a shot in the arm. After we embraced, I asked about Merle, and my friend said a neighbor was babysitting her. I had brought my wheelchair for any museums or other sightseeing trips. She and Joe lived in a two-bedroom apartment, but when I entered I panicked—a long flight of stairs greeted me. I wanted to run back to the plane. I had never been faced with this challenge because John had always carried me up the stairs.

Shirley turned white when she saw my face and confessed, "Nita, I didn't want to tell you about the steps for fear you would not come."

I tried to remain calm. "Somehow I'll manage if you can handle my wheelchair."

"Sure. Don't you worry. I'm a pro. I bring Merle's carriage up and down a couple of times a day. Shall I take your chair up before you try the stairs? I'll open the door to the apartment so you can go right in."

"Yes, please," I took a deep breath, I gritted my teeth, got out of my chair to transfer to the first step, inhaled deeply and proceeded to hike myself up step by step until I reached the top. As soon as I reached the landing, I rested a minute, then hiked myself into my chair, stood up and swung through into her home, which was decorated with secondhand colorful and comfortable furniture. Shirley said she would return quickly, and when she did I found myself staring into the face of the most gorgeous child I had seen in a long time. Merle was not only beautiful with compelling hazel brown eyes and a head of soft brown curly hair, but her winsome personality was a delight. I was totally fascinated when Shirley and Merle said prayers before every meal. At first the child frowned at me until I quickly uttered the Hebrew prayers with them. Joe Bernstein and Shirley fit together like a glove; not only was her husband handsome, but he also possessed a keen sense of humor and was caring and sensitive.

On my second day, Shirley announced that we were going to the loop. She drove into the city Monday morning, pulled into a parking lot and we headed into a local radio station. When she presented the tickets, one of the ushers looked at me, "Miss Bloom?"

"Me?" I asked rather dubiously. The young man nodded. I was surprised and looked at Shirley, whose innocent expression didn't fool me. Something odd was going on.

"Please come with me," the usher directed as he pushed my wheelchair over to the right aisle and down toward the front of the theatre.

Promptly at eleven o'clock the curtains were opened and a stocky young man came to the front of the stage with a microphone in his hand to introduce the "Welcome Traveler's Show," a nationally known radio program that I had heard several times. In a few minutes the usher and a helper lifted me up the steps on to the stage and wheeled me over to the host.

"Welcome, Miss Bloom. You're not aware of the circumstances that brought you to this program, are you?" I shook my head. He proceeded to explain that Shirley had written to him about me to request that I appear on his broadcast that day as a guest from New York State. The emcee quickly put me at ease, then proceeded to ask relevant questions about my injury, my years at NYU and my love life. I kept the conversation on the light side, not going into lengthy discussions. I cited the incident when I felt a fly on my leg for the first time. The audience loved it. At the end of my discourse, I was presented with a multitude of gifts including an overnight suitcase filled with several pieces of jewelry and an invitation to lunch at the famous Pump Room. Shirley and I had the time of our lives.

I left for LaGuardia on Sunday and was enveloped in John's safe strong arms and warm kisses. He asked about the trip and almost flipped when I told him about the stairs, but I detected a certain distance in him. I said nothing. Suddenly he pulled off the highway onto the emergency exit. John didn't say a word. He put his face in his hands and kept shaking his head. Cars were whizzing by.

"Hon, what is it?"

"I've done a terrible thing."

"You? What do you mean?"

"You know I hired a new secretary some months ago?" I nodded. "Well, the woman had a lot of domestic problems. She needed a shoulder to lean on. I felt since we had similar marital problems perhaps I could help her. We met several times at the Green Room in the Hotel Lafayette."

"I don't understand. What was terrible?"

"The principal of the Suffern High School, where The Rockland County Center for the Physically Handicapped was housed, called me into his office and told me if I didn't stop meeting with a married woman, I wouldn't be allowed in the school system."

My hands became clammy. I stared at John incredulously. I wondered how long this had been going on? How often he had met with his secretary? Was this something more serious?

"Please, Neet. . ."

"I think we better go before a policeman comes over." He pulled onto the highway. "You haven't finished your story, have you?" I asked curtly. "Just how long have you been seeing this woman? This isn't something new. Since I was away. This has been going on for quite some time, hasn't it?"

"I was hoping to help her. She has serious marital problems— children and all. She needed help. Please, Pupsie, I acted without thinking of the consequences. Mostly the pain to you," covering his face with his hands again.

"John, I've been concerned—and not only about what you just told me. Your drinking habits again. Don't think I haven't noticed. I'm not comfortable at all. John, I think we need breathing space. I really want to go home now." I was drained. This wonderful person had too many problems. I couldn't cope. I needed time alone.

John looked at me unbelievingly. "Pupsie, I love you more than life. I don't ever want you out of my life—my heart—my soul. I did a foolish thing. I meant well. I tried to do a good deed, but it backfired. I beg you. Please forgive me. Please."

John's suffering was more than I could bear. I reached over to pat his hand. "God knows how much you have done for me. We all make mistakes. I'm first on the list. I love you too, and I'm sorry you had this miserable experience." He drove into New York and, at the first opportunity, pulled me to him. We clung to each other like two magnets and he took me to the Broadway Central. I knew he had to get back to Suffern, but he insisted that we have a light supper, and shortly after I bid him goodnight.

When John left, I went into the bathroom, but before entering I looked into the mirror on the door of the bathroom. Before that day it never crossed my mind that John could be unfaithful. But then I saw another side of our situation, a more realistic one: a sad reflection faced me. Face the truth, I mumbled, you're not a woman, not a whole person, and you'll never be fully independent. You'll always have to depend on someone to help you. No matter how well groomed I was, that goddamned wheelchair was the first thing anyone saw. Yes, I was a "cripple." What right did I have to expect anyone to be loyal forever? I had put up a guard by placing limits on our sex life. It was only natural that a normal person might stray once in a while. God help me, I begged, to become more understanding and less critical. I should be thankful for his dedication and love and above all—all that he had done for me."

Chapter 43

After summer classes were over, I was advised to transfer to Hunter College to take the required specialized courses necessary to become a speech therapist. John and I drove to Hunter College on the upper East side; I was pleased to find a smaller college and one much less crowded. I enrolled in the fall of 1951.

Again I was a loner; again I had the discomfort of eating alone. Although the transition was difficult, I had developed much more patience with curious students who asked personal questions and professors who had a problem coping with my condition. I learned that I had to be an educator. I also learned to ask for help when I needed it if I thought I might lose my balance or fall. The school was much more academic and expected a lot more individual participation. In a few weeks I became acclimated and began to enjoy the new environment. The cost, however, was painful: the taxi fares going uptown and back were depleting my budget.

In mid November I received bad news. The New York Chapter of the National Council of Jewish Women regretted that they could not continue to send any more money after that semester. What would I do? Where would I live? John flew along the highway into the city that night. I was a mess. Nothing he said convinced me of anything positive in my life.

"Sweetheart, please don't get depressed. I know somehow you'll find a way. If it isn't this Jewish guild, you'll find another good fairy. Just be patient. By the way, I've asked Bob Martin to check your legs. It's been almost a year since you've been wearing the night braces."

I didn't give a darn about the damned braces. In late November John brought Dr. Bob into the city to examine my legs. Nothing had changed. "Nita," he advised, "in my opinion we have to proceed with the remedial surgery. There will be two procedures: one is called a triple orthodesis, which is a heel cord lengthening; the other is a stabilization of your metatarsal arches. These procedures will be done on both legs and will allow you to stand flat on the floor. As far as I know this has never been done on any adult—only on children." He smiled slyly, "Would you mind being a guinea pig?"

I looked at John, who was watching me with a knowing smile, and turned back to the doctor. "Bob. I'll do anything to improve. I'd be very grateful for the good old try. When do you want to operate?"

" January is tight. I would like to set a date early in February, 1952. "

"Do you have any idea how long the recuperation period will be?"

"Not really. Your legs will be in short legged casts for at least six weeks."

I shook my head sadly.

"What's wrong, hon?" John looked puzzled.

"I'll have to stop going to Hunter. I don't even know if the VA will pay for this operation. It's experimental. I doubt it." I was disgusted with everything.

John took my hand. "Your day will come. Don't worry about anything. The bill will get paid. Think how much happier you'll be to be able to stand on your own two feet."

Tears rolled down my cheeks. "I love Hunter. I'm getting a fine education toward becoming a speech therapist." I was torn between my desire to have the operation or to apply to another organization for college funds.

"I know, Pupsie. Try to be patient a little longer." He lit two cigarettes, handing one to me. "Bob wants to examine your feet again."

"Hey," Bob interrupted, "we have time for that. I'm hungry. How about you guys? I know a hell of a good Chinese restaurant. Have you been to Chinatown yet?"

I perked up. "We went once and loved it. Be ready in a jif."

The three of us went downtown to a great restaurant and I enviously watched Bob deftly manipulate his chopsticks, regretting I would never master that art, being the klutz I was, and even relishing that John couldn't do it either.

When we returned to the Broadway Central we went up to my room. Bob briefly examined my legs, and tactfully said "Good Night,"saying he would wait for John in the lobby. "Johnny," I moaned, "where will I recuperate? Darn, when is my life going to be less complicated?"

John embraced me, kissing my face, my tears, my lips. "When we're together. I don't think it will be long. I heard that Rose is dating now. " That revelation surprised me. "You'll see, it won't be long before she meets someone she wants to marry. And then, and then," my love picking me up into his arms, with his eyes shining brilliantly, "we can get married."

"Oh, John, do you really think so? You really think it will happen?"

"Goddamned sure. You'll see."

I knew there was only one place for me to recuperate after the surgery. I was compelled to ask my parents. The following Saturday, John drove me to Suffern, parking in front of my dad's shop while he waited in the car. I swung through into my parents' store. Luckily both Mom and Dad were there. "Hi."

Dad came running over with a chair. Mom was silent, her eyes brimmed over with tears. "Aneeda, did you break up with the shaygetz?"

"No, Dad," taking a deep breath, "please, can we skip that subject for a moment? I have something very important to tell you. Dr. Martin, the orthopedist at Camp Jawonio," not wanting to mention John, "recommended surgery on both of my legs."

"What for?" Dad looked puzzled.

"Look at my legs," raising my skirt to show my short legged braces, although I knew it didn't mean anything to either of them. "I had been wearing long-legged braces with a waistband around my waist. I don't need it anymore. I wore short legged night braces for a year but they didn't work and I need surgery in order to bring my heels flat on the floor so I won't stand on my toes like I'm doing now." After a few more questions and explanations, I came to the point. "I came to ask if I could recuperate at home until I'm better, if it's okay with you?"

My parents looked at each other helplessly. "Aneeda, I don't want to see that shaygetz in my house. Where are you going to be operated?"

"Way out in Brooklyn. I'll only be there a short time. You and

Mom won't have to visit. Dad, I promise the only time you'll ever see John is when he comes to pick me up. Will that be okay?"

My father nodded his head sadly. There was no other place for me to recuperate. I had to make the best of the situation and be thankful I could come home.

Nearing the end of 1951, I was introduced to Mr. E. S. Ronk of Stewart, Dougall and Associates, Inc., who was friendly with J. Thomas Schneider, chairman of Personnel Policy Board, office of the Secretary of Defense. Mr. Ronk wrote him a lengthy letter giving a detailed description of my history, adding "I believe Bill HR 6085 has been denied for reasons that I do not know, but it appears to me that there must be some way, some method, whereby the tremendous amount of intricate governmental machinery and red tape can be overcome in order to afford Miss Bloom the right to live rather than exist. The key to the whole situation, as I see it, is in recognizing this girl as a veteran of the U. S. Army." The chairman then replied to Mr. Ronk stating that he was passing on the information to a member of his staff with the request that it be investigated and recommendations made as to what, if anything, could be done.

Our toasts for the coming year were somewhat brighter: the pending surgery, the possibility that John could get his divorce, the continued hopeful signs for the new Bills—all gave John and me reason to believe 1952 would be a significant year.

On February 15, 1952 at the Norwegian Hospital in Brooklyn, New York, Dr. Bob performed the remedial surgery on my legs. From the moment I came out of the anaesthesia and for many days following the surgery, I suffered unbearable pain and intense spasms in my legs. I did not encourage visitors because the hospital was too inconvenient and, furthermore, I didn't want anyone to see me in that uncomfortable condition. John was an angel and drove into Brooklyn almost every night to see his unhappy camper.

Despite the discomfort, he brought me home a week later to Suffern with my legs enclosed in short legged casts from my knees down to my toes. I was thankful my parents were in the store when I arrived. John gave me the necessary instructions on how to take care of myself.

Living in my parents' house was not going to be easy. I had never lived in this particular house before. A long narrow hall with drab linoleum was separated from the rest of the house with a small bedroom where I slept; the bathroom across the hall was so small that it barely accommodated my wheelchair, and I could not close the door. This restrictive area, separated from the rest of the house, was the only saving grace in that it did afford me cherished privacy. The back room was six feet wide by eight feet long—hardly a room for someone in a wheelchair. Faded flowered wallpaper lined the walls; a second-hand Simmons sleep sofa butted against the back wall; an old Singer Sewing Machine perched under the window; a torn shade adorned two flimsy curtains much shorter than the windowsill, and a small closet crammed against the wall holding my clothes made it impossible for anyone to walk around the room. If the door was open, only the invisible man could navigate. When my parents stayed in their bedroom, I couldn't hear a sound.

It caused me grief to see my Mom and Dad witness my suffering but I couldn't conceal my pain and I didn't want to continue the pain killers. It was a wonder my teeth didn't fall out from grinding them constantly. The excessive spasms in my legs caused them to jerk right off my wheelchair pedal. After several weeks the pain subsided, but not enough for me to go out socially. John visited daily, but always left before Mom and Dad came home. Several friends came over to keep me company, but oh how I missed Mar. Her sense of humor would have been a tonic. I read copiously and listened to my favorite New York classical music station. Was I ever happy the day Dad brought home a small television. Lucy and Desi provided the humor I desperately needed.

During my recuperation, I received a reply to a letter I had written to Katherine St. George concerning the fact that I 'd lost my source of funds. She wrote: "If in the event you have any difficulty in your dealings with the Federal Security Agency, I hope you will write me, as I shall certainly be happy to cooperate with you in the matter in every way I can." One of the blessings I had during this period was time. I devoted much of my leisure hours to contacting as many representatives and interested parties as possible.

Almost every day I was confronted with the same problem: my parents did not have an automatic hot water heater in their apartment. If they forgot to go to the basement and turn on the heater, there was no hot water. One morning before washing the breakfast dishes, I put a kettle of water on the stove to boil and while carrying it back to the sink, damned if the kettle didn't fall and spill all over me, down into the cast and onto my right leg. I couldn't move. I couldn't get to the phone. I screamed bloody murder: "Help somebody, help."

A woman's voice shouted, "Just a minute. I'll be right in." An attractive young woman flew into the house. "Pearl Schuller, my God, what happened? What can I do, you poor dear?"

I was panting like a dog. "You're sent from heaven. I don't think you should do anything to me right now but if you'll kindly call this number and ask for John Muller, I'm sure he'll come right over and take care of what has to be done." She made the call immediately and then I introduced myself adding, "I don't know how to thank you."

"I heard your screams while I was walking my son. You must be in terrible pain?"

I shook my head affirmatively, struggling to gain control of myself. "My friend will see that I get the proper care."

"Can I get you a coke?"

"No thanks, but a glass of water would be great. I don't know what I would have done if you hadn't come by. I recently had surgery on my legs. I'm a paraplegic."

"I've heard all about you—the gorgeous young woman in our neighborhood."

I blushed, "I've never met her."

"You're just modest. My husband Jack and our two children, Barbara and Craig, moved here from Queens, New York a couple of months ago." Pearl laughed, "This small town is quite a change from the big city where we left our parents and our friends."

"Oh, I'm sure a lovely young woman like you won't have difficulty making new friends soon. Hey, you better see to your baby. I'll be okay. John will be here in a few minutes. I'll be eternally grateful for your help."

"Oh, that's okay. I'll stop in to see you again." She looked at me quizzically, "Are you sure you're okay?"

"Yes, I've calmed down. Bye now. Thanks for being my life-saver."

A few minutes later John raced into the house. "Oh, darling, I'm so sorry. The doctor will be coming any minute. Luckily I was able to find an orthopedist just as he was leaving the hospital."

The local physician arrived shortly and recommended that

the casts be removed immediately. I was thankful my legs were not burned too severely. He recommended an ointment to use daily. I was petrified. John called Bob Martin who concurred despite the fact that the casts were supposed to remain on a few weeks longer. I was lucky the burn aspect was minor, I tried not to become too stressed and prayed the operation would still be successful. John came over every day for over a month to exercise my weakened legs while I moaned and groaned from the dastardly pain. I was weak and exhausted, just plain miserable, but I had to hold on because John had the utmost faith in me.

I kept telling myself it was only one more obstacle I had to overcome.

Chapter 44

M y parents' home was far from paradise, but difficult as it was, with the bathroom in the back hall, steps in and out of the house and John an unwelcome guest, it did serve its purpose. Miraculously, I recovered from the surgery, but I had to wait until I had physical therapy before I knew if the operations were successful. My one salvation was when John took me out for a few hours. If he happened to come when Dad was home, my father would hide behind a newspaper or utter a mumbled "hello." John, bless his heart, took Dad's rudeness in stride, always confident that soon that situation would change.

Slowly I became weight bearing again, ever thankful that when I stood for the first time, my legs were planted firmly on the floor. When summer camp opened, John picked me up daily at my parents' home and took me to Jawonio where I practiced ambulating up and down the parallel bars; I exercised on the mats doing push ups and sit ups and swam every day. John was living at Camp Jawonio during the summer. When I became tired, I would rest in the cabin where John and I would most likely spend the summers when we got married.

John hired a new physical therapist, the same man who had worked with me at the Burnt Mills School. Woody had matured considerably and proved an able assistant to John.

The beginning of camp was always hectic, and that first day in particular John was under a great strain.

"Hon, Aunt Jen asked me to come to Paterson for the weekend. Perhaps I should spend a little time with her and spare you the burden of rushing over here to bring me to camp I'll do my exercises on my Aunt Jen's floor." I stroked his cheek. "Try to be patient. Everything will fall into place."

John shrugged his shoulders. "Pupsie, I have an idea. When

you go to your aunt's house, do you think I might discuss my marital situation with Saul?" My uncle was a leading attorney in Paterson.

Early Friday John drove me to my aunt's and I enjoyed a pleasant few days. Every morning and after breakfast I did exercises on her floor, I would play on her baby grand piano for an hour or more. I loved to improvise and also play all her simple sonatas. My uncle and aunt had two young children who were of school age and we would play when they came home. One afternoon Aunt Jen and I went shopping. I got my hair cut. On Saturday night we went to a concert at the YMHA where I had been a volunteer for the USO before I went into the service.

Before John came for Sunday brunch, I had asked my uncle Saul if he would spend a few minutes discussing our problem and he was very amenable. John explained the difficulty he was having, getting his wife to grant him a divorce.

Uncle Saul took a long drag on his cigar blowing a circle of smoke that almost caused me to choke. "John, your wife is a practicing Catholic, is she not?"

"Yes."

My uncle shook his head from side to side. "She will never give you a divorce. You're batting zero," giving me a stare that stung like an arrow. John didn't respond to this pronouncement but thanked my uncle and turned the conversation to other subjects.

After we bid farewell to Aunt Jen and her family and got settled in the car, I extended my hand to John. "This is it. The end of the road. I can't go on with this kind of a relationship any longer."

John looked at me in disbelief. "Do you honestly think that Saul's words are cast in stone?" He lit two cigarettes and handed one to me. Speaking emphatically, he said, "I'm telling you, I *will* get a divorce. Sooner than you think. I didn't want to get you too excited but there are rumblings that she is going with someone. I am almost 100% certain, Nita, that before the year is over, Nita Bloom and John Muller will be married." I looked at him adoringly. I trusted him with my life. John had never let me down.

Camp Jawonio began. There were hugs and kisses from many of the former counselors. I assisted during orientation week and later on worked with the campers in many different areas. Mollie, the camp nurse who had worked at Burnt Mills came on board. Camp opened and went into full swing.

Everything was improving, but there were too many nights I just couldn't fall asleep. One night at my parents' home, I was dwelling on having sex with John. One afternoon at camp, I asked John if I could take his specially equipped car for a couple of hours. I drove to the Bronx VA where I had made an appointment to see a young neurologist, Dr. Faluti, who came to the VA shortly before I left in 1946, to see if he had any free time for me.

We made small conversation, I informed him about my recent surgery and he was pleased. After several minutes, the good doctor asked, "Well, Nita, what brings you here today?"

"I plan to be married in the not too distant future, Dr. Faluti. I'm concerned that I'll be depriving John of a complete sex life. Is it possible for you to test me or. . . can you give me any information?" I bit my lips. He smiled. "I guess I sound immature but I want to know more specifically."

"What happens with sex now?"

"We haven't had intercourse. I have warm sexy sensations but I don't know what will happen when I'm put to the test."

"Can you get undressed and get on the table, or should I help?"

"No thanks, I can manage."

"Here's a paper covering to put over your abdomen."

I took off my clothes and got on the low table, putting the large paper across my abdomen and closing my eyes while Dr. Faluti took an instrument and passed it around the vaginal area.

"Girl," he said excitedly, "you are A-one okay." Hugging me, "You'll be just fine. Your vagina contracted and with foreplay to arouse you, penetration will not be difficult. I'm very happy for both of you."

Another obstacle gone! That treasure I would keep to myself and won't John be surprised!

About the third week into camp, just before parent's visiting day, one of the twelve-year old girl campers became seriously ill, ran a high fever and had to be rushed by ambulance to the nearest hospital in Nyack. I stayed behind to answer the phone. A half hour later, the phone rang.

John's voice sounded desperate, "God, Neet. Clare didn't make it. She died on the way to the hospital."

"Oh, my God."

"She had polio. Do you know what religion she was? I think she's Jewish," he said frantically.

"John, I don't know." My stomach twisted into a thousand knots. "I think she's Catholic."

"All right, I'll get a priest to give her the last rites. Get me her parent's phone number. I have to get in touch with them immediately. Will you tell Woody immediately, and for Gods' sake, please keep everything quiet until I return. Pandemonium could break out."

"Yes, darling. I'm so sorry." I gulped, "Lord, there could be an epidemic."

"I have a call into Bob as well as our camp physician. Bye."

I began shaking like a leaf. Me and my demand for religious tolerance. I had insisted that no one give their religion because I never wanted anyone to be turned away because of race, religion or creed. Mercifully we learned that the stricken parents had blessed John for, indeed, the family was Catholic. The camp questionnaire was changed immediately. That tragedy was followed by another catastrophe: Mollie, the camp nurse, had to resign because of a death in her family and had to return at once to Florida. John called Marilyn and asked if she would take the nursing job. Fortunately she was not working. She, Harold and the two children, drove up from North Carolina to New City. Amazingly, camp went forward without too much panic. A couple of the counselors were hysterical, but John spent hours with them discussing the tragedy and gave more time for those who continued to suffer from psychological problems. The entire staff held nightly prayer meetings because Dr. Bob warned that it would take a week before we would know whether or not an epidemic would break out. No one even thought about Marilyn's children. We were all so caught up in the trauma of the whole situation. Thankfully the week passed without further incident, and we were spared another tragedy that could take a child's life at the age of twelve. My opinion of John rose even more. He had been absolutely splendid in his ability to handle this most difficult crisis.

Marilyn was a great asset to the camp. Her nursing capabilities were outstanding. The children adored her. Ellen and Naomi learned to feed the children. The most precious sight was to see four-year-old Ellen and two year old Naomi encouraging the chil-

dren while they were exercising during physical therapy. I taught
Ellen how to swim, and when her father came the following weekend she proudly jumped in the water to show off her accomplishment by swimming across the pool from side to side.

Camp ended on a happy note. All campers participated in
"Oklahoma" at the end of the camp season. Mom and Dad came
out. I thought my father would have a cow when he saw Ellen's
little boyfriend: a precious black three year old she had adopted
as her own.

On a brisk, cool October 14th, just before John's 33rd birthday,
I was at my parents home reading when the phone rang. John said
abruptly. "I'll be over shortly. Sit tight. Don't fly away."

"What's up?" Plunk. "Hello, hello?" Darn him.

A half hour later, the front door opened and John raced in.
"Wow," I giggled as he lifted me higher than ever before, "What's—
?"

John was bombarding kisses all over my face. "Pupsie, she's
getting married. Oh my God, Rose's getting married."

Tears blinded my eyes.

"We'll go out to dinner tonight "

I kept shaking my head unbelievably. "I'm too excited to
eat."

We went to a small inn in New Jersey for a light supper. We
had a cocktail first and another with our turkey club sandwiches.
"I'll have to talk to a lawyer and find a state where I can get a
quickie divorce." John's hand covered mine."Why don't you call
Aunt Jen? Maybe Saul knows someone. I'd rather keep our private
affairs out of Suffern."

"I agree. But when is your wife getting remarried?"

"I think it's the end of this month. Hon," John said sheepishly, "can we stop at a motel this evening? I want to be alone with
you."

"I do, too."

I called Aunt Jen to casually say that John wanted to talk to
Saul again, and she invited us to join them for a Sabbath meal the
following Friday night. At the end of the dinner Saul and John
went for a walk. We stayed for a while, thanked them and drove
back to Suffern.

"Tell me, tell me, what did my uncle say? May I have a

cigarette?" Neither of us smoked in my relatives' home on the Sabbath.

John lit two cigarettes, handing me one, taking a deep drag on his. "He said the only way to make peace with your folks was for me to become Jewish. He'll speak to your father, but advised us to say nothing until he talks to him first."

"Oh, no, I could never ask that of you. It isn't fair." I sighed deeply. "I love you just the way you are. Asking you to convert would. . ."

"Pupsie," John interrupted, "I once told you I would do anything to make peace. You know you would be miserable if your parents stopped seeing you again and there's no other way. I want everyone to be happy. I wouldn't mind being Jewish. I never told you that one Saturday morning I went to a synagogue in Spring Valley. I didn't care for the service because it was Orthodox, and I didn't understand one word. Everyone was friendly, the music was pleasant, but I didn't like the fact that women were separated from the men."

"I'd be bored out of my wits, too. If anything, I would prefer a Reform service. We don't have to worry about that immediately. You have to get your divorce first. Did Saul give you any advice?"

"Yes, he gave me the name of a lawyer in Georgia. As soon as I get my divorce and I hear that Rose is married we can make our plans."

"Lord, what will your mother say?"

"Let's not worry about anything, or anyone. First things first."

In mid-November John got his one day divorce and his ex-wife got married shortly afterwards. He began meeting with my rabbi to prepare for his conversion. We set our wedding date for December 25 and decided to tell my parents the week before the wedding. The ceremony would be held in their home and include only the two witnesses necessary to sign the marriage contract. It broke my heart not to include my sister. John didn't invite his parents because of the conversion and because they were getting on in years. He felt it wasn't necessary to tell them right away.

I was sure I'd be struck by lightening before I became Mrs. John Muller.

Chapter 45

December 25, 1952. The day I would become Mrs. John Muller. The sun shone in all its glory. At long last peace reigned. John was converting to Judaism. My father was ecstatic, carrying on as though he had always loved John. Rabbi Moses Rosenthal, John, two cronies of Dad's and our mutual friend, Ben Pakula, would be witnesses for the ceremony.

Lord, I know I'll pee all over the living room floor. My bladder was playing havoc. All morning long I wheeled back and forth to the bathroom.

"Honey," Mom urged from the kitchen, "have a piece of toast and a cup of coffee. You haven't taken a thing."

"No thanks, Ma. I really don't want to eat. Too excited. I don't want to take any fluids, but thanks." My poor mother didn't understand about intake and output. "Please be a love and hand me my dress."

Dear Mom. How I pitied her. I wanted so much for us to be close like the old days, but she was completely submissive to my father and never contradicted him. My John was kind and understanding. Whenever we made decisions, it was by mutual consent. His primary concern was for me to become a completely independent woman. I always wondered what kind of a woman my mom might have been, married to a less demanding person. Mom was still a very attractive woman: her jet black hair now sprinkled with tones of soft grays, giving it a salt and pepper look. Her complexion was clear and soft and her figure still pleasantly zaftig. I rarely lost my patience with my mom, and if I did, I always felt guilty. Worst of all, everyone postulated that I was the spitting image of Mom, which was both flattering and frightening.

I had saved enough money from my part time job at the Broadway Central Hotel for my trousseau. Midge shopped with

me the day I bought my wedding dress and shoes to match. She
had been a pillar of strength throughout the entire ordeal, especially since Mar had moved to Durham. The dress was simple but
elegant—an off-white taffeta sleeveless with a jeweled neck collar
of tiny colored rhinestones and a gold braid around the neckline.
I had decided against the more traditional long white dress because of John's previous marriage.

"Mom, "I said as I stood up, "please be a love and zip me
up." I sat down after she finished so she could come around and
see me.

"Neet, you look gorgeous. The dress fits like a glove."

"Thanks, Mom. I hope Johnny will like it. If anyone comes,
please close the kitchen door, especially if it's him. It's bad luck for
anyone to see the bride before the ceremony, isn't it?" I was struggling to make conversation. Mom had been left out of all the
planning because we had given my parents such short notice.

I rolled toward the back window, sitting quietly in the sunlight. A lovely cool, crisp December day. Merry Christmas, world.
So Jews don't celebrate Christmas. I'll celebrate any holiday I damn
well please. I'll marry anyone I damn well please. I don't think any
more of John because he converted simply to bring peace into our
lives. I forced myself to stop thinking these thoughts and concentrate on the happiness of my wedding day. Today Cinderella will
marry her Prince. The sun shineth on the happy bride and groom.
"Sh'ma Y'Israel . . ." Oh, please, long may they live. And dwell in
peace. Oh, how I wanted to live in peace, love and be loved.

"Nita, dear, here's Rabbi Rosenthal."

The slight, frail man came around to the front of my wheelchair, bending down to place a kiss on my forehead. "I wanted a
word with. . ."

"Please, Rabbi," I interrupted, "I beg of you, please make
your speech short. For the past six weeks I have been practicing
walking up and down in the parallel bars in the hall. Today I'm
going to ambulate to the ceremony without braces. John doesn't
even know because I practiced in the halls when no one was home.
You know how proud he'll be, but I can only stand about ten
minutes at the most."

"Bless your heart, my child. I can't believe you're all grown
up and ready to assume one of life's greatest challenges." Pausing
he continued, "John is a fine man. It's just too bad he didn't take

the time to learn Hebrew because he memorized all the necessary prayers very quickly."

I didn't respond. I knew why John stopped his lessons: because the Rabbi told him it was my father who insisted that he learn Hebrew—and that finished that.

The little man kissed the top of my forehead again. "Don't worry your pretty little self about anything."

"Will you be ready soon, Rabbi?" I had to put my hat on properly. Yikes. Forgot to practice ambulating wearing my hat. What if the veil blurred my vision? What if . . . let's get on with the power of positive thinking. "Everything's up to date in Kansas City."

"Dad and the men are setting up the chuppah. We'll see you shortly, dear," Mom closed the kitchen door.

I took special care in lifting the small off-white taffeta pillbox hat out of its patent container and backed into the hall, opening the bathroom door to see my appearance. I adjusted the hat on back of my head, gently framing the veil around my face. My good bladder had calmed down. My reflection returned my approving smile. No trace of the hectic last few weeks: completed one semester of my junior year at Hunter College, the on-again-off again marriage of Johnny's ex-wife, even working like a demon to improve my physical condition for today's near miracle and at long last, everything fell into place. The tears, sleepless nights, terrible confrontations of all the years. No trace today. Omnia vincit amor.

Actually, my physical appearance hadn't changed much since I became paralyzed nine years ago. True, my legs had atrophied appreciably, but I maintained the same weight of 110 pounds at five feet-two and a half inches, my dark brown wavy shoulder length hair hadn't fallen out; I almost looked the same without those darn braces. Footsteps were approaching, "Mom, you look sensational." The resemblance was undeniable. Salesmen frequently asked Dad if either of his daughters was in the store. I doubt if those remarks pleased him. A half smile on my mother's face. Mom, please be happy for me.

"You look gorgeous, dear." Mom hesitated, "Anita," she looked like a scared rabbit.

"Oh, please, Mom. I'll be fine. You don't have to worry one

bit. John is a gem of a human being." Blew her a kiss. "Please get my crutches while I back my chair so I can stand."

"Oh my darling John," I said to myself, "I can't wait to surprise you." I had spent long strenuous hours ambulating in between the old parallel bars John had brought and kept in the dreary front hall. The remedial surgery I had almost a year ago enabled me to stand and navigate without braces. Once or twice John had tried to assist me in ambulating outside of the bars with my crutches but it hadn't gone too well. Every chance I had, I practiced between the parallel bars. If I lost my balance, I could grab the bars for support.

Today was the most important day of my life. I was determined to "walk" for the man that I would be grateful to forevermore. Lord, I'm counting on you. Together, let's make it the miracle of 1952.

I reached down, lifting one foot off the right foot pedal, then the other. Damn hat shifted and I hurriedly set it straight. "Mom, will you please open my pedals so I can stand."

I ignored her panic-stricken expression." Thanks, you're a doll." Placed the crutches on either side of the chair, pushing hard on the hand rims of the crutches. Up. Up. Down. Good, Lord.

"Don't you want to use your chair?"

"Dad, please," I said, lowering my eyes.

Up legs. I pressed harder on the hand rims of my crutches that enabled my hips to rise and I could extend my legs to a full standing position. I was fortunate that my paralysis was the spastic type, not flaccid, thereby using the extensor spasms to their best advantage—something John had taught me early on. I shifted my weight on to the left foot, hiked my right leg, placing the right crutch forward. One step. Dad was breathing heavily, not being the most patient man. Sorry, this might take some time. A spasm lurched me forward. Dad started to grab me. Glared at him until he removed his hand. Where was he going to put his hand? What did he know about my condition? Did he ever ask John to explain anything in all these years? Stop thinking these ugly thoughts.

Dad looked like a millionaire today in his deep brown suit and light brown abstract tie. "Dad," I said calmly, "please let me do this alone. Thanks."

I needed plenty of room. Shifted to my other leg which shot forward nicely. I never took my eyes off my gams because sensation in the lower extremities was almost minimal. I started to shake. Beads of perspiration dripped down my forehead. Echoes of high school cheerleading: go, go, go. Another step, feet flat on the floor. Bless you, God. I will remain ever faithful. My wrists are killing me. Thirty or more feet to go. I can't go on. Stop a minute. Take long breaths. Dull linoleum floor—thankfully unwaxed. Another step. I can't move. Hushed stillness throughout the house. Anxious guests. Warm rays of sunshine. Yes, I hear You. Renewed energy. Wait for me, John. One step. Passed gas stove. Clean white tablecloth. Each thump resounded like a robot's gait. What was that? An obstacle course? The rise between the kitchen and living room. Here's where I would make a grand entrance—smack on the floor!

Slowly I placed one crutch over the hump. Raised my eyes for a second. Wow, they were transfixed. I was on a tightrope, the game of balancing. Looked up to see an adoring look on John's face, glancing at a dark navy silk suit. I'll make it, sweetheart. Don't anyone move or breathe. They can't. They're hypnotized. Tried the left leg. No, too high. Sweet Jesus. Panting like a long distance runner. Go, go. Another attempt. And another. And over. Right leg was always better.

John. John. My beloved. I looked up again. Tears in his eyes. My wrists must be ankylosed. Slowly I dragged each leg over to the blue canopy but my feet wouldn't move. In a fog saw four weary men clutching the posts as though they were being tortured. I had to move next to John. My ankles could not rotate. The old two step, dearie. Inch by inch, until I edged against him safely. My heart pounded like a kettle drum. Pressed the hand grips harder and harder until I was frozen to the spot.

". . .the people of Israel shall be proud to receive. . ." and on and on and on.

Lord, he did it again. John's strong grip around my waist. Clutched my crutches. My arms would turn purple. My mouth felt like dry cotton. My legs wobbled. I was sure to faint on top of the rabbi. One of my dad's friends mopped his brow. Stop, my eyes beseeched; the Rabbi continued ". . . and our beloved children will be fine outstanding Jews . . ."

Oh, Lord, Rabbi was still punishing me for the first time when I told him Herm would convert, and he told me I dare not marry him. Pushed on my legs. Pushed. John's firm arm around my waist for support.

At last the contract . . . Hebrew . . .English . . .the broken glass—"Mazel tov," shrieked everyone. Down went my crutches. John caught me, lifting me high into his arms, our lips melted into a long kiss. A chair for me. Midge, Pearl and her husband Jack burst into the house and embraced me.

"You dood it, Neet," Midge happily proclaimed.

"You mean, *we* dood it. What a gal. How can I ever thank you?"

"Honey, this marriage was heaven made." So many years, but we would always remember the time neither of us would dare defy our parents by marrying a "goy."

"Jack and I are very happy for you, Nita," said Pearl as she bent down to kiss me. Her husband waited his turn as did the other guests. They had sent me a tray for dinner the night before with condoms that I hid in my suitcase.

Mom passed a tray filled with tiny Knish. "How sweet," drawing her toward me for a kiss and hug.

Ben kissed me. "Have you found a place to live?" This was the man who had persuaded John to leave his former job and come to Suffern as the new director of the center.

"Yes, we rented a three-room summer cottage in Monsey. Thank heavens it's a heated cabin, and really the place has a lot of charm. As soon as we're settled, we'd love for you and Ann to be among our first guests."

"I'm thrilled for you, honey. Ann and I can't tell you how much we wish for you. Two of the finest people we know." Our hands clung in a tight clasp. Sandy, their twelve-year-old daughter, was a victim of cerebral palsy. No one had helped her as much as John, who was responsible for getting her to ambulate on braces and crutches. They thought the sun rose and set on my John, as did everyone else who met him.

The eldest of my father's cronies sat stiffly on the upholstered chair. Mr. Pailet had known our family ever since we came to Suffern more than thirty years earlier. He came from a very wealthy family. Dad had always encouraged me to date his son in hopes that we would all have charmed lives. Not only Mr. Pailet, but anyone in the small town of Suffern, N.Y. who knew me before I was paralyzed, looked at me as if they didn't know me. Mr. Pailet kept shaking his head from side to side as if to say, no child of his would ever marry a gentile, or they'd be disowned.

An hour later, John put his hand on my shoulder. "Pupsie, we'd better get started. It's a long ride to my folks." I shuddered from the whiskey odor and prayed that Christmas at his house wouldn't be too tortuous.

"I want to call Marilyn before we go." My heart broke because my sister couldn't be with us. John and I had compromised, only inviting the essential witnesses for the ceremony at my parents' house but agreeing to let my mother attend because I might need her help. ". . . ..yes, Mar I did, I walked. Stood for twenty minutes, so help me. Save the details. We're off to the Mullers' for Christmas. Tonight the bridal suite at the Waldorf. Right, same as you and Har did. Kisses to the dolls. Love ya. Mar, thanks for understanding. " Always a stalwart, what a sister.

John took my wheelchair and my suitcases, returning to carry me into the shiny bright red Buick convertible for which he had traded his old Chevy. Dad held my crutches. Lips pressed hard against mine. Tears against tears. Loud voices quickly diminished. Cries of "Good luck, good health and happiness," followed by a pelting of rice. Smiles faded like vivid colors bleached in hot water.

Dad and I had not spoken one word. I had seen my father looking at John and I knew he had seen John's bloodshot eyes. I blew a kiss to him.

"Bye," Dad called, his arms tightly around Mom. Tears locked in our throats. The car moved forward.

"Have a grand time," Midge called.

"Don't do anything I wouldn't do," gibed Pearl.

Expressions turned sad. Bodies receded. Slowly I rolled up my window.

John and I had not uttered a sound. I covered my left hand, opening and closing my fingers, playing peek a boo with the exquisite gold band engraved with orange blossoms and set with small garnet stones that John had selected from an antique wedding shop in Greenwich Village. As soon as he turned the corner at the end of our street, John pulled over to the curb and stopped. "Nita, darling," his enormous arms held me tight.

"Hi, husband." Moved closer, looked up, suppressing my discomfort over his bloodshot eyes. "John . . ."

"Gonna screw my baby . . . "

"Sweetheart, you're exhausted."

"Gonna get me some . . ."

Brushed his lips over mine. He had never used vile language to me.

"Please let me drive. You must be tired from taking this trip yesterday—telling your folks—the ordeal of today. Please, dear, take a nap." To my relief, he nodded willingly. I moved over to resume the driving. John stretched out, laying his head on my wheelchair pillow and fell asleep instantly. I took my hand off the wheel for a second, giving his head a tender pat. The man was entitled to a few drinks with all he had endured.

I drove through the underpass beneath the Erie Railroad, heading toward south Jersey on Route #202. Mounds of pink lavender clouds formed happy faces. Rows of pine trees stood like cadets in front of St. John's seminary. A gentle wind muted tones: Nita Boom Boom, as Joey's father used to prophecy, Nita Bloom was going to marry Joey; Nita Bloom was never going to get married. Grins tickled my whole body.

Stole a peek at my husband. All six feet of him stretched out. What a guy! Our romance was a fairy story. We had conquered all our obstacles. Nothing but nothing could compare to all the obstacles we had faced and overcome over the past four and a half years.

I took the curves slowly. We were going to be late. His mother would be angry; his father would throw a fit. My hope was we wouldn't have to stay too long. What if they knew John had converted? My clammy hands gripped the wheel tighter. I was suddenly exhausted. Loud snores interrupted the music in my head. I nudged his shoulders. He grunted and turned on his side. We now approached Oakland, New Jersey, another hour to go. Christmas wreaths on all the doors. Snowbirds lined the telephone poles. Bare branches swooned in a brisk wind. I turned on the classical station to hear an orchestration of my favorite carol, "O Holy Night," singing softly "fall on your knees. . ." remembering the years when carols were forbidden. Remembering Marguerite's deep contralto and my introduction to the carols. Perhaps one day, after all the hassles, our parents would forgive and be happy for us?

"What's your name?"

Beaming, I happily answered, "Mrs. John Muller, your wife. Did you have a good nap?"

"Yes, my dearest wife, pull over when you can. I need some sugar. Lots of it."

"Johnny, we're late. I'm somewhat nervous. Are you sure your parents took everything in stride?"

John was silent. "Pupsie, I have to confess. I didn't tell them. I didn't have the opportunity."

My stomach churned. I inhaled deeply. "I'm sure Charley told them. Everything will be just fine," patting my leg. "We belong to each other until eternity and don't you forget it. Anything else is petty crap. Promise you won't get upset? Hon, pull over there. I'll bring her in now." He gently kissed my lips. We changed places and I dozed until we reached his parents' house

I barely had time to fix my hair when Mr. Muller, Charley and Eleanor, the children, and Emily Lance, Eleanor's mother, who was widowed last year, all came out with cheerful greetings of "Merry Christmas."

Eleanor kissed me, "Nana's in the kitchen doing last minute fixings. Nita, God, you look stunning."

"Thanks. Everyone looks grand. Merry Christmas to all." No congratulations from anyone. I remembered the Mullers didn't know. The shock would come soon enough. Mrs. Muller came into the living room just as Charley who had insisted, was pushing my chair into the house. "Hello, Mrs. Muller, Merry Christmas."

"What's merry about it?"

Immediately John spoke up, "Mom, we're married."

Sadly his mother responded, "Yes, I know. And I suppose ye weren't married in the church?" A deep sigh, then she calmly muttered, "Oh well, ye'll be having dinner soon. Here's somethin' for ye," handing John an envelope."

John kissed his mother. "Thanks, Mom."

"Thanks, Mrs. Muller, it's very kind of you."

"Oh, ye'll be calling me 'Mom' now, won't she, Sonny?"

My husband smiled, "Of course."

"Well, come to me table now. We'll open the gifts after."

The meal was outstanding. Mrs. Muller prepared the traditional holiday food with all the fixings, chestnut stuffing and cold celery sticks that "Jewish people liked." There was an assortment of pies. I had never tasted mince pie. I liked it, but oh, there was nothing to compare with her scrumptious apple pie. I was determined to have John's mother give me her recipe one day.

The children went wild opening their gifts. Eleanor and Charley gave us a magnificent antique tray. My gift from the Mullers, three linen white handkerchiefs, had my name on it, with the name of the original recipient scratched out. John, his father, brother, and Eleanor drank plenty of Christmas cheer. We left about 7:00 P.M. amid good wishes from all.

I was totally wiped out. Happy to let John drive. The drink had settled my bladder until we arrived at the Waldorf Astoria about 9:00 P.M.

"Hon," John asked as soon as we arrived in our luxurious suite, "do you mind if I call Miss Hawkins (the woman who was responsible for getting Camp Jawonio) and her live-in companion Jeanette to join us for a drink? Good for public relations." My husband never stopped thinking of what was good for the Center.

"John, I'm exhausted. Do you mind if I don't join you this time? It's kind of late for a last minute call, isn't it?"

"Either they'll accept or they won't." Oh, well, why not?

Shortly after Miss Hawkins and Jeanette came over, John ordered hor d'oeuvres and drinks. They congratulated us profusely, I made small talk, then excused myself to prepare for my wedding night. One of my friends had surprised me with a bridal shower and two of my friends had given me a sheer pink nightgown with a matching peignoir. I went into the large bathroom, undressed, put on the gown, then carried my bedpan placing it under the bed. Before too long, I heard John say "good night" and within minutes he came into our bedroom, with bloodshot eyes and smiling like he swallowed a forbidden sweet.

"God, you look gorgeous. Damn, forgot the camera. You're like a vision that will be imprinted in my heart forever."

"You're making me blush."

"Hon . . . Never mind. Be right back. Keep the bed warm." I heard him splashing around, brushing his teeth and like lightening he was back. "Hon, I'm taking this bedpan away. I don't want you to use it anymore. You have good sensation. I think you can get up and go to the bathroom just like any other person."

"Hey, I'm willing to try whatever you say."

"You mean it?" I knew I was blushing. John gingerly helped me out of my nightgown taking time to fondle and kiss, slowly fondling, then arousing me to great passion until I left this earth to fly into the land of ecstasy.

Dr. Faluti. He was 100% right!

Chapter 46

On Monday morning, I was awakened by a tender kiss from my husband. "Good morning, my gorgeous bride." John peppered my face with light kisses.

"Oh, darling," I murmured lazily. "Yum, I smell freshly brewed coffee."

"Pupsie, the bellboy just brought our breakfast. Come, get up; we've got places to go and things to do."

"Really?"

"Yes, Mrs. Muller, how'd you like to see Marilyn?"

"How wonderful. You're very thoughtful, darling."

"Soon as we get out of here, we're off and running. It's a six hour drive."

"I'm going right to the phone."

"Why don't we surprise her?"

"Well, if you think so. I can hardly wait."

"We can stop at one of those wonderful barbeque pork places on our way."

"At your command, my dear husband." We talked about John's future plans for the camp and the clinic. His work consumed his every waking moment.

We drove almost to Durham, stopped in South Hill and had the most delicious barbeque pork sandwich I ever had. Then on to Durham, going to Marilyn's. I learned a lesson I never forgot for the rest of my life: never, but never, did I ever take anyone else by surprise.

Poor Marilyn. Harold was out of town. She had been planning to do her shopping Tuesday morning and didn't have a thing in the house. My sister practically slammed the door in John's face, then quickly collected herself, welcoming us with open arms, then settled for borrowing beer and eggs from a neighbor.

"Darn you," Mar lamented, "I had a feeling you were coming to Durham. I was going to bake a wedding cake first thing in the morning. God, I'm so embarrassed."

My poor sister. Why had I allowed John . . . "You're embarrassed?" John looked totally ashamed. "*We're* embarrassed to death. From the bottom of my heart I apologize a million times. Mar, I assure you we'll never do that again—to anyone. Please forgive us."

Mar came around the table to kiss both of us. "I'm so happy you're here." Marilyn and Harold were renting a little house that was sparsely decorated with only the bare necessities, but the warmth she exuded obliterated any material or physical inconveniences. We sat around the table while she prepared the small supper.

John had fully regained his composure and was regaling her with funny incidents about our wedding, the rabbi, Miss Hawkins, Christmas, and his family antics. Soon we were all hysterical and becoming boisterous. I hushed them for fear of waking the children.

The first thing in the morning Ellen and 'Nomi,' squealing with delight, raced into our room. John took Mar to the grocery store while I thoroughly enjoyed playing with my adorable nieces whom I hadn't seen since summer camp. They were developing beautifully, Ellen had grown since I saw her, still talking a mile a minute, while Nomi, who was more bashful, traipsed along. They entertained me with funny little stories, then brought me into their room to show me all the wonderful gifts they had received at Chanukah a couple of weeks earlier. When John and Mar returned she made us a scrumptious breakfast: hot buns, sunnyside eggs, freshly made apple fritters, and coffee. Afterwards we drove over to Duke University to tour the campus and marvel at the splendid Gothic architecture, the Chapel, the noted Duke Hospital, ending our short trip back at Mar's. We sent our regrets to Harold, and after tons of hugs and kisses, we headed back home. Six hours later, when John pulled into the driveway of our little bungalow in Monsey, I was more than thankful to the landlord for turning on the heat.

In my mother's opinion, I ought to hire a houseworker at least three times a week, but I decided against it. First of all, we didn't have the money. Besides, I had to prove I was capable of

taking care of my household. The first few days I spent the whole
morning struggling to make the bed, tidying up the dishes, sweep-
ing the floors, studying my new cookbooks, and making grocery
lists for John. Somehow we survived. The third week of our marriage John had to attend a conference that required him to be
away for almost a week. I told my sister and she called back to say
Harold would bring her and the girls up to stay with me. Although there were five steps going into the house, I managed fine
with John or Mar.

The days were bitter cold; Mar, the kids and I slept in our
bed under the electric blanket. The second night I awoke, and it
was especially cold. I tapped Mar and she got out to check the
thermostat.

"Neet," she whispered, "the electricity is off. We have to wake
the kids, put their coats on and put more covers on the bed." I was
thankful I had bought a couple of extra blankets. I stayed awake
most of the night praying all the food John bought wouldn't spoil
because I didn't trust the cabin's old refrigerator. The next morning the electricity came on and two of us spent the whole day
combing through my 'Better Homes' cookbook, preparing all kinds
of food neither of us had ever made and didn't stop until all the
meat was cooked because we were petrified that it would spoil.
John had bought foods that were foreign to us in my mother's
kosher home. He was willing to keep kosher with one condition:
if we did, that was the end of eating out. It was either all or
nothing with John, for as he said, "We have only one stomach." I
had eaten non-kosher foods for many years and I had no intention
of continuing the tradition, but he brought pork loin, pork chops,
and other assorted meats that were totally unfamiliar to my sister
and me. In fact I had never really cooked before. All I knew how
to prepare was cold tuna, chicken, egg, or pea salad. We ended
our cooking charade baking a batch of cookies and allowing the
girls to do their share in stirring the batter. When John came home,
he was feted like a king.

On January 6, 1953, Mrs. St. George put two new Bills in
the hopper: Bill HR 1188, which would award me the flat sum of
$25,000. I was not pleased with this action because it would not
grant me veteran's status, but my representative informed me that
her intent was to bring further attention to my plight. The other
Bill, HR 1078, would make all members of the original WAAC

bona fide veterans of the United States Armed Forces. She urged members of the Committee on Veteran's Affairs to support both Bills, encouraging me to do the same. Mrs. St. George mentioned that she and Mrs. Rogers had gotten together about the possibility of early hearings. My mom forwarded a letter from my friend Bob Frost, who had been actively championing my plight, and he enclosed a letter from a politically influential friend, Michael Leo Looney, who worked for the government in Washington, D. C., stating, "First of all, the Army and the VA had recommended against passage of the aforementioned bills stating that 'it would have much more chance of success if we prepared a new Bill and then went back to the Army and the VA and work with them to get a favorable recommendation in order that the committee will have some support."

Mr. Looney continued, "I have talked to a great many persons who have shown interest, and sometime later in the fall I am going to get commitments from them with respect to a new Bill. There is no point in doing this, however, until after the election, as we don't know who will be back. Everything I have learned since my return confirms what I told you, that, since the Army and the VA do not want the members of the WAAC covered by legislation, it will be an uphill fight. If sympathy were votes, I could assure you now that a new Bill would pass. . .. Tell Miss Bloom not to be discouraged, and I will do everything possible to get her covered by the legislation affecting women veterans."

Early in March. letters came from both St. George and Mrs. Rogers saying that Rogers had introduced a new Bill, HR 56, which would extend benefits to all former members of the WAAC. St. George's letter mentioned that she had been in frequent contact with Mrs. Rogers about her Bill, HR 1078, and furthermore, stated ". . .that Mrs. Rogers's Bill would not give me protection, at least as it was written. An amendment could correct it, but I frankly feel that the safest course for me to take, is for me to push for my own Bill." Letters of support continued, but again, there was no action.

In mid-May I became very despondent and found myself unable to sleep night after night. The actions of the Bills regarding my fight to become a veteran all seemed so hopeless. I wrote to Katherine St. George informing her of my deep concern and she replied that she could readily understand my impatience. She added that the VA had not made a recommendation on my Bill and that I should approach Mrs. Rogers as chairman of the House Veteran's committee who could certainly expedite the report.

Summer camp at Jawonio proved to be just the right medicine for me. Mar continued as camp nurse, and of course brought the girls. The campers and day campers had increased substantially. Most of the counselors from the previous year returned. Mar sent Ellen and Naomi to a nearby day camp. Activities were in full swing. Even Harold, who had been timid with the severely disabled children, broke down by assisting several youngsters and taking them into the water.

One afternoon Ellen, dragging a tearful Nomi behind her, came straggling into camp. "We want to stay at Jawonio with our friends and help them." Although we were stunned that the children had simply left the day camp and walked down the hill to Jawonio. We welcomed them with open arms. Marilyn immediately called the day camp and the director understood, saying they would return her money.

We spent a rewarding summer; all the children were high spirited. Camp Jawonio had earned a fine reputation. John Muller's name flourished as a prominent figure throughout New York State.

I really enjoyed being close to Marilyn's children, but I was plagued with headaches over the thought that I would never obtain my veteran's rights. I found myself crying everytime the thought entered my mind. My constant brooding caused me to become lethargic. I couldn't shake the feeling no matter how hard I tried. John tried to keep me occupied with work, but that only lasted for a short time and I would go back to brooding. I felt panicky thinking that I would end up with the same depressions as my mom. I prayed for news that would take me out of these awful doldrums.

I did receive a letter from St. George that perked me up somewhat. She stated that there might be a hearing on her new Bill, HR 1078, during the 83rd Congress. This Bill was very much like the Bill she introduced in the 81st Congress. It would, if passed, provide veteran's benefits based upon service as a member of the Women's Army Auxiliary Corps. She further stated that I should appear as a witness before the subcommittee because she felt "it is in your best interest to present your case yourself since it is your right to make such a request." She suggested that I write to Edmund

P. Radwan, who was the Chairman of the House Subcommittee of Compensation and Pensions.

I did write to Mr. Radwan, crying as I pored my heart out trying to explain how extremely important this legistlation was for me.

Just as I had written to President Truman concerning St. George's previous Bill, I wrote to President Eisenhower. I felt it was a propitious time.

Later in the summer I received a letter from Mr. G. H. Birdsall, in answer to my letter to President Eisenhower. His letter was neither encouraging nor discouraging. "What the final determination of the 83rd Congress will be on this matter when it reconvenes, we are unable to predict."

On August 26, my friend Morris G. McGee, executive secretary of the PVA, appealed to President Eisenhower on my behalf. "If you can do anything to expedite this matter with congressional leaders of your party, we will greatly appreciate it, for this organization recognizes Mrs. Anita Bloom Muller as a full-fledged veteran." How could I be depressed with so many influential and kind human beings who continued to stand by me and champion my cause? One day it had to come to pass. I had to keep faith.

When we arrived at camp from our bungalow, we knew we had to find a more permanent home. John and I found a two-family house on Maple Avenue in New City not too far from the camp, borrowed the down payment from Aunt Jen and Uncle Saul and, by hook or crook, eked out the monthly payments. We hoped to rent out the second floor apartment. The house was directly behind the Catholic church. After summer camp was over, we moved to our new home, well aware that more construction work was required, including a long ramp on the side of the house to eliminate the steps. I had no entrance or exit when we moved in. The bathroom also required certain adjustments to make it more accessible for me. The carpenter was busy; the house was always full of dust.

On our third night there I was standing, leaning against the kitchen sink, washing some vegetables before dinner when I heard the door open—but no other sound. I sat down, turned my chair around to see my husband standing in the doorway with a silly smile pasted on his face. I didn't see anything funny until I glanced all the way down his overcoat.

"Oh, no!" In the pocket of his coat was the snout of a black dachshund puppy. "Out, out," I said excitedly.

"Look, Neet, don't get all riled up," as indeed I started to emote again, "the puppy's owner said I could return him tomorrow if you didn't like him. Just one night, hon."

"Get him out of my sight. Do you hear? I thought we had a deal. No children, no dogs." John paled, quickly putting the puppy in the second bathroom. I broke our pledge of never going to sleep angry.

"Pupsie," he said in the morning, "if you don't want the puppy when I come home tonight he goes back, I promise."

The next morning after our friend Ed, a carpenter, came to do his work, John took the puppy outside before he left for work. The little dog came snooping in the kitchen. I asked Ed if he would mind taking care of the dog. "Please put it in the bathroom. There's so much dust around here. Can you imagine bringing a dog into the house when you're still in the middle of construction?"

"He'll be a lot of company for you, Nita."

"No, I don't like dogs. I was bitten by a mad dog when I was two years old. One day our next door neighbor's German Shepard flew down the steps foaming at the mouth and bit my leg as I started shrieking. You could hear my shrieks a hundred miles away. Luckily I wasn't hurt badly, but that fixed me for dogs. I don't want any dog. Period."

Soon the puppy began to whimper out loud. I knew he was hungry. I opened the can of dog food and opened the bathroom door. 'It' dashed over to the dish—I moved it away, dead certain he was going to bite my legs. He just kept looking at me with his sad eyes and continued to whine. Finally I moved back, allowing him to devour the meat. As soon as he finished, he came back to me, looking up with his sad eyes, begging to be picked up. Ed saw the puppy, came over and put the dog in my lap. I froze, but the dog stayed for the longest time until he fell asleep. He was such a cutey pie. My heart went out to him. For the rest of the afternoon, wherever I went, he followed, sometimes putting his little paws on my pedals begging to be picked up, and I now happily accommodated him. Ed left, very much aware that I had fallen in love with 'it.'

John came home to find me reading with the dog on my lap. He simply smiled. No words were necessary. I finally called the dog Baron Von Schnooper because he was always poking his head into everything.

In 1953 New City was beginning to emerge from an insignificant town, and became the recognized Capital of Rockland County. The Tappan Zee bridge connecting Westchester County to Nyack brought an influx of people to the area. Housing construction tripled; traffic was now becoming heavier in the capital of Rockland County. I had joined the local Women's Club, the synagogue where services were held in the basement of the Methodist church, and volunteered to become a 4H leader for adolescent girls to teach basic skills in cooking and sewing. John bought me an old piano and I began taking piano lessons in classical and jazz music. On one of those rare days, Mom came over to have lunch with me. I told her about my activities.

"Nita, don't take on any position in the Women's Club because you'll only be hurt."

"I don't understand. The women are all friendly."

"I was asked to be an officer once; the women I thought were my good friends blackballed me. It really hurt because I knew it was only because I was Jewish and these were my so-called good friends."

"Oh, I'm so sorry, Mom, but you know, that was years ago. Things have changed since then."

"I hope so. I wouldn't want you to be hurt."

Mom's prediction was wrong. I went on to assume many offices, eventually becoming president of the Clarkstown Women's Club. I was proud that I'd inherited my dad's leadership abilities.

One Sunday afternoon, after speaking to his parents, John asked me to accompany him to Jersey. "Dad sounds distressed. He hasn't been pleased with the new supervisor of the Dillon's estate and wants to leave."

"Where would they go?"

"I hate like hell for them to go back to their home in Bedminster and put Charley and Eleanor out."

I was noncommittal, getting that gut feeling of what was coming next.

"Neet, do you think I can offer them the apartment upstairs? We wouldn't have to charge them much rent and it would make things a hell of a lot easier."

I knew my husband was pleading. I could hardly say no. My

mom always told me that living in one room was better than living with anyone in the family. I dreaded the possibility of my in-laws living right on top of us, but I couldn't bear to hurt my husband who had given more than anyone could ask of one human being.

In a couple of months the elder Mullers were settled in their new abode, and Mom Muller was delighted to be living right above John and directly in back of the Catholic church. We had our first altercation a few weeks after the move. Early one morning I had to drive to the Veteran's Hospital for a checkup. Upon my return, and to my dismay, I found my bed had been made and my dishes washed and dried and placed neatly on the counter top. I inhaled deeply, put the kettle on and called to my mother-in-law from the bottom of her landing. "How about coming down for a cup of tea, Mom?"

"Sure! I'll be right down."

We had the tea and each of us took a brownie I had made the day before. "Mom, I appreciate that you knew I left early this morning and came down to make my bed as well as tidy up a bit." Mom's face lit up like a candle all aglow. "Mom, you're an independent woman. So am I. Johnny's greatest pleasure was to see me completely independent. True, I had to leave early and didn't have time to make the bed, but there will be other occasions when I choose not to tidy my house. I want to be frank with you. I prefer that you don't come into our apartment when I'm not here. John and I value our privacy just like you and Dad."

Tension filled the room. I waited for an explosion. Both of us stared at each other.

"Needa, that's what I like about you. You have something to say, you say it. The others pussy foot around and think I'm too stupid to understand. I understand you completely and that's the end of that."

Whew. We got along famously after our chat. I used to die laughing when she would come running down the stairs on a hot day, racing over to the car, "Dearie, you get the sickness of yer life if ye don't put a sweater over yer shoulders." The temperature was only in the high eighties. However, even with Mom's platitudes, I wasn't happy. On many occasions I felt the intrusions and spying were more than I could tolerate. I said nothing, hoping the day would come when we might find a home just for the two of us.

One evening John came home to find me quite distressed. I had received many letters from Congressmen only to find more promises but no action. Mrs. St. George wrote of her continued concern, assuring me that she would find a way to work on a Bill that would offer me veterans' recognition. But those words did not solve the problems that we had with our meager income. My spirits remained low.

"Neet, you are getting too distraught about this problem. I agree with your father. It would take a miracle for any Bill to pass. Please give it up. I'll probably get an increase soon. We won't be desperate for the money. Please hon, I don't want you to get sick."

No, you weren't the one in the camp. "John, this awful nightmare happened to me." I had to be careful not to hurt John's feelings because he had not served due to his essential war job. Deep in my heart I knew I would never ever give up on my country's obligation to those of us who volunteered when our country needed us. I simply wouldn't talk about it anymore.

Chapter 47

John and I took great pleasure in how beautiful our apartment looked. Whenever we entertained, we received glowing comments about our unusual decor. I had bought an old sewing machine to make drapes out of the lavender material I had purchased and trimmed with a deep purple rope binding. For the living room we had selected a contemporary pale green upholstered sectional sofa and purchased a cherry wood dining room piece. It looked like a cabinet when placed against the wall but when it opened it became a table that could seat ten. We found a stunning black and white sleep sofa and a cherry red leather lounge chair for John that we put in the den. My husband went hunting occasionally. He had a specially made cabinet to hold several guns that I insisted were to be kept under lock and key and empty at all times. My sewing machine, an old upholstered second hand couch, and a couple of colorful hand-me-down chairs that were adequate for the seldom-used enclosed porch completed our furniture collection.

The only roadblock was having my in-laws directly above us. I knew there were nights when John stopped up to see them first and that his mother would ply him with an extra drink or two to make him stay longer. Occasionally, his father would barge into our apartment while I still had my nightgown on and I would bite my tongue to restrain my anger. We had dinner with them occasionally and I, of course, reciprocated. I tried to befriend them, knowing how much it would hurt John if I ever offended them. Intuitively I knew his mother was eavesdropping on our hall steps listening to all my phone calls or worse, and she could hear anything and everything at night. When would the miracle happen? When would I be entitled to GI benefits? It was the only way John and I could ever move. What a difference it would make in our lives.

John and I had many occasions to celebrate: our 3rd anniversary, many holiday parties, Christmas with Charley and Eleanor, and a glorious New Year's Eve with my friends from Suffern.

On a cold day in January 1954, Baron von Schnooper ran away and headed for town, only to enter the open door of a bar. Some smart aleck gave him a schnapps and the poor thing wobbled home swaying like a drunk. When I picked him up for a sympathetic cuddle, all he did was whine.

"Oh, my shnookums, what have they done to you? You poor Baron. Oh, my poor little baby." Then it struck me, and I felt not only paralyzed from the waist down, but from the top of my head to the tip of my toes as well. What a dope! Of course—I wanted a baby. God almighty. I wanted a baby badly. Tears flowed like Niagara Falls.

John came home for dinner that evening, bringing his usual keen intuition. "Pupsie, what is it? What happened, Neet?"

I hesitated before answering. "John, someone gave the Baron a drink today and he came home wobbling like a drunk."

My husband roared. "Well, he's over it now. He's lapping up his dinner like a pro."

As if that was that. Well, it wasn't. "He was in great distress. I picked up the poor baby to cuddle him. All of a sudden it hit me."

"What hit you?"

Lowering my eyes I said quietly, "John, I want a baby. Our baby." Looking up shyly, I added, "Don't you?"

My husband nodded, "Our baby? Yes, I do, sweetheart," coming over to embrace me. "I've wanted to say something ever since I watched you with Baron. I knew I wanted a child of our own. I didn't know if you were ready." He looked at me wickedly, "Shall we start now?"

"Oh, hon, I made dinner . . . "

"Leave it in the fridge. Let's go out to celebrate."

"Oh, darling, we do read each other's thoughts, don't we?"

That same winter, Mrs. St. George's secretary wrote asking me to meet with the Congresswoman in Washington to discuss what further plans were possible. She told me that Congressman Radwan from Albany, New York, had introduced HR 8041 to provide benefits under the laws administered by the VA based upon service in the WAAC under certain conditions. The Bill stated "that any person who served for at least ninety days in the WAAC who prior to establishment of the WAC was honorably discharged for disability rendering her physically unfit to perform further service in the WAAC or in the WAC shall be deemed to have been in the active military service during such period of service for the purposes of laws administered by the Veteran's Administration. No monetary benefits shall accrue by reason of this act for any period prior to the date of enactment and compensation or pension shall not be payable by virtue of this act concurrently with United States Employees' Compensation based on the same service. Any person eligible for compensation or pension by reason of this act who was also eligible for compensation benefits provided by the United States Compensation Act of l917, as amended, shall elect which benefit she shall receive." The Bill would not be retroactive. Well if that was the way the cookie crumbled—just let it happen, I prayed.

That Bill, in my opinion, represented my desire more closely than any of the previously introduced bills because it did not spell out my name per se but it would provide, if enacted, for all honorably discharged WAACs to be deemed to have been in the active military service. Once again I pleaded with the influential persons I had met to use their influence concerning any of the relevant bills, particularly Congressman Radwan's new Bill. I was advised to write to Senator Herbert H. Lehman to ask for any help he could provide. His executive assistant wrote that the Senator would watch out for this legislation. The subcommittee on Compensation and Pension had scheduled hearings in March. Many Congressmen reassured me of their wholehearted support. Unfortunately, I could not attend.

Mrs. St. George appeared before the subcommittee on Compensation and Pension, speaking eloquently on my behalf. She kindly sent me a copy of the 83rd Congressional Record which included the entire hearing. She pointed out to the subcommittee that the Veteran's Administration had denied her Bill, HR 1078, because it did not make very clear that if the Bill was passed, it would merely grant benefits requiring service connected to diseases or injury, and the VA stated that an appropriate amendatory clarification could seem to be required. She mentioned that this subcommittee was also considering HR 8041, introduced by the Chairman Congressman Radwan. This Bill, she empahsized, would do exactly what the Veteran's Administration had desired in their criticism of HR 1078. She further pointed out to the subcommittee that the amount of money involved would be negligible because it did not apply to very many women.

A few days after the subcommittee met, I received a letter from Joyce Martin, research director of the New York Democratic party. I had requested their help with Bill HR 1078. Their response was that everything possible that could be done had already been done as far as my case was concerned. "Naturally, the Democrats are not in a position to influence the course of legislation and your contact with the Republicans was the wisest course you could take."

The message from Ms. Martin was obviously telling me that my chances would be enhanced if I was a Republican. As soon as John came home that night, I thrust the letter at him. He shrugged his shoulders but I couldn't control my temper. "John, is she saying that I should become a Republican?"

My husband spoke firmly. "Nita, do you want your Bill passed? You know, with President Eisenhower in office, this is a Republican administration. You must become a Republican."

"No," I said loudly and defiantly. Baron flew into the room. "No, I won't do it!" John didn't say a word. Tearfully I mumbled, "It's a must isn't it?" He shook his head up and down.

I could not get out of the doldrums. The subcommittee had not completed their results. All our efforts to become pregnant proved unsuccessful. I made an appointment to see my gynecologist and he suggested that John and I be tested to see if there was any reason why I wasn't conceiving. After the tests, which found no problems, the doctor suggested that we take periodic short vacations. Even though John was busier than ever drawing plans for a new center, he did take the time to get away for a day or two every so often.

John, Ben and a few members of the Board met many nights exchanging ideas and several times I joined them. One evening in early April, John's brother Charley paid us a visit. We were sitting in the living room having a drink. Charley appeared to be jumpy and he finally blurted, "I have something to tell you. Eleanor and I have bought a new home. It's her heart's desire — a country club environment with all the amenities on the property," taking a long swig of his drink.

"What's the problem, Charley?" I asked. "No Jews or blacks allowed?"

John turned ashen. "Goddamnit, Charley."

"It's only the country club, John . . ."

"I don't give a—"

I interjected, "People do what they have to do, Charley. We will visit you. You'll be raising your children in that environment, not mine."

"I'm so sorry, Nita, you're the last person in the world we would hurt. We hate the rule. You know that don't you?"

"I'll be goddamned if I ever . . . "

"Hush, sweetheart. It's not necessary that we go to their club." Wishing to change the subject I said, "Shall we invite Mom and Dad down for dessert?" The look I gave my husband ended that conversation.

When they left, I said to John, "We're talking about your brother, dear, I'm sure it was a terrible ordeal for him to make the long drive with that load on his mind. I wouldn't like to be in his shoes. No way."

Every day I raced out to the mailbox hoping for news from the subcommittee on Veterans' Affairs. The first positive sign was the letter I received from Katherine St. George on April 28th. She wrote, "I am very glad to be able to tell you that Congressman Radwan's Bill, HR 8041, was reported by the subcommittee to the full committee on Veteran's Affairs." I immediately wrote to Mrs. Rogers asking her if she thought it was advisable for me to appear. She wrote back immediately to state ". . . the subcommittee reported favorably HR 8041 to the full committee and they will assemble in an executive session to take action on the bills reported to it." She further stated that "no testimony is heard during an executive session other than from committee members themselves." Other than John, no one knew about the latest happening and I asked him to keep mum. I prayed day and night!

My prediction about the Clarkstown New City Women's Club not being prejudiced was right and they asked me to run for president in the fall. John, proud of all my accomplishments in the group, encouraged me to accept. It was my hope that the office would offer an opportunity to broaden the organization's base to include assistance to Camp Jowanio and other charitable institutions.

In a few weeks we left for camp. In early May, a Western Union telegram arrived from Katherine St. George, "*H.R 8041 was reported to the House by the Veterans' Affairs Committee Today.*"

I was so excited I thought I'd drop dead. For the next few

weeks, I waited on pins and needles. Finally, on June 7th, another telegram came from St. George: *"I am very happy to report that I succeeded in getting favorable action on your Bill in the House today."* Now it had to go to the Senate.

My attendance to a synagogue had been very limited, but I felt compelled to attend. John accompanied me the following Friday night.

A week later, responding to my call, Senator Ives verified that he had been alerted to HR 8041. "This Bill has come before the Senate Committee on Finance but, inasmuch as it was just referred to the House committee on June 8 no action has been taken to date. However I shall be very glad to do whatever possible in behalf of any legislation on your behalf." I immediately alerted other Senators urging their support.

Senator Wallace F. Bennett responded to my wire urging his support on the Radwan Bill. "You will be happy to know that the Senate Finance Committee reported this Bill out to the Senate yesterday. There is every reason to believe that this will receive favorable Senate action this session."

The following day I was called to the phone in our cabin. "Nita," Robert Moss, president of the Eastern Paralyzed Association shouted, "Bill HR 8041 just passed the House and is now in the Senate. The American Legion is backing a major Bill giving all veterans an increase in their pension and they're pushing for their Bill with their powerful lobby behind the scenes. The only way your Bill HR 8041 will go through is if a senator attaches your Bill as a rider. It won't be easy, believe me. The American Legion lobby is powerful; they won't want anything to interfere with their major Bill. If you have pull with any Senator, get on the ball at once! The rider must be carefully worded so that anyone in the Senate who supports the Bill on behalf of the American Legion would not veto the attached rider. Do you hear me? At once, like—now!"

"Oh, my God. Thanks, Bob."

I wheeled into our private quarters without saying a word to anyone, wheeling up and down the room, back up and back down. Who to call? I didn't know any Senator that I could call spontaneously. I had written to Senator Ives and he expressed sympathy but I didn't feel he was the one to approach. I stared out the window watching the children at play. And then it dawned on me.

But of course—Senator Herbert Lehman of New York, known for his compassion and humanitarianism. I dialed information and the next thing I knew I was transferred to Senator Lehman's executive secretary Julius Edelstein, to whom I related the bare facts. Mr. Edelstein assured me he would relay the information to the Senator and give me his answer as soon as possible.

I immediately dialed Katherine St. George's office and she sounded delighted, reassuring me that she would do everything in her power to spread the word. The next day, Mr. Edelstein called back to say the Senator would help. My excitement was at an all new high!

On August 11, 1954, I received a wire, *"I am pleased to inform you that HR 8041 was passed by the Senate today, Irving M. Ives."* I was beside myself waiting for the final move.

Eleven days later, at 3:40 P.M., I received the most important telegram of my life: *"President Eisenhower signed Bill. Congratulations. You must know how happy I am to have been able to accomplish this for you. Katherine St. George."*

"John, Marilyn, come here! It happened! The Miracle! The miracle of 1954!" Flags suddenly appeared. Marilyn pushed me into the center of the large field and John, my nieces, all the counselors, all the able bodies and those children in wheelchairs were given little flags and marched around me singing "God Bless America."

Yes, oh yes, it was worth all the heartache, all the years of desperation. The wrong was righted. All those wonderful people who had fought my battle. I would be indebted to them forever. The country I loved passionately came through despite all the odds. I knew that one day the Congress of the United States would award the same benefits to all the women who had joined the Women's Army Auxiliary Corps. "God bless America," I sang, louder than ever before in my life. My struggle was over!

When the realization of all the benefits I was to receive fully dawned on me, I was truly humble. In acknowledgment of the awful tragedy that befell me when I was in the WAAC, my government had at long last recognized me as a service connected spinal cord veteran and I was overwhelmed with pride.

John and I put the $10,000 I received from the VA as a down payment on a Dutch Colonial country estate on ten acres about three miles away from where we lived in New City. Fortunately our living quarters were on the first floor, which met with the VA Housing regulations. A three hundred foot driveway led to the entrance of the home. In addition we acquired two magnificent looking collies, Honey and Beauty, who won the love of Baron immediately. If one put his or her foot flat on the ground outside our property the toes were on Germonds Avenue, New City, and the heel was in West Nyack. John and I chose the latter as our mailing address for the home we named 'Germonds.' The house was over two hundred years old and was flanked on either side with tremendous weeping willow trees and two large ponds that were a natural habitat to hundreds and hundreds of ducks. Many times, when I looked through the double door in the living room, I would find an artist sitting at the edge of the property with an easel.

Everything was perfect.

Even my in-laws were happy for us. Mom Muller was in all her glory because they had moved downstairs into our apartment and two priests from the Catholic Church had rented the one upstairs. I was certain I was about to live a Cinderella's life at long last. I was thoroughly relaxed, thinking about going back to college, becoming more active in the community, and was excited by the possibility that I might even, one day, become pregnant.

"Only in America," Dad always said.

"God Bless America!" I shouted at the top of my lungs.

Epilogue

On November 2, 1957, John died suddenly at the age of thirty-eight. The diagnosis was acute hemorrhagic pancreatitis caused by overwork, overeating, and overdrinking. I continued to live alone on our ten-acre property, supported only by my veteran's pension. I managed the large house, drove to and from town, and gradually became more active in the community.

After I was widowed, Theodore J. Friedman (TJ) came to visit from his home in Catskill, New York, where he owned a real estate business. He was still a bachelor, but to my surprise, he had matured considerably. We were married in March, 1959. Our marriage was sweet, but unfortunately very short. We had hardly been married a year when TJ died of a heart attack at the age of forty-nine.

When John had died, he had left me almost no resources. Of course, the physical independence he had given me could never be measured financially. TJ left me the beneficiary of his estate, and for the first time I would be spared any financial burdens.

In the late 50's, both my parents died of heart conditions. I had been very angry at Dad and it took many years before that anger abated. I can now understand and forgive his frustrations and reconcile myself to his treatment of me.

On September 9, 1960, I lost my best friend when my sister Marilyn died at the age of thirty-four of peritonitis, brought on by an unsuccessful operation. Afterwards, I spent a great deal of time with Marilyn and Harold's girls, Ellen and Naomi, trying to staunch their grief and help the family get back to normal. Harold proposed, asking me to be a mother to his girls, and we were married in December, 1960. Going from favorite aunt to stepmother was much too difficult, though, and sadly, much dissension arose among all four of us. A decade later, after both Ellen and Naomi were married, Harold and I divorced.

In 1968, I had enrolled in a two-year course to become a mental health technician, and in 1971 I received my BA in Psychology from Loyola College in Baltimore. I worked in one of the State Mental Hospitals and became the first president of the newly formed Mental Health Association of Maryland.

Harold and I saw each other occasionally over the next few months, and after he and I had spent time together without any of our former tension, we discovered that not only did we share a mutual love of our children (whom I had legally adopted after Marilyn's death), we also shared many other common interests. By then, it didn't take long to realize that we truly loved each other and we were remarried on June 2, 1972. Harold insisted we have a big party to celebrate, since our first marriage had started on such a sad note.

Today, Ellen and Naomi are attractive, intelligent, productive women, married to wonderful men. Hal and I boast five of the most beautiful, brilliant grandchildren in the world!

Hal and I have come full circle in a relationship that began as a result of a crisis. We have found a place so special and glorious that together we can solve any problem we encounter.

We have traveled extensively and have been fortunate to maintain homes in Florida and Maryland. I have been Hal's caretaker when necessary and he has been mine. I am fortunate to have him as my dearest partner on earth.

I had to have a triple bypass operation in the summer of 1998 and I must admit it was very tough to overcome, but with the help of some wonderful doctors, therapists and friends, I did.

In September 2001, Hal and I decided to move permanently to Boca Raton, Florida, where we purchased a lovely condo facing the intracoastal waters, but in October my life again changed for the worse. I was stricken with a major stroke affecting my left side, and the independence that I treasured was threatened.

Once again, I drew upon the lessons that John had taught me. It has been difficult, but I am leading a somewhat active life.

At the age of eighty-one, I have experienced sixty years in a wheelchair.

I hope that my life and the challenges that I have faced will inspire others, especially young men and women, to overcome adversity and go forward in life with a positive attitude to conquer any misfortune.